No More National Debt

by

Bill Still

Reinhardt and Still Publishers / The Still Foundation, Inc.
St. Petersburg, FL 33701

Contributors

My sincere thanks go out to the 152 "backers" who contributed to the writing of this book in a financial way through KickStarter.com:

Greenbacker Contributors
Gary Boorse
Rondi Olson

Platinum Contributors
SwarmUSA

Gold Contributors
Frank Maggio
James S Corr
Rick
Eric Ackerly
Angela Summers
For Amber's future. Love Dad x
Eric Jorgensen
Dan Thompson
B Avery
Lance Kolada
Paul Cox
Tom Millard
Tristan Olive
Mark Wolfson
Patrick Henry Reidt
Kaarle StÃ¥hlberg
Moe Kinney
Thomas Lasco
no1ninja
Barnett Eades
Stephen Fabo
Robin Miller
Brian Hedges
Steve Farnum
Robert Jerrells
Raymond Knoflach
Michael Buehler
David Middleton
Gray Oliver
Jonathan Lizotte
Dave Braatz
Greg Hickey
Colin Duesterhaus
Jeffrey G. Baker
Tom Zdra
Jerry Zimmer
Beth Beckmann
Alex Parody
Kale
Henri Sweers
Glenn Reed
steven ciaccio

Jim Buske

Silver 3 Contributors
Craig DeForest
J Phillips
Dan Osborne
tedraiter
Alan
LARRY GRZEMKOWSKI
Dan M
Jim Johnson
John Edwards
Thomas Winter
David Piller
russell2349
Danny Tosolini
Tom Winter
Christopher Schweizer
Nelson Bonner
Chuck Mincey
Ellen Sandles
Pedro Palos

Silver 2 Contributors
Jay Spencer
Stephen McIntyre
turtle
Timothy Sadler
Steven J Pratt
Robert French
Terry Kinder
Aaron Cranston
Jeanine & John
David Wood
Dwight Carmichael
beydo
Daniel Lillqvist
CriticalThinker
Brendhan Pelot
Jarrod Peterson
Christopher Ness
Jan Seemann
McGregor Scott
Douglas Anderson
Spencer MacDonald
Jim Kuczkowski
Oaken
Tony Mainella
Harvey Kivel
John Steven Bianucci

Patrick Fischer
John White
Howard Lichtman
Dawn Brosius
Bill Kennedy
Christopher Forgione
David Hagersten

Silver Contributors
Charles Jones
TXin1880
Michael Voeltz
andyb
Louis Cannino Sr
Scott Benzing
tsadana
Jim Martin
John Taylor
Tony Auguste
Mark S. Kenzer
John Bozak
Walt Longyear

Bronze Contributors
TomS
Jonatan Flodin
Mark Halsel
StarTrader1968
Fred Peachman
Vicki Kerman
Jim Sutton
Asif Punjwani
Simon Tesfamariam
tim stefanco
Jonathon Hilditch
Caleb Payne

Copper Contributors
Seleste Skinner
Ivan Martin
Jan Wouters
Michael Tyler
Matthew Piner
Mark Aaftink
Kamran Munawar

First Printing – March 2011
2nd Printing – April 2011

Copyright © 2011 by The Still Foundation, Inc.

All rights reserved. No part of this book may be reproduced or transmitted in any form or by any means without written permission from the publisher, except by a reviewer who may quote brief passages in a review; nor may any part of this book be reproduced, stored in a retrieval system or copied by mechanical, photocopying, recording or other means, without permission from the publisher.

Reinhardt and Still Publishers / The Still Foundation, Inc.
St. Petersburg, FL 33701

Contact us: stillfoundation@gmail.com

Cover art by Dara C. Still

ISBN 978-0-9640485-5-3 (Paperback)
ISBN 978-0-9640485-2-2 (Hardcover)

All hyperlinks, whether via footnote, reference, or HyperScan®, may lead to 'linked content' generated or authored by others. This content may be governed by foreign or domestic copyright laws, and the author of this book does not claim authorship of said content.

Printed in the US, Canada, and UK

Table of Contents

ABOUT HyperScan· QR CODES vi
Foreword.. ix
Introduction 1
Chapter 1 – The Magic Isle of Guernsey... 2
Chapter 2 – Thought Experiment 8
Chapter 3 – Stone Money 12
Chapter 4 - Economic Myths 17
Chapter 5 – Problem With *End The Fed* 24
Chapter 6 - The False Solution 38
Chapter 7 - How Did I Get Into This?.. 46
Chapter 8 – Ancient Greece 58
Chapter 9 – Carthage 62
Chapter 10 - Rome 65
Chapter 11 – The Biblical View.. 69
Chapter 12 – England 74
Chapter 13 – Colonial America.. 78
Chapter 14 – American Central Banking 90
Chapter 15 – 2nd BUS.. 109
Chapter 16 – Abe Lincoln 126
Chapter 17 – The Crime of '73 144
Chapter 18 – William Jennings Bryan... 159
Chapter 19 – Silver Money 165
Chapter 20 - The Aldrich Bill... 169
Chapter 21 – The Jekyll Island Caper.. 178
Chapter 22 - The Election of 1912.. 185
Chapter 23 - Birth of the Federal Reserve 200
Chapter 24 – The Crash of 1929 225
Chapter 25 – Program for Monetary Reform 238
Chapter 26 - State Level Solutions 248
Chapter 27 – Sound Money Initiatives 262
Chapter 28 – U.S. National Solutions 265
Chapter 29 – Competing Currencies 277
Chapter 30 - Karl Denninger on MERS 284
Chapter 31 –Kennedy Assassination Myth... 286
Chapter 32 - Fake Quotes 288
Chapter 33 –International Solutions 297

Chapter 34 – Economic Disinformation 322
Chapter 35 - Bonus Videos Online 336
Appendix – More about HyperScan 339
Index... 341

ABOUT HyperScan® QR CODES

Congratulations – in your hands, you have the world's first book to be powered by HyperScan QR codes. By using most camera-enabled smart phones, readers of this book are able to 1) load a QR-code scanning application, 2) hold the camera to the HyperScan code, and 3) experience pictures, video, sound, and graphics that leap off the page.

HyperScan QR codes look unlike any other "QR" ("quick response") code, yet, unlike all other proprietary QR codes (which require proprietary readers), HyperScan QR codes can be read by almost any QR code reader, across all smart phone platforms. While a special HyperScan QR code scanning app is scheduled for release in 2011, if you have already have a QR scanner on your phone, you should be "good to go."

If you would like to be notified when the special HyperScan reader app becomes available, or when the author of this book has important updates to share with you, please scan this HyperScan code and provide your contact information and platform in the simple onscreen form provided:

URL: 7.tv/0bea

WHAT HAPPENS WHEN I "HYPERSCAN IT" ?

Most QR codes expedite, among other things, the process of opening browsers, typing (or retyping) long web addresses, and waiting for the browser to visit a web page. Your camera and phone's onboard software translates the "little black squares", or modules, within the HyperScan code, into a shortened URL code (i.e. address for a web site). TO INSURE THAT HYPERSCAN QR CODES ARE AS SMALL, AND YET AS READABLE, AS POSSIBLE, HYPERSCAN CODES RESOLVE TO THE SHORTEST URL IN THE WORLD – www.7.tv . At 7.TV's state-of-the-art data center, the HyperScan code is then immediately directed to a web site or page, based on a data base table managed exclusively by the author of this book.

About HyperScan QR Codes

WHICH QR CODE SCANNING APP SHOULD I USE?

Most QR code readers, on most smart phones, are able to quickly read HyperScan QR codes. Many of these apps are free, or may sell for as little as $.99. Blackberry and some Symbian phones come preloaded with an app optimized for their phones.

HyperScan recommends users download scanning applications that provide two levels of security and privacy:

1) Before the HyperScan QR code redirects you to any website, the QR scanning app should first ask you for permission. Some apps may allow you to disable this function, but visually insuring that you are familiar with the web site address **before** visiting is an important step in safely scanning QR codes. **HyperScan, LLC does NOT recommend QR scanning applications that do not allow users to visually and plainly see the URL before directing a phone's browser to a web site.**

2) The QR scanning application should NOT direct a browser to an interim web site before going to the 7.TV URL embedded in each authentic HyperScan QR code. Look closely at your phone's browser after scanning a HyperScan QR code - the first URL should start with either "7.TV" or "HyperScan.IT," with a "/" followed by 1-6 characters. Then, after you review and approve it, the browser should then be directed to the site selected by this book's author. However, some "free" and even paid QR scanning applications find ways to utilize information about user scanning behavior, location, and other data when a code is scanned. We therefore only recommend QR scanning apps that go DIRECTLY to the address within the QR code (and then to the designated site). If you are using a QR scanning app that visits a site BEFORE displaying the 7.TV site designated by the HyperScan code, we suggest you stop using this application and download one that does not engage in this behavior.

At this time, we only recommend **QuickMark** for a code scanning app. This reader does an exceptional job reading HyperScan codes. For more details, please visit www.HyperScanIt.com and select "Recommended Applications" from the site.

For more information about HyperScan, please see the Appendix.

HyperScan® is a registered trademark of Media IP Holdings, LLC. For further information about HyperScan, please visit www.HyperScanIt.com, or email questions to info@HyperScanIt.com.

Foreword

February 12, 2011

Like most of us, I first learned about Bill Still when a friend advised me about the 1995 film, "The MoneyMasters." Actually, he whispered it to me, in a secretive tone not meant for prying ears; two sideways glances, a hand covering his mouth so that nobody could read his lips, and the words escaped – "Check out the 'MoneyMasters.' Google it. It's the best way for you to understand what's REALLY going on."

This one piece of advice began a painful journey of discovery of what really happened to the $1.2 billion of approved real estate projects I once thought I controlled, which were gradually seized and "redistributed," as the hidden rules of money creation were unveiled to me.

The sooner we learn the rules of this larger, economic game, the sooner we, as a people and nation, can get back on our feet, and live the free, sovereign lives for which our forefathers died.

THE ECONOMIC GAME

Our economy is a massively multi-player game, and every person in every nation must play. The game's byproduct is an invention called money, and with little exception, it gravitates to the rule makers. Today, an elite banking class, referred to by many as the Money Masters, the Money Changers, or the Money Trust, writes these rules.

Central banking is their trade, and here are their tools:

- Persuasion and influence -- using an infinite supply of money as the bait.
- Distraction -- enabling economists, bankers, and academia to overcomplicate our understanding of how money is quite simply created out of thin air.
- Sleight of hand – to force us to blame each other, and not the Bankers, when the money supply expands and then shrinks, and markets crash around us.
- And, finally, raw monopoly power.

Foreword

Ironically, money in the world economy is very much like that found in a game like *Monopoly*®. In the *Monopoly* board game, each player starts the game with $1500 of <u>worthless pieces of paper, backed by nothing</u>, which are <u>given to all players,</u> purely as a means of seeding the economy. The game is fair, and this "unbacked," fiat paper money works just fine. The rules are the same for every player, favoring nobody, and, in the long run, better players tend to win, because they have mastered the rules of "finance," and interpersonal relationships, that apply in this fictional economy.

BUT – this fair, open game, with printed, open rules, is NOT how our economy truly works. And, to illustrate much of the picture that Bill Still paints in this book, <u>you need only change two rules.</u> Play a game of Monopoly with these two new, "secret" rules, and the outcome will be dramatically different:

- SECRET RULE 1: *Instead of each player starting with free access to $1,500 of money, each player must BORROW this money from the Bank, and pay 5% interest on his or her money to the BANK, every time they pass "GO."* This mirrors a version of the Federal Reserve Banking System, and Federal Income Tax (both of which were spawned, weeks apart, in 1913.)
- SECRET RULE 2: *The Banker can play and compete in the game, by using the money the Banker "earns" from charging interest on the use of the paper money - and can allow new players to enter the game to compete, using the Banker's earnings, whenever the Banker elects.* This mirrors what happens when Banks foreclose on properties, or sell loan documents to vulture capitalists (many of them clients of the banks), allowing them to legally pilfer property for pennies on the dollar - often with loans made by the very same Bank.

With these secret rules in place, prices for properties will fluctuate widely; one-time winners can become losers quickly; and a steady flow of new players enters the game, particularly when "losers" have their properties liquidated during the bankruptcy process, or when available properties are auctioned during periods when the balance of players are already highly leveraged (and therefore, cash-poor).

You'll also notice that the game takes on a decidedly chilly environment; negotiations between players are rare – one party is heavy on "demands," and the other party is apologetic, meek, and often desperate.

To develop this analogy a bit more, in this new, perverse form of Monopoly, it's usually only the Banker who is aware of these secret rules at the very beginning of the game. The other players keep playing along, oblivious to these secret rules, throughout their entire game. Some may win, but most lose.

Finally, should a player inform the other players of these secret rules, boldly suggesting that the game be restarted with fair rules, they are often treated as outsiders, presumably instigating trouble to get back in the game, or covering up their own financial shortcomings. And, those players who are faring well under this system, even if still oblivious to the secret rules, will do little to support the instigators. After all, why rock the boat? Lastly, a third class of players – the banker class, or the Money Trust – are fully aware of these rules, and the advantages they glean from them, so they do little to even acknowledge the rules exist, let alone support any effort to start the game over without these secret rules in place.

BACK TO BASICS

There are many ways one may become aware of the secret rules that are now beginning to decimate the U.S. and global economies. Those who hunger for freedom and a fair system, recognize the need to stop this game, and start over, with new rules that advantage nobody. The longer we wait, the more of our remaining, real assets will be taken from us, and given to the Bankers, and their friends.

The number of us who now know that <u>something</u> must be done is likely in the millions. We come from every walk of life, belief system, and nation. Almost every one of us has a horror story to share, and a litany of evidence that validates how sick the monetary system has become.

Despite the volume of <u>evidence</u>, very few people or organizations have valid <u>solutions</u>. Although many are sincere, they would have us believe that governments can't be trusted, and that money must be tied to a commodity such as silver or gold.

Bill Still's goal is to use evidence drawn from money systems throughout history, to establish two simple guidelines for truly sound money, and then, he proposes a simple, HOPEFUL mantra to get the populace on the road to real recovery:

1. We, the people, through a democratically elected, honest republican (small "r") government, should control the issuance, quantity, and quality of our money.
2. This money MUST NOT be based on, or bonded by, any commodity, since "commodity bondage" ultimately subjects a sovereign nation to the whims of those who create, control, corner, or counterfeit that commodity - be it silver, gold, oil, wheat, silicon chips, or cow chips.

Bill's trumpet call is clear: Sound money must be controlled by, and backed by, we the people. It should be SPENT into existence, and not LENT into existence.

Indeed, the new mantra for this 21st century human rights movement should be: NO MORE NATIONAL DEBT.

- Frank Maggio, St. Petersburg, Florida. FSMaggio@gmail.com

Introduction

For those of you who are a little pressed for time, I'm going to tell you what this book is all about in 60 seconds. Start the clock.

Brace yourselves; you aren't going to like this: Despite what some politicians have told you, our problem is <u>not</u> the Federal Reserve System. Our problem is the big banks using the Fed as their foil to keep us perpetually confused. The Fed is just there to make us <u>think</u> it is part of the government and therefore the government is keeping the big banks honest. The truth is that the Fed and the big banks work together to obfuscate the real problem and confuse us. They do EVERYTHING possible to make us look the wrong way -- or even better -- give up entirely. The Fed is NOT the government. It is <u>disguised</u> as the government. Federal court rulings and the U.S. Supreme Court have confirmed this. But more importantly, if you eradicated the Fed tomorrow along with every other central bank in the world, <u>none</u> of our problem would be fixed – zero! The Fed is not the problem.

Here are the two problems:
1. National debt – government borrowing, and

2. Big banks get to counterfeit our money, then loan it to us at interest. It's called "fractional reserve lending". There are only 2 basic choices for who issues a nation's money:

- We the people – through our government. (Most people think this is the way it's done.); or
- Borrow it, mostly from banks.

The second alternative -- believe it or not -- is the case today -- for nearly every nation on earth. Think about this. Which do you want? The issuance of the nation's money is the most important power – even the very definition of sovereignty. Without this power:

- A nation CANNOT be sovereign.
- A nation must borrow all its money – mostly from bankers -- and yes, they do charge interest on it.
- A nation <u>must</u> eventually collapse.

Under this system, who do you think has control? Remember what Proverbs warns:

"... The borrower is servant to the lender."

That's why nations can never get out of debt under this system, because all our money – except for coins -- is borrowed, and the banks love it. Under this system, reducing the National Debt is impossible. Why? Because all our money is created as this debt. To reduce the national debt is to reduce the national money supply. No politician ever says this in public. Maybe they don't know. Maybe they do.

Governmental "austerity" measures will not work. Why? **It's the interest** – the interest on the National Debt of every nation is growing faster than any likely cutbacks in spending. This never-reported fact is what is overwhelming every governmental budget everywhere around the planet.

It doesn't have to be this way. We can fix it – you and I -- just average people with no special training – can understand what the problem is and insist on change. That's what they are so scared of – that we will figure this out.

Self Government

So what is the general political tone of this book? That's important to know – right-left, anarchist-monopolist, libertarian? The following was taken (and modified) from my Reforum. Yes, that's how we spell it. The HyperScan link is at the end of this section, but remember, it's all text and text doesn't work too well on the small screen.

This book is about re-invigorating the self-governance concept. Freedom isn't free. Government NEVER grants it. You have to strive for it. More importantly, we have to teach our children that they have to teach their children that you have to perpetually strive for it. Once you stop the striving, (and notice I did not say "fight" for it) then freedom will simply vanish, sucked into the octopus of the modern-day Money Trust.

I have been blessed with a large international audience. I write from an American-centered viewpoint because that's what I know best, but I'm always trying to find how people in other countries are dealing with their monetary problems and frame concepts in a way that are relevant to people around the world.

These people are interested in freedom. So what is freedom all about? It's humankind's thousand-year struggle to escape serfdom. It's about de-consolidation of power. We've come a long way, but unless we understand that our hard-won freedoms will soon be lost to folks who want to re-consolidate power, all our efforts to maintain freedom will be in vain.

Self-government is all we've got. It's the only thing that allows us to band together and through united effort effectively counter this money monopoly monster that is rapidly dominating every aspect of life, pillaging every nation to the point of extinction. That's why the one thing that angers me more than any other issue – even the money issue – is a growing and general distrust of self government to the point of believing it is no longer valid. I understand why, but I sense Washington, Jefferson, Madison and Henry are all screaming in our ears "Turn this around!"

Self-government is all we've got! A million Americans have given their blood -- their entire lives -- defending this concept. They are all screaming, "What's wrong with you Internet boobs! Get off your keyboards and work, lest our sacrifice be held in vain!"

Here's an example: this guy self-named "USBankruptcy" made a comment on one of my YouTubes which, I'm sure, he felt was mildly supportive:

> Can't get any worse? Congress will print and give it away. But not to you or I.

Well, I'm also sure he didn't expect to be blasted:

> Friend, understand this essential component of human freedom: WE ARE CONGRESS! We get elected every 2 years. WE can fix this. Folks like you who view CONGRESS like the Wizard of Oz -- some remote, intractable, all-powerful body -- will never get anything done. You either understand and believe in self-governance; or you believe in powerless Internet whining leading straight to serfdom. There is no in between. I don't want CONGRESS to give me ANYTHING -- but a stable money system yielding a level playing field -- and a smart salute when I give them an order.

Whether he knows it or not, Mr. *USBankruptcy* is regurgitating an essentially anarchist line. Anarchists are dangerous. The communists and monopolists you can identify. They are just different faces of the same coin – further consolidation of power. History has shown that it's these guys – the anarchists -- who claim to want no power over them who -- when they get their way -- end up having the most repressive powers of all Lord it over them.

It's All About De-Consolidation of Power

Again, government is all we've got to de-consolidate power -- to give some power to us, we, the people. Self-government is a gift of God. Nothing else but our combined effort insisting on the rule of law and a piece of the power pie within the rule of law can possibly maintain just our current level of human freedom. If we want that level of freedom to advance, we have to take back the money power as well.

But no government will ever just <u>grant</u> you power. We have to do it ourselves. We have to teach your children to strive for it. We have to teach them to teach their children. We have to make our government. We have to make our freedom. No one is going to give it to us. We have to claw it back -- continually. The monopolist guys just buy it. They always will. But we have this precious system where we can strive for it -- within the law -- and win it. We can substitute our work for their money. It's a pretty fair deal. But without this governmental framework, no amount of work can substitute for their money.

I'm not a statist, I'm probably -- if anything -- a moderate libertarian. I want minimal government, but I want EVERY BIT of it in my -- in our -- control.

Now we can't all go to Congress, though maybe in the future we can electronically, but if it were up to me, I'd have Congressional elections every weekend. But in lieu of that, every two years is probably good enough.

IMPORTANT NOTE on HyperScan QR:

Some of these HyperScan QR codes (see the two on the next page) are linked to text files that will be very difficult to read on a cell phone screen. If you would prefer to view the HyperScan-enabled content on a PC or Internet-connected TV, or if you have a phone that is web-enabled but

Introduction

has no camera, then simply type into your browser, 7.tv/_ _ _ _, where the four placeholder characters represent the 4 case-sensitive HyperScan QR code characters below each code following "7.tv/". For example, this HyperScan QR code can either be scanned, or typed into your browser: 7.tv/1a23.

URL: 7.tv/1a23

NOTE: We recommend browsers that support geolocation requests, such as *Google Chrome*, *Firefox*, and *Safari*. If you are using Microsoft *Internet Explorer*, you may need to adjust your security settings, or enable Google Toolbar's "My Location" or similar services. Because HyperScan codes are optimized for mobile phones, failure to enable geo-location services may generate a blank page on your PC screen.

Karl Denninger's Annual "Predictions"

So what going happen? How is all this going to unfold? Are we looking at hyperinflation or a deflationary depression? These are tough questions so let's go to one of the experts. Each year, Karl Denninger, founder of "The Market Ticker" (http://market-ticker.org/) issues his annual prediction for the coming calendar year:

URL: 7.tv/1a41   URL: 7.tv/1f2

Above right is an additional HyperScan QR code reserved for additional information from Karl. If nothing shows up, no additional information has yet been provided.

Chapter 1 – The Magic Isle of Guernsey

Once upon a time, there was a little island in the English Channel – much closer to France than to England – called Guernsey. Yes, that's where the Guernsey cow came from. Guernsey cows are famous because their milk has a golden color due to an exceptionally high content of beta-carotene, a source of Vitamin A. And you thought this was to be a book about money? Hold on, we are getting there.

Despite the fact that the island of Guernsey has only 30 square miles and a population of only 65,000 people and very little in the way of natural resources except cows, their per capita income is $40,000 per year, 9th highest among the 200 or so countries of the world. What gives? Guernsey has used a money system since 1817 that can serve as a model for the rest of the world to use to escape the ongoing great depression of 21st century.

To see a map of Guernsey, HyperScan here:

URL: 7.tv/7a83

Despite its proximity to France, Guernsey is actually a British Crown Dependency and, to its credit, has never joined the European Union. After the Napoleonic Wars, Guernsey was in dire economic straits. The island's roads were mere cart tracks, only 54-inches wide. In wet weather they were virtually impassable. There was not a vehicle for hire of any kind on the island. There was no trade, nor much hope of employment among the poor. The sea was washing away large tracts of land due to the sorry state of the dykes.

Guernsey, like most nations at that time (as well as today) had borrowed heavily from banks. The States Debt was £19,137 with an annual interest charge of £2,390, but the gross national revenue of the entire island was only £3,000, leaving only a paltry £610 per annum to run the entire island. In other words, interest paid to banks consumed 80% of the GDP, thus reducing the populace to a state of pitiful serfdom.

In 1815, a Committee of well-respected, public-spirited elders was assembled to finance the building of a Public Market near the main harbor, Saint Peter Port, so the farmers could more easily sell their products for export. The cost of the new facility would be £6,000. In addition, fixing the dykes would cost an additional £10,000.

Further taxation of the impoverished island was impossible. Borrowing the money from the banks would result in even higher interest charges that could never be paid. The Committee made a historic recommendation to remedy this dire situation.

> The Committee recommends that the expense should be met by the issue of States Notes of 1£ Sterling to the value of £6,000 … and that these notes will be available not only for the payment of the new market, but also for Torteval Church, roads to construct, and other expenses of the States….[1]

The Committee argued that there was little to fear from inflation because the local banks already had £50,000 of their money (Notes) in circulation. As a further protection against inflation, the overly cautious citizens of Guernsey placed redemption dates on the notes of April 1817, October 1817, and April 1818. In other words these notes were good for payment of taxes and good as regular money in circulation until the expiration date was reached. At that time, the notes would no longer be legal tender and the State would destroy them.

> In this manner, without increasing the States' debt, it will be possible to finish these works, leaving sufficient money in the Exchequer for other needs."[2]

Once the good citizens realized that these notes would work without the skies falling on the gentle island, additional issues took place in 1820 and 1821. By 1821, some £10,000 of Guernsey Notes was in circulation, all created without debt.

---

[1] Grubiak, Olive and Jan; *The Guernsey Experiment* (1960, 1999 reprint, Bloomfield Books, Sudbury, England), p. 8.
[2] Ibid

> [It was] the most advantageous method of meeting debts, from the point of view both of the public and the States finances. Indeed, the public seemed to realize this fact, and, far from being averse to taking the notes, they sought them out eagerly.

The citizenry clearly understood that these Guernsey Notes were clearly government financing in the public interest. They also realized that if there were to be any inflation as a result, at least it was better than no money at all, and at least they would all shoulder the inflation equally.

In 1824, another £5,000 notes were issued for the markets, and in 1826 £20,000 to erect Elizabeth College and certain other schools.

By 1829, £48,000 worth of Guernsey debt-free Notes was in circulation, and by 1837, over £55,000.

> In the Billet d'Etat it was a frequent subject for congratulation; and it was stated over and over again by eminent men of those times that without the issue of States' notes, important public works, such as roads and buildings could not possibly have been carried out. Yet by means of the States' issue, not only were these works accomplished, but also the Island was not a penny the poorer in interest charges. Indeed, the improvements had stimulated the flow of visitors to the island, and with increased trade, the island enjoyed its newfound prosperity.[3]

In 1826, however, the first signs of opposition by the banking community began. A complaint was lodged with the British Privy Council that Guernsey had no right to issue debt-free notes. However the Guernsey (also known as the "States") Financial Committee explained the situation to the satisfaction of all, and the matter was closed.

The next year, 1827, surprise, surprise, a new commercial bank opened, called "Old Bank". They began printing up private bank notes in such quantity that the island became flooded with money. Soon, Guernsey feared that inflation would set in – or worse – that their own debt-free money experiment would be blamed for the inflation. So a Committee was appointed to confer with the banks. What went on in these meetings remains a mystery to this day; but the result was that £15,000 of Guernsey Notes would be withdrawn from circulation and the government

---

[3] Ibid, p. 8-9

Chapter 1: The Magic Isle of Guernsey

would be limited to issuing a grand total of only £40,000 of their own notes. This agreement remained in force until World War I.

In the wake of World War I, the banks came under severe restrictions on how much money they could issue. All bank money was being directed towards the war effort. But Guernsey was under no such restriction, probably because its experiment was unique, and perhaps forgotten.

Guernsey made good use of her opportunity. By the end of the war, in 1918, Guernsey had issued £142,000, and 40 years later, that had grown to £542,765. Today, private bank notes no longer exist. British money circulates side by side with State Notes.

> Naturally, there is a greater demand for the States Notes; no sane citizen of Guernsey wishes to have his taxes increased to pay debt charges! To enlarge on this theme: In 1937 the States Note money, about £175,000, cost the States only £450 for printing and handling. A loan of the same dimensions would have cost about £11,383 annually. So can you blame the Guernsey taxpayers for preferring their own money since, under their sensible and benevolent financial system they pay hardly any income tax.[4]

> During the entire experiment in Guernsey, from 1817 to date, there has at no time been a threat of inflation from the creation of States Notes. At all times, the States were very careful in the issue and cancellation of notes according to their ability and requirements.[5]

In other words they carefully controlled the quantity of their money in circulation.

> Any visitor to Guernsey is immediately impressed by the vast difference in prices between the island and the mainland in Britain. Thanks to the exceptionally low taxation and import duties, Guernsey enjoys low prices, plenty of money, and a high standard of living. In fact, Guernsey can afford to leave worries about inflation to the debt-ridden mainland![6]

Today, Guernsey remains an island of prosperity. As author Ellen Brown puts it:

---

[4] Ibid, p. 11
[5] Ibid, p. 11-12
[6] Ibid, p. 12

Chapter 1: The Magic Isle of Guernsey

> Guernsey has an income tax, but the tax is relatively low (a "flat" 20 percent), and it is simple and loophole-free. It has no inheritance tax, no capital gains tax, and *no federal debt*. Commercial banks service private [lending], but the government itself never goes into debt. When it wants to create some public work or service, it just issues the money it needs to pay for the work. The Guernsey government has been issuing its own money for nearly two centuries. During that time, the money supply has mushroomed to about 25 times its original size; yet the economy has not been troubled by price inflation, and it has remained prosperous and stable.[7]

Once you understand the Guernsey story, you have to admire the modesty of their website:

> Guernsey's ability to look after its own fiscal affairs has meant that it has been able to foster a favourable tax climate. This has led to many offshore banks, fund managers and insurance companies establishing here. Whilst the traditional industries of flower growing, fishing and dairy farming still play an important part, contributing both to the varied economy and to the island's character.

> Guernsey also has its own stamps and currency, and while British pounds can be used on the island, Guernsey pounds cannot be used in the UK.

But the question may arise, what keeps them from printing too much. They watch inflation closely, and the calculations are all completely transparent, run by a committee of citizens, and open for all to see on their website.

URL: 7.tv/6da2

That's all they care about. Is this causing inflation? They can expand as much as they want as long as it causes no inflation. They don't care about

---

[7] Brown, Ellen H., *Web of Debt*, (Baton Rouge, Louisiana, Third Millennium Press, 2007), p. 100-101.

theory. Born out of desperate need, they found out the secret of money and have quietly gone about using it and thereby have a high standard of living with very low taxes.

Fortunately, the Guernsey experiment is not an aberration. It has been tried time and time again, and when the quantity is controlled in the public interest, always with success. The bankers, however, inevitably attack these in-the-public-interest, debt-free government issues of money. Debt-free money is in everyone's interest except bankers'. Typically, they will use their money and influence to create some financial emergency, then bribe sufficient politicians to convince them to vote for legislation giving the bankers a monopoly on issuing all the nation's money as a loan, thereby stripping the nation of its ability to issue its own money debt free.

This will be a recurring theme in this book. There is a way for citizens and their governments to take back the money-creation power of the banks. Yes, bankers are experts with money, but they are experts in maximizing their profit and rarely have much interest in the public interest. Freeing your government from borrowing money from bankers is the first, and most important step for national freedom and prosperity. It is also THE most important step to limiting governmental overspending. If a government cannot borrow, it MUST live within its means.

Debt-free, government issued money -- where the quantity is properly controlled in the public interest -- has always worked to promote low taxation and maximize freedom for the majority of a nation.

Chapter 2 – Thought Experiment

Dr. Bob Welham is not an economist. By training he is a mathematician and expert in Artificial Intelligence. He loves to demystify the overly complex economics jargon that keeps everyone in a constant state of confusion on this topic of money. I cannot write anything better than the following, authored by Bob:

> To see more clearly the fundamental difference between our current system of debt-based, commercially issued money and the proposed system of debt-free, publicly issued money, many have found it useful to think initially on a smaller scale. The following thought experiment is a variation on the similarly illustrative stories told in *Salvation Island* by Louis Even and *Holocaust Island* by James Gibb Stuart.

Imagine a trading community that organizes its own means of exchange by agreeing mutually that certain authorized, but intrinsically worthless tokens should be used as money. For example, these tokens might be metal coins, hard-to-counterfeit pieces of paper or, if we assume the necessary technology, electronic digits within ultra-secure computer systems. The medium itself doesn't really matter, so long as the money system functions conveniently, safely, transparently and honestly and enables efficient trade in real goods and services to flourish. Importantly, it should not be to the advantage of any special, privileged sector of the community, but should operate in a manner neutral to all economic participants.

As necessary and appropriate, the imagined community increases its money stock by collectively -- and publicly -- creating and spending into circulation new tokens. This is the only way in which new money is created. Any suitable communal infrastructure project or public service provision (e.g. public roads, defence, education, health) that the community agrees upon can be funded using this new money. The creation of new money is carefully and transparently controlled by an accountable public body to be broadly in lockstep with the growth of real wealth, therefore systemic price inflation is not a problem.

Thus the trading community provides itself with an adequate and effective means of exchange with which to conduct its business. No one in particular gains financially from the existence of, or from the nature of, the money stock, and the essential means of exchange for the community. It is a

Chapter 2: Thought Experiment

shared utility, brought into being collectively, which thereafter circulates permanently for the benefit and convenience of all.

Of course, once in circulation, the money might then be lent and borrowed amongst the trading population, as they see fit. However, its origination, its issuance, is not dependent upon it being borrowed into existence. It is issued debt-free by the people, for the people.

The primary functions of banks in this community are then two.

First, they act as custodians of their customers' money, just as the car-parking company at an airport looks after and safeguards cars left in its care.

Second, they act as intermediaries between borrowers and lenders, bringing the parties together and facilitating arrangements between them. They have no power to increase or decrease the quantity of money in circulation – no power to make counterfeit money.

Now, imagine that one day someone, let's call him Mr. Banker, offers to replace, like for like, all the trading community's collectively issued and persistently circulating money-tokens with ones which he alone will henceforth provide. Somehow or other he convinces everyone that his money-tokens are preferable to those currently in use. All that is different is that he lends the money-tokens to members of the community, and charges each borrower interest. This system is called debt-based money, meaning that the money does not enter circulation -- it does not exist -- until someone borrows it, at interest, from Mr. Banker. Rather than provide itself with a permanently circulating money supply, the community now effectively rents its currency from Mr. Banker.

The money stock is the same size as before and economic activity and trading within the community proceed as usual. The big change is that each money-token now comes into circulation only if someone initially borrows it at interest from Mr. Banker. This is the exclusive way in which it enters circulation under his debt-based system. So, for each money-token now in use, someone, somewhere within the community, is paying interest on it to Mr. Banker.

What is the net effect of this new system on the community as a whole? Real wealth production is the same, but Mr. Banker, who now exclusively and profitably issues and lends into circulation the means of exchange, is enjoying a large income from the interest charged. He spends some of his profits and thus consumes a portion of the community's production, hence the sum of everyone else's consumption is correspondingly reduced, though they work and produce just as before. Also he accumulates wealth by retaining and investing some of his income. Under this system there is a built-in and continuous transfer of wealth from the money users to the money issuer-lender, namely Mr. Banker. He also exerts great influence over the economy by deciding who may borrow from him, and how much they may borrow, and <u>inexorably</u> his power within the community grows. To justify this power he professes great expertise in the efficient allocation of money, and claims that his great income is well deserved because he facilitates and promotes real wealth creation as no one else can. Not everyone is so sure and some think that he has merely annexed, monopolized and exploited an essential function formerly performed by the people for themselves at almost no cost.

The money supply has been privatized, and consequently the governing body of the community, which previously used to issue and spend into circulation the money supply for the public good, must now itself borrow at interest the difference between its tax revenue and its expenditure. The autonomy of the now indebted community is severely compromised. It is now subject to the interests of its creditors. Over time, the public debt grows as politicians compete to bribe the electorate with ever more extravagant spending commitments. And who should be consistently at the head of the queue to lend to the government but Mr. Banker? He knows that the government has the power to confiscate money from the economy through taxation, indefinitely into the future, so who better to lend to? Gradually his political influence increases and after a while it seems that the whole economy is being run mainly to service the debts owed to him, rather than primarily to provide the real goods and services that the people need. The financial tail is now wagging the productive dog.

Reality is of course far more complicated and sophisticated than the little scenario above. But the principle is clear – any community or nation that cherishes and wishes to safeguard its sovereignty, its autonomy, must issue its own money, and control the quantity. Handing over these essential functions to profit-motivated private bankers entails a heavy price for society to pay for its means of exchange, a convenience and utility that it could and should provide readily for itself at negligible cost. Also, it cedes enormous political power to the vested interests of the money issuer-lenders, and self-determination is lost.

The Babysitting Circle

Just to drive home the fundamental choice of monetary system with an example on an even smaller scale, imagine a babysitting circle whose member's use mutually agreed but intrinsically worthless tokens to pay each other for babysitting services. The obvious and cost-free way for the circle to issue the tokens is simply to allocate a suitable number of permanently circulating tokens to each member and then let 'trade' proceed. This would obviously work just fine, the tokens could even be lent and borrowed amongst the members if need arose. But now suppose that a couple within the circle comes up with the alternative system that they exclusively should issue the tokens and lend them to all the other members at interest. The system operates more or less as before, but the members notice that, for the bother of a bit of record keeping, the new token issuer-lenders receive back as interest all the tokens that they themselves could possibly need, plus they even accumulate an excess of tokens. By monopolizing the issuance of tokens, and by allowing them into circulation only as interest bearing loans, the couple has secured for themselves an easily earned 'living', not to mention an increasing store of 'wealth'. They themselves have no need to do any actual babysitting and all their own needs are more than covered by the interest payments they receive from the other circle members. At this scale, the unnecessarily expensive and parasitic nature of a debt-based, commercially issued means of exchange is glaringly obvious, and no self-respecting group of babysitters would fall for it. Unfortunately, the same cannot be said at the national level.

Bill Still's new book *No More National Debt* shows how this battle over who controls the money supply has been conducted for real and in deadly earnest throughout the history of banking in the USA. With the passage of the Federal Reserve Act of 1913, it was game, set and match to the private bankers. However, nearly a century later, with the help of the Internet as a medium of mass communication and education, and through the dedicated efforts of Bill and many other money reformers worldwide, there is now a resurgence of interest and understanding of the fundamental problems that come with adopting a debt-based, commercially issued money supply. It appears that because of the exponential growth of debt, the world is now fast approaching a global financial meltdown, and this is concentrating minds. But it really doesn't have to be this way.

Chapter 3 – Stone Money

Our friends in the metallic money crowd tell us that only gold or silver can be money. But what if your nation had no gold or silver? This is a difficult question for the goldbugs to answer. The following little story told by Milton Friedman is about a nation with no access to gold or silver coin, yet a need for a money system beyond barter. Although good arguments can be developed from this story to support both sides of the value-backed question, the astonishing conclusion shows just how short-lived an effective money system can really be.

In 1903, an American anthropologist named William Henry Furness spent several months on the island of Uap (now called Yap), in the Caroline Islands, Micronesia, then a German colony. For a Yap map, HyperScan:

URL: 7.tv/6e34

Upon his return, he reported his interesting findings on the money system of the natives in his book, The Island of Stone Money (1910). Notice how Furness defines money as a "representation of labour".

> As their island yields no metal, they have had recourse to stone; stone, on which labour in fetching and fashioning has been expended, is as truly a representation of labour as the mined and minted coins of civilisation.[8]

> Their medium of exchange they call fei, and it consists of large, solid, thick, stone wheels, ranging in diameter from a foot to twelve feet, having in the centre a hole varying in size with the diameter of the stone, wherein a pole may be inserted sufficiently large and strong to bear the weight and facilitate transportation. These stone "coins" were made from limestone found on an island some four hundred miles distant. They were originally quarried and

---

[8] Friedman, Milton: Money Mischief. (Orlando, FL, Harcourt Brace, 1994), p. 14. Note: the first letter in this sentence – the capital "A" -- is bracketed in Friedman's book. I excluded this distinction for ease of reading.

Chapter 3: Stone Money

shaped [on that island and the product] brought to Uap by some venturesome native navigators, in canoes and on rafts....

A noteworthy feature of this stone currency — is that it is not necessary for its owner to reduce it to possession.[9] After concluding a bargain which involves the price of a fei too large to be conveniently moved, its new owner is quite content to accept the bare acknowledgment of ownership and without so much as a mark to indicate the exchange, the coin remains undisturbed on the former owner's premises.

My faithful old friend, Fatumak, assured me that there was in the village near-by a family whose wealth was unquestioned—acknowledged by every one—and yet no one, not even the family itself, had ever laid eye or hand on this wealth; it consisted of an enormous fei, whereof the size is known only by tradition; for the past two or three generations it had been, and at that very time it was lying at the bottom of the sea! Many years ago an ancestor of this family, on an expedition after fei, secured this remarkably large and exceedingly valuable stone, which was placed on a raft to be towed homeward. A violent storm arose, and the party, to save their lives, were obliged to cut the raft adrift, and the stone sank out of sight. When they reached home, they all testified that the fei was of magnificent proportions and of extraordinary quality, and that it was lost through no fault of the owner, thereupon it was universally conceded in their simple faith that the mere accident of its loss overboard was too trifling to mention, and that a few hundred feet of water off shore ought not to affect its marketable value, since it was all chipped out in proper form. The purchasing power of that stone remains, therefore, as valid as if it were leaning visibly against the side of the owner's house. . . .

For a photo of the Stone Money of Yap, HyperScan:

URL: 7.tv/7dfc

---

[9] Ibid, p. 4

> There are no wheeled vehicles on Uap and, consequently, no cart roads; but there have always been clearly defined paths communicating with the different settlements When the German Government assumed the ownership of The Caroline Islands, after the purchase of them from Spain in 1898, many of these paths or highways were in bad condition, and the chiefs of the several districts were told that they must have them repaired and put in good order. The roughly dressed blocks of coral were, however, quite good enough for the bare feet of the natives; and many were the repetitions of the command, which still remained un-heeded. At last it was decided to impose a fine for disobedience on the chiefs of the districts. In what shape was the fine to be levied? ... At last, by a happy thought, the fine was exacted by sending a man to every failu and pabai throughout the disobedient districts, where he simply marked a certain number of the most valuable fei with a cross in black paint to show that the stones were claimed by the government. This instantly worked like a charm; the people, thus dolefully impoverished, turned to and repaired the highways to such good effect from one end of the island to the other, that they are now like park drives. Then the government dispatched its agents and erased the crosses. Presto! the fine was paid, the happy failus resumed possession of their capital stock, and rolled in wealth, (pp. 93, 96-100)."[10]

Dr. Friedman then goes on to explain how modern versions of money are similarly ephemeral.

> The ordinary reader's reaction, like my own, will be: "How silly. How can people be so illogical?" However, before we criticize too severely the innocent people of Yap, it is worth contemplating an episode in the United States to which the islanders might well have that same reaction. In 1932-33, the Bank of France feared that the United States was not going to stick to the gold standard at the traditional price of $20.67 an ounce of gold. Accordingly, the French bank asked the Federal Reserve Bank of New York to convert into gold a major part of the dollar assets that it had in the United States. To avoid the necessity of shipping the gold across the ocean, the Federal Reserve Bank was requested simply to store the gold on the Bank of France's account. In response, officials of the Federal Reserve Bank went to their gold vault, put in separate drawers the correct amount of gold ingots, and put a label, or mark, on those drawers indicating that the contents were the property of the French. For all it matters, the drawers could have been

---

[10] Ibid, p. 4-5.

Chapter 3: Stone Money

marked "with a cross in black paint," just as the Germans had marked the stones.

The result was headlines in the financial newspapers about "the loss of gold," the threat to the American financial system, and the like. U.S. gold reserves were down, French gold reserves up. The markets regarded the U.S. dollar as weaker, the French franc as stronger. The so-called drain of gold by France from the United States was one of the factors that ultimately led to the banking panic of 1933.

Is there really a difference between the Federal Reserve Bank's believing that it was in a weaker monetary position because of some marks on drawers in its basement and the Yap islanders' belief that they were poorer because of some marks on their stone money? Or between the Bank of France's belief that it was in a stronger monetary position because of some marks on drawers in a basement more than three thousand miles away and the Yap family's conviction that it was rich because of a stone under the water some hundred or so miles away? For that matter, how many of us have literal personal direct assurance of the existence of most of the items we regard as constituting our wealth? What we more likely have are entries in a bank account, property certified by pieces of paper called shares of stocks, and so on and on.

The Yap islanders regarded as a concrete manifestation of their wealth stones quarried and shaped on a distant island and brought to their own. For a century and more, the civilized world regarded as a concrete manifestation of its wealth a metal dug from deep in the ground, refined at great labor, transported great distances, and buried again in elaborate vaults deep in the ground. Is the one practice really more rational than the other?[11]

What both examples—and numerous additional ones that could be listed—illustrate is how important appearance or illusion or "myth," given unquestioned belief, becomes in monetary matters. Our own money, the money we have grown up with, the system under which it is controlled, these appear "real" and "rational" to us. Yet the money of other countries often seems to us like paper or worthless metal, even when the purchasing power of individual units is high.

---

[11] Ibid, p. 5-7.

Chapter 3: Stone Money

According to Dr. Ralph Byrns, Professor of Economics at the University of North Carolina Chapel Hill the limestone wheels of Yap – known as Rai stones -- are still used today for traditional transactions such as dowries and land transactions and have been used for over 15 centuries:

> The Yap money supply is easily the most stable anywhere in the world – despite demands from foreign collectors and museums, about 6,600 of the stones remain on the island. But there are disadvantages. Conventional bankers are unwilling to deal with the stones, so stone money cannot earn interest.[12]

Value-money advocates claim that only precious metals can represent the labor of the citizens, and colorful paper receipts cannot. Obviously this is not the case. Wouldn't the agreement of the citizens of Guernsey to print additional colorful paper notes based on nothing but the good faith and credit of the nation, be a representation of the national labor as well? Obviously they worked just as well or better than paint marks on an immovable rock.

The argument is that the quantity of these rocks is easy to control because they take so much labor to produce. So then, the question becomes, "is humanity -- under any conditions -- capable of controlling the quantity of a money system?" Or even more fundamentally, "is humanity capable of self governance at all" or are we simply doomed to be ruled by economic tyrants. If the latter is the case, then we might as well dissolve Parliaments worldwide right now and be resigned to our fate. Or would you prefer to teach your children of the importance of keeping the struggle for freedom alive?

History has shown that humans are capable of controlling their economic destinies, but not unless they understand that the money system is the PRIMARY and BASIC attack point of those who would enslave us all.

---

[12] Copyright 2011, EconomicsInteractive.com. Used with permission of Dr. Ralph Byrns from: http://www.unc.edu/depts/econ/byrns_web/Economicae/Essays/Focus/Comm_Money.htm

Chapter 4 - Economic Myths

There is absolutely no hope of fixing the U.S. economy -- or for that matter that of any other nation – primarily because of three great misconceptions. The economic problems that most people became aware of in the fall of 2008 are not reversing. Unemployment is still rising. Foreclosures are still rising. The world's economic death spiral into a deflationary depression must continue until the real problem is addressed.

Our entire global economic system is at a tipping point and nothing – nothing – can rescue it short of the basic reforms presented in this book. Nothing less than the survival of our species depends on this:

URL: 7.tv/8e1f

When it finally becomes apparent that the previously employed solutions will not work, people in every nation will demand new solutions – solutions outside the economic thinking that governments have tried to keep us focused on since the "Great Depression" of the 1930s.

If you only read two more pages of this book, let me set you straight on these three great misconceptions, because until a majority of the voters of any nation understands that these three popular notions are false, we cannot hope to fix our economies:

- Reducing our governmental spending is NOT a politically viable solution. Any reductions will be temporary because the national debt is now compounding at an unsustainable rate. A far more important and more basic change is needed.
- Ending the Fed is NOT the solution.
- Returning to gold-backed money is NOT the solution.

Briefly, here's why.

Misconception #1: Spending Reductions – Austerity

Every day you hear it a dozen times on television: we must reduce government spending. While reducing governmental spending is important, it is only a symptom of the real problem. The problem is that all of our money is created out of debt – every bit of it. Every dollar in your pocket, every dime spent by any government anywhere is created as an interest-bearing debt. The stark reality is that if we could reduce our debt -- since all our money is debt – we would be reducing our money supply, and no politician is going to do anything to further reduce the amount of money in the system in the middle of a deflationary depression.

Reducing our budget deficit to zero – a balanced budget -- is a laudable goal, even if politically impossible, but the reason it is good is that it minimizes the growth of the interest on the rapidly accumulating national debt. That's the 800-pound gorilla in the room that nobody talks about, because no one understands what it is or how it got there. So, in order to make things more clear, we need to focus on the interest that debt generates – and the control that the interest payments generate. Even the conservative estimates of the Congressional Budget Office predict that interest payments on the U.S. national debt will exceed $1 trillion per year in the near future. That's about what the entire discretionary budget of Congress is today.

As we will show, those interest payments are ENTIRELY UNNECESSARY!

Misconception #2: Ending the Fed

When we were editing my first film on the economy in 1995, *The MoneyMasters*, I decided that I really should have a professor of economics take a look at it to be sure I hadn't made any significant mistakes. I've been a reporter all my life and so I know how to get in touch with university professors for comments.

So I dialed up the Stanford University Press Office and told them I had a documentary on economics and needed a comment from Nobel Prize winning economist, Professor Milton Friedman. The next day, *ring, ring*; it

Chapter 4: Economic Myths

was Milton Friedman – then aged 84 -- on the phone. He graciously gave me his home address and I overnighted him the first cut of the film.

A couple of days later, *ring, ring*; Milton Friedman called back. I'll never forget his first words: "Boy, if you kill the Fed and don't kill fractional reserve lending, you've done nothing."

He, of course, understood the problem much more deeply than I ever will. He explained that it wasn't the Fed that was the problem; it was the money creation power of the commercial banks. He told me to put more emphasis on stabilizing the quantity. His preferred method was to have the amount of money tied to the population, but if there was some way to peg it reliably to GDP, that would suffice. More on this later.

Here is the Friedman quote we used on *The MoneyMasters* website:

> As you know, I am entirely sympathetic with the objectives of your Monetary Reform Act...You deserve a great deal of credit for carrying through so thoroughly on your own conception...
>
> Best wishes, Milton Friedman, Nobel Laureate in Economics; Senior Fellow, Hoover Institution on War, Revolution and Peace[13]

Misconception #3: Gold-Backed Money

Gold is not the answer. Gold is the problem. Invest in gold all you want, but don't tie your national money to it. History has clearly shown that doesn't work. It has ALWAYS worked against freedom and governance by self-determination. There has never been a time in the last thousand years when gold money has worked to enrich the middle class, reduce serfdom, and empower freedom.

Is gold reliable and free from manipulation? Heck no! Ask anyone who follows that market regularly. It is awash in manipulation, and even out and out fraud.

Some will argue that silver-backed money is the answer because that's what William Jennings Bryan campaigned on in 1896. Silver was a BETTER solution at that time, but as we will show, what was in place was

---

[13] http://www.themoneymasters.com/

a gold-backed system, which was horrible. Backing a national money with anything of value, known as "metalism", only allows the richest folks, the biggest bankers, to corner the market on that commodity. Look what the Hunt Brothers did in 1979-80. See Chapter 16 for details.

I respect Ron Paul. He has correctly identified some of the problems with the economy – big bankers are in control of the QUANTITY of money in our system; but his solution – a return to gold backing for our money -- is wrong and will lead us to yet another disaster. We were on the "gold standard" during the Great Depression of the 1930s. As you will see in later chapters, leading economists banded together and tried to warn President Roosevelt, but he ignored their pleas. That allowed the big bankers to prolong the suffering as they bought up America's assets for pennies on the dollar. Sound familiar? The same thing happened with the previous major depression in the U.S. – the post-Civil-War depression -- which was twice as deep and 3 times as long. When will we ever learn?

Milton Friedman on Money

> What determines the particular item that will be used as money? We have no satisfactory general answer to that simple question....
>
> When most money consisted of silver or gold or some other item that had a nonmonetary use ... the "metallist" fallacy arose that "it is logically essential for money to consist of, or be 'covered' by, some commodity so that the logical source of the exchange value or purchasing power of money is the exchange value or purchasing power of that commodity, considered independently of its monetary role" (Schumpeter 1954, p. 288}.
>
> The examples of the stone money of Yap, of cigarettes in Germany after World War II, and of paper money currently make clear that this "metallist" view is a fallacy.[14]

Remember, gold is *concentrated* wealth.

Albert Einstein on Gold Money

On November 7, 1931, German physicist Albert Einstein wrote a letter to the editor of the prestigious German-language, anti-Nazi newspaper *Berliner Tageblatt*. Though it was never published, the letter resides in the

---

[14] Friedman, Milton: *Money Mischief*. (Orlando, FL, Harcourt Brace, 1994), p. 14.

Chapter 4: Economic Myths

Einstein Archives. Einstein had won the 1921 Nobel Prize in Physics and at this time was a professor at the Berlin Academy of Sciences. Einstein's "general theory of relativity" is symbolized by the 20th century's best-known equation: $E=mc^2$. His name – Einstein -- became synonymous with genius.

Seeing the depression deepen worldwide, Einstein had deduced that gold money was the problem and even proposed – in basic form -- the correct solution:

> The gold standard has, in my opinion, the serious disadvantage that a shortage in the supply of gold automatically leads to a contraction of credit and also of the amount of currency in circulation....
>
> The natural remedies to our troubles are, in my opinion.... Control of the amount of money in circulation and of the volume of credit in such a way as to keep the price level steady, abolishing any monetary standard.[15]

Exactly right! Only 18 months later, In May 1933 Einstein, a non-practicing Jew, had his books burned in the Nazi book burnings, as Nazi propaganda minister Joseph Goebbles proclaimed, "Jewish intellectualism is dead." Einstein learned that his name was on a list of assassination targets, with a "$5,000 bounty on his head".

> One German magazine included him in a list of enemies of the German regime with the phrase, "not yet hanged".[16]

Einstein fled Germany in 1933 along with 14 other Nobel laureates and settled in at Princeton University. He was instrumental in convincing FDR that Hitler was working on an atomic bomb.

The World Is Crying Out for a Solution

It never ceases to amaze me how much folks around the world study the history of America's struggle against this debt money system of the big

---

[15] Rowe, David E. & Shulmann, Robert J.: *Einstein on Politics* (Princeton, New Jersey, Princeton University Press, 1977), p. 418.
[16] Isaacson, Walter: *Einstein: His Life and the Universe.* (New York, Simon & Schuster, 2007), p. 407-410.

Chapter 4: Economic Myths

banks. They still look to the U.S. to lead them out of the financial wilderness to freedom.

The problem with the economy of every nation on earth has the same root – national debt – debt that is totally unnecessary. The good citizens of Sweden, Germany and Iceland recently invited me to speak in their nations. Here is a bumper sticker design and a t-shirt design we made for my Iceland trip of June 2010.

Don't get me wrong; I'm not into debt repudiation, though it can be done. It worked in Argentina in the late 1980s, but it is probably not necessary in the U.S. All nations can get out of debt and not incur any more debt. Any nation that did this would immediately stabilize their economic situation -- that is, incur neither significant inflation, nor deflation – by design. Human societies run best on stability – a stable economic platform – one that can be predicted in the long term. Once the money power is taken away from the big banks and returned into the hands of we, the people, then economic common sense can return, and the nation's legislature can once again become responsive to the voting electorate instead of to the bankers. Once that is achieved, especially in a large nation, others will soon follow.

One additional set of benefits; this solution would fix most of the following world problems:

- Hunger
- Poverty
- Misery, and
- Disease

Chapter 4: Economic Myths

In other words, what we need is a new human rights movement for the next generation based upon No More National Debt.

Chapter 5 – Problem With *End The Fed*

Congressman Ron Paul believes the cure for keeping America out of a depression is to end the Federal Reserve System and replace it with a return to gold-backed money.

URL: 7.tv/23db

I have met Dr. Paul, as you can see from this picture (HyperScan above) taken in Oct. 2009. Personally and professionally, I think he's an honest man, a man of principle. He is a man who has struggled nearly alone in Congress against this monster that theoretically "controls" how much money there is in our system.

However, his latest book, *End The Fed*, contains some crucial errors that will not steer our system away from its inevitable economic death spiral. These errors cannot be allowed to stand unchallenged in the popular literature or we will be dooming our children to remake the same mistakes made by earlier generations. Again, as Milton Friedman said:

> If you end the Fed and don't do something about fractional reserve banking, you've done nothing.

What does that mean? It took me quite a while to figure it out. It means that the focus shouldn't be on the Fed. It should be on the National Debt. If you kill the Fed and don't kill the National Debt, you've done nothing. If you kill the National Debt problem, you will automatically have to bring full attention to fixing the fractional reserve lending problem. Eliminating National Debt means issuing debt-free U.S. Notes once again. Once the nation sees that it can create its own money without debt, it will become obvious that we no longer need to borrow it from banks.

Dr. Paul also wants to return America to a gold money system. But haven't we tried that before? Yes. It's been tried time and time again both

Chapter 5: Problem With *End The Fed*

in the U.S. and in other nations. It fixes nothing. It doesn't work. It does not support stability. It does not support sovereignty. It does not support freedom.

Dr. Paul is also for "sound money." I am for sound money, too. But sound money doesn't have to be gold or silver. "Sound money" really means that the quantity is controlled by the government in the public interest. In economics, it's all about stability. Dr. Paul appears to sincerely believe that gold money will control the quantity. I think American monetary history alone shows this to be false.

So, it's not <u>what</u> backs our money that is important; it's <u>who</u> controls its quantity. When deciding who will control the quantity of money, there are only two choices:

1. Private banks (the system we have today); or
2. You – the voting electorate – by electing your representatives.

Right now commercial banks get to issue the vast majority of our money – except for coins – as a debt. Other than coins, and a few U.S. Notes (Lincoln's old Greenbacks) – which are still legal tender, by the way -- we don't have a debt-free national money. We rent our money – at interest -- from banks.

History has shown that civilizations just can't endure this type of money system for long. That's why the Sumerians created the Jubilee Year. Every 50 years debts were forgiven. It resets the debt clock and allows civilization to NOT be crushed by debt.

For more information on the Jubilee Year, HyperScan this:

URL: 7.tv/31b6

When Gold is Money

History has also shown time and time again that when gold is money, that hasn't fixed this debt problem.

- We were on a gold-backed system just before the American Revolution, during the Stamp Act depression.
- We were on a gold-backed system during the deepest depression in American history, the 30-year-long, post-Civil-War depression.
- We were on a gold-backed system during the crash of 1929.

In a gold money system, bankers own most of the gold and they just manipulate the amount of gold they loan out, thereby controlling the quantity of money and the politics of the nation as well.

Remember, gold is *concentrated* wealth.

Winston Churchill - 1932

Winston Churchill, as Chancellor of the Exchequer, reintroduced the gold standard in 1925. In 1932, Churchill testified the following, before the House of Commons:

> When I was moved by many arguments and forces in 1925 to return to the gold standard, I was assured by the highest experts, and our experts are men of great ability and of indisputable integrity and sincerity, that we were anchoring ourselves to reality and stability, and I accepted their advice. I take for myself and my colleagues of other days whatever degree of blame and burden for having accepted their advice.

> But what happened? We have had no reality, no stability. The price of gold has risen since then by more than 70 per cent. That is as if a 12-inch foot rule had been stretched to 19 or 20 inches.... Look at what this has meant to everybody who has been compelled to execute their contracts upon this irrationally enhanced scale. Look at the gross unfairness of such distortion to all producers of new wealth, and to all that labour and science and enterprise can give us. Look at the enormously increased volume of commodities which have to be created in order to pay off the same mortgage debt or loan. Minor fluctuation might well be ignored, but I say quite seriously that this monetary convulsion has now reached a pitch where

Chapter 5: Problem With *End The Fed*

I am persuaded that the producers of new wealth will not tolerate indefinitely so hideous an oppression. . . .

I therefore point to this evil, and to the search for the method's of remedying it as the first, second and third of all the problems which should command and rivet our thoughts.[17]

So, our real economic problem is a quantity issue – who controls the quantity. Where Dr. Paul and I agree is that Dr. Paul and the supporters of gold-backed money have correctly identified this as the problem – that the QUANTITY of money is being manipulated for the benefit of bankers, not for the benefit of we, the people.

Where we differ is how to fix it. That's what this book is all about.

NO MORE NATIONAL DEBT

If governments couldn't borrow, they would have to control their spending. Every time they wanted to spend more, they would have to suffer the wrath of the voters by either immediately:

1. Raising taxes to pay for the extra spending, or by
2. Cutting current spending so that money could be freed up for the new spending, or
3. By printing additional debt-free government-issued money. This, of course, would be done with the full knowledge of the American people as it would increase the supply of money and thereby reduce the value of everyone's money.

Simple!

In today's system, politicians can kick the can down the road by borrowing – by increasing the national debt – and passing the repayment problem (along with the compounding interest) along to the next generation.

If governments couldn't borrow, they would have to issue their own money without incurring debt, instead of borrowing the national money into existence, as we do today. Since the inception of the Federal

---

[17] House of Commons, 1944, vol. 399, Parliamentary Debates, Great Britain. Parliament.

Reserve, the government only creates about 3% of the nation's money – the coins. Coins are the only form of debt-free money today. What government can't raise in taxes, it must borrow – primarily from banks.

The truth is that governments don't need to borrow. Throughout history, nations have discovered this secret – sovereign governments can just create their money, debt free, and unless they are suicidal, control the quantity themselves. Ending the national debt system will put the money power squarely in the hands of Congress. The only reasonable argument against this system is that Congress – if given this, the MOST IMPORTANT power of any sovereign – will abuse it – by printing and spending too much money.

So the question is, "Once Congress has this power, how do we control their spending?" Different people have different ideas on how to control the appetite of Congress, but to say that Congress is too corrupt to have this, the mightiest power of a sovereign nation – is to not believe in the basic concept of an elected government at all. You would either have to believe in anarchy – no government at all – or plutocracy – government by banks – essentially the system we have today.

If you believe in our system - a Constitutional Republic - you have to believe that the money power must go into the hands of we, the people, via our closest elected representatives; an elected government that is then held accountable by we, the people.

Therefore, we have no alternative but to take back the money power away from the Fed and restore it into the hands of Congress, where it properly belongs. This power is specifically granted to Congress, and Congress alone, in *Article 1, Section 8* of the U.S. Constitution:

> The Congress shall have Power ... To coin Money, regulate the Value thereof....

If that money is actual gold or silver metal, then regulating its value could mean being sure of the purity and weight of the coin money; but as we will see in *Chapter 14*, the term "coin" had a much broader definition 200 years ago: for example the term "to coin a phrase." Clearly the term "coin" refers to a broader definition of money than the "metalists" would have us believe. The founding fathers of that era were familiar with many different

Chapter 5: Problem With *End The Fed*

kinds of money; precious metal coin, copper, bronze, zinc, several different kinds of paper money, bank account entries, and now, electronic money -- and there is only one way to regulate the value of these many forms of money – by controlling its quantity. This is the case I will make in this book.

In Search of Dr. Paul

In the past year, I've made several attempts to get Dr. Paul to sit down and talk, so that we could come to a consensus on what should be done to fix the problem. I've been to his office and left messages and even emailed his staffers. No luck.

In October of 2009, I attended the 35th anniversary of the Conservative Caucus, held in Rosslyn, Virginia. Dr. Paul would be speaking, and I hoped to finally meet him there.

URL: 7.tv/04c4

I was successful. He graciously posed for the picture above. I asked for a follow-up meeting and he handed me his card, but it took six months before his staffer finally responded:

March 31, 2010

Mr. Still,

I received a copy of an email you had sent to Dr. Paul requesting a meeting about the Audit the Fed movement. You had hoped to try to get on the same page as Dr. Paul regarding auditing the Fed, and I was wondering if there were any questions you might have that I could answer.

Chapter 5: Problem With *End The Fed*

Paul-Martin Foss
Legislative Assistant
Office of Congressman Ron Paul
203 Cannon HOB
Washington, DC 20515

Here was my response:

March 31, 2010

Mr. Foss,

I hold Dr. Paul in high esteem. My wife -- who is also a physician -- and I met Dr. Paul at the 35th Anniversary Gala of the Conservative Caucus. I asked him for an appointment so that we could discuss our differences. I know that at some point we are going to bump heads on this issue. I'd like to make that bump as congenial as possible. For example, I believe we are speaking at a function put on by Baylor University together -- but Dr. Paul will speak the day before I will.

My line is "Goldbugs are our friends. They have correctly identified the problem -- that the quantity of money is out of control. They just think gold will control that quantity and it won't."

My take is that gold money systems only put control of the quantity in the hands of the biggest bankers -- the largest owners of gold. It has NEVER done anything to promote true freedom for the average Joe, and help continue humankind's escape from serfdom. My latest documentary "The Secret of Oz" focuses on proving this point.

Critics try to claim that my solution is to provide the world with an endless supply of non-gold-backed, inflationary money, which Dr. Paul refers to as "fiat" money. Of course, the real meaning of "fiat" is derived from the Latin root meaning, "let it be done." In other words ANY money declared to be money by the state is, by definition, fiat money. Most government-issued gold coins are fiat money.

This criticism of my position is not correct. My solution is simple and two-fold:

Chapter 5: Problem With *End The Fed*

U.S. money in the form of U.S. Notes should be created by the state, debt-free. Federal Reserve Notes -- and their electronic equivalents -- debt money -- would be abolished. This, of course, would mean the money creation powers of the commercial banks and the Fed would be abolished.

Government borrowing would also be abolished. If governments wanted to spend, they would have to tax, not kick the can down the road for future generations. This would have to be specifically prohibited by Constitutional amendment, repealing the specific language of Article 1, Section 8 of the Constitution: "To borrow Money on the credit of the United States".

But now with the money power firmly in the hands of Congress, how could we keep Congress from creating and spending too much money?

By one of three basic methods:

- By Constitutional Amendment. The quantity of money per capita would be stated. That means the money supply would increase only with population; or
- The quantity would be controlled by we, the people through our closest federally elected representatives of our Republic -- namely, Congress. This would mean that this quantity issue would have to become the primary issue in every Congressional election; or
- An independent board or Monetary Authority comprised of elected representatives from each of the 50 states would receive inflation targets set by Congress and then print enough money for Congress to spend into existence as to fall within these targets. Congress would not determine the quantity. It would only determine the amount of growth that should be a target. This would separate the money power in line with the separation of powers concept inherent in the rest of the U.S. Constitution.

Now, Dr. Paul makes justifiable arguments against giving this power to Congress. He fears Congress can't be controlled from printing too much, particularly in order to help themselves gain perpetual re-election. His argument is understandable; however if we are going to have an elected government, then, by definition, we have to control it. We can do it. We must do it! Congress is all we've got. If you don't trust yourself to control the most important power of a sovereign, then whom will you trust? The market? That's what gold advocates typically say. What they don't seem to understand is that a privately controlled quantity of money is essentially what we've had since 1913, and it has brought this Republic to the brink of financial ruination.

Ron Paul's Book, "End The Fed"

Dr. Paul makes some EXCELLENT points in his book; yet, some are not so good, including a horrible misinterpretation of the Constitution. I won't go through them all, but here are just the first few examples:

> Page 2: "...civilizations literally rise and fall based on the quality of their money...."
>
> **Response**: No. It's only the QUANTITY and who is controlling that quantity. Ideally, money should be valueless and ubiquitous. That's the only way to prevent the largest banks and commodity traders from buying up the "basis" of a commodity-backed money.
>
> Page 7: "Without the Fed, the federal government would have to live within its means."
>
> **Response**: No, it's not the Fed. The money creation power HAS to be taken away from the commercial banks. As Prof. Milton Friedman told me in a phone call he made providing guidance for my first documentary, *The MoneyMasters*: "Boy, if you end the Fed and do nothing about fractional reserve banking, you've done nothing."
>
> Page 8: Dr. Paul frequently says things like this: "... the illusory world created by the unlimited printing of money."
>
> **Response**: Money is not simply printed. If that were true, our problems would be easier to solve. Our money is borrowed into existence, not from the Fed, but from the largest commercial banks and central banks in the world.
>
> Page 14: "... privatized profits and socialized losses."
>
> **Response**: Yes! Couldn't agree more.

Chapter 5: Problem With *End The Fed*

Page 18: "It also explains why the Constitution placed a ban on paper money and permitted only gold and silver as money."

Response: This is the most egregious error in this book -- a complete misinterpretation of the Constitution. Paul completely leaves out that paying in gold and silver coin was only for State governments -- and on top of that, this section has been completely ignored over the years. There is NO PLACE in the Constitution that places a ban on paper money and the U.S. Supreme Court has ruled as much.

To see the definitive ruling, Julliard v. Greenman, 1884:

URL: 7.tv/26bc

So that's just a sample. I want to be as kind as possible to Dr. Paul. For many years he has been the only one in Congress who has the gall to attack the Fed openly. He's the ONLY one who has stood in the breach for years and years. I do not want to hurt him or diminish his credibility. I just want to discuss our differences face to face, or in an open forum, and come to as much consensus as possible.

I think the crux of our difference is that Dr. Paul thinks gold can control the quantity and no form of self-government can. I think history belies this belief. I think only Congress can perform this, the most important of functions of a sovereign nation – probably through an independent Monetary Authority that would oversee the actual creation and maintenance of the quantity of money in the system. Additionally, until you recognize that the core of the problem as the impact of compounding interest from the National Debt, you can't possibly propose a correct solution. Additionally, if you don't end the private money creation power of the big New York money center banks, then you have accomplished nothing.

My letter to Mr. Foss was never answered. It may be that as the system continues to collapse, Dr. Paul may yet get his way with a gold-backed money – at least on the international level. Here we see that World Bank President Robert Zoellick, is certainly calling for it.

World Bank President Supports Gold Backing

Reuters 1:44am EST, November 8, 2010

SINGAPORE (Reuters) - Leading economies should consider readopting a modified global gold standard to guide currency movements, said World Bank president Robert Zoellick.

Writing in the *Financial Times*, Zoellick said a "Bretton Woods II" system of floating currencies is needed to replace the Bretton Woods fixed-exchange rate regime that broke down in the early 1970s.

Zoellick called for a system that "is likely to need to involve the dollar, the euro, the yen, the pound and (Yuan) that moves towards internationalisation and then an open capital account."

He added: "The system should also consider employing gold as an international reference point of market expectations about inflation, deflation and future currency values."

I wonder if this pleases Dr. Paul, or any of his followers, to know that their fondest dreams are now supported at the international level, by the President of the World Bank?

Ron Paulisms – Updated

- December 14, 2010 – CNBC:

URL: 7.tv/28cf

Chapter 5: Problem With *End The Fed*

Cong. Ron Paul:

"The Federal Reserve is a cartel. They get to print the money.... The Constitution really doesn't give them that authority. The Constitution says that only gold and silver can be legal tender."

Comment: Absolutely incredible! Just how many completely false statements does a politician have to make per minute before a news anchor – especially a financial news anchor -- will challenge you? Obviously more than three. Doesn't this CNBC anchor even understand the meaning of the only two, short sections in the Constitution that pertain to money?

Until the so-called "quantitative easing" where the Fed started "buying" U.S. Treasury securities with electronic digits created literally out of thin air, the Fed did not "print" – or create -- money. The Fed's job is to try to control how much money the banks create and make it appear that they have that situation under control. Well, how's that working out for us -- we, the people?

As far as Dr. Paul's interpretation of the Constitution, the Fed is not given the authority to "print" money, but the U.S. Government certainly is, according to several U.S. Supreme Court rulings. The Constitution was written in 1787, 126 years before the passage of the Federal Reserve Act. But, privately owned central banks – which is exactly what the Fed is – were chartered by Congress three times before the Fed came into existence:

- 1781 – the Bank of North America
- 1790 with the First Bank of the United States, and
- 1812 with the Second Bank of the United States.

As far as Dr. Paul's oft-repeated claim that only gold and silver can be legal tender, that is just patently untrue. See the Julliard v. Greenman decision of 1884, earlier. Dr. Paul knows this. Why he insists on claiming that gold and silver are the only choices for legal tender becomes increasingly difficult to understand.

Alan Greenspan Supports Gold-Backed Money

Metalists have another supporter, former Federal Reserve Chairman Alan Greenspan.

In the interview, the host, David Asman, asked Greenspan:

Asman: So then, why do we need a central bank?

> Greenspan: Well, the question is a very interesting one. We have at this particular stage a fiat money, which is essentially money printed by a government, and it's usually the central bank which is authorized to do so...."

Wrong, Mr. Greenspan! Although one might be able to argue that Ron Paul really doesn't understand the system, that cannot be said for Mr. Greenspan. The vast majority of American money – except for coins and Federal Reserve notes -- is not printed by the government. It is created as electronic digits by commercial banks. Well over 95% of all money is created this way – all done completely outside of effective Congressional control. Furthermore, until 2010, the central bank did not create (or "print") U.S. money. Their function – theoretically -- was to attempt to regulate how much money the commercial banks were creating electronically. In 2010, that changed when the Federal Reserve announced that it was "monetizing the debt". In other words, they began creating money directly by buying U.S. bonds in the open market and paying for them with their own electronic digits created entirely out of nothing.

Now, let's return to Mr. Greenspan's comments:

> Some mechanism has got to be in place that restricts the amount of money which is produced – either a gold standard, a currency board, or something of that nature, because unless you do that, all of history suggests that inflation will take hold with very deleterious effects on economic activity....

What is VERY interesting in this sentence is that Mr. Greenspan correctly identifies another alternative – the alternative which we in the monetary reform community support – "a currency board" – as he puts it. But putting that aside for the moment, let's go on with his pronouncement regarding the effectiveness of gold backing for money:

> There are numbers of us, myself included, who strongly believe that we did very well in the 1870 to 1914 period with an international gold standard.

But "very well" for whom? Yes, it did control the quantity of money. It worked great for bankers, but the broad, general population suffered horribly for lack of money to supply the rapidly expanding population and rapidly expanding American economy as the nation industrialized. We will go into greater detail, in later chapters of this book. You can watch the entire 107-second Greenspan interview at:

URL: 7.tv/25be

Gresham's Law

Metalists love to cite Gresham's Law as a reason why gold should be money. Monetary reformer Dr. Bob Welham explains:

> Gresham's Law states that commodity currency of relatively low intrinsic value ("bad money") will drive out commodity currency of higher intrinsic value ("good money"), if they are of equal nominal value. Coins are clipped, faked, forged and so on and, if there is scope for such profitable cheating, then invariably it will happen. The way completely to avoid Gresham's Law is to have non-commodity currency with zero intrinsic value, backed by strong anti-counterfeiting laws and enforcement to safeguard its integrity. Gresham's Law weighs in favour of an intrinsically valueless currency – no further reduction in intrinsic value from zero is possible.[18]

---

[18] Personal email dated Dec. 24, 2010.

Chapter 6 - The False Solution

The Austrian Solution and Ludwig von Mises

At the core of the gold-backed money crowd is the Ludwig von Mises Institute. Mises was an Austrian economist who had a profound influence on the free-market libertarian crowd in the United States. Now there is nothing wrong with free markets, if they are really free – certainly not what we have today, and especially not what we have had for the last 10 years. There is nothing wrong with what's called "classical libertarianism," a movement that supports the minimal amount of government interference that is practical to still hold anarchy and chaos at bay.

The problem with Mises is most, but not all, of what he said was true. In fact, he is credited with ripping socialist economic systems to shreds and with the fall of the Polish socialist economic system in the 1980s, Mises was hailed as having been right all along by former socialist economists. Prominent socialists, such as Robert Heilbroner, admitted publicly that "Mises was right" all along (the phrase "Mises was Right" was the title of a panel at the annual 1990 meeting of the Southern Economic Association at New Orleans).

In his 1922 work, *Socialism: An Economic and Sociological Analysis*, Mises stated:

> The only certain fact about Russian affairs under the Soviet regime with regard to which all people agree is: that the standard of living of the Russian masses is much lower than that of the masses in the country which is universally considered as the paragon of capitalism, the United States of America. If we were to regard the Soviet regime as an experiment, we would have to say that the experiment has clearly demonstrated the superiority of capitalism and the inferiority of socialism.[19]

So, this is good stuff, and exactly correct. In addition, Mises warned the world that the widely trumpeted "New Era" of permanent prosperity of the "Roaring 1920s" was merely a bubble created by too much money being

---

[19] "Socialism: An Economic and Sociological Analysis" by Ludwig von Mises. *Biography of Ludwig von Mises*

Chapter 6: The False Solution

created by banks and that it would result in a bank panic and depression. All this he predicted 20 years before he came to America.

What Mises should have seen was that America was already on a gold money standard, so it should have been obvious that gold money was not the answer for control of the national money supply in the public interest. Also, his view of the American system is premised upon a near fairy-tale notion of the existence of a "free" market, when, as we will show in this book, the "Money Trust" monopoly has completely dominated the "free" market since the American Civil War.

Mises also opposed solutions like propping up prices or wage rates, rightly saying they would make the situation worse. He opposed encouragement of consumer spending as a curative, saying that the real problem was under-saving and over-consumption and proposed thrift and less government spending as the cure.

> If socialism was an economic catastrophe, government inter-vention could not work, and would tend to lead inevitably to socialism. Mises elaborated these insights in his *Critique of Interventionism* (1929), and set forth his political philosophy of laissez-faire liberalism in his *Liberalism* (1927).[20]

Of course, during the Great Depression of the 1930s, these theories fell on deaf ears. President Franklin Roosevelt convinced a desperate nation that only a massive increase in government spending – a re-inflation of the bubble with borrowed money – the Keynesian theory - would fix the problem, exactly what the current administration in 2011 is trying to do.

So the two alternatives of the day were:

- Massive Keynesian spending by the state – statism -- which forever after would depend on an ever-increasing economy – I call it the "housing-start economy", or
- The Mises cure, featuring free-market deflation and austerity in the hopes of somehow stimulating less consumption and more saving. Does it strike anyone else that this seems impossible?

---

[20] Rothbard, Murray N.: *Biography of Ludwig von Mises (1881-1973)*, as published by the Ludwig von Mises Institute, http://mises.org/resources/3248

But today we can see that these are BOTH false choices – the same choice being offered to the world in 2011.

The real cure at that point was true monetary reform – the repeal of the Federal Reserve Act of 1913 – which, remember, was then only 20 years old -- and a return of the money power into the hands of we, the people so that it could be administered in the public interest. In other words, a return to Lincoln's Greenback solution, but with strict controls on the QUANTITY of money.

Libertarianism is great EXCEPT when it comes to this, the most important and fearsome power of a sovereign nation. There are only two choices; the money power must be in the hands of:

- We, the people, controlled strictly in the public interest, OR, it will surely be ceded to
- The Big Banker class, to be run solely in their interest.

There is no middle ground. Apparently, their theory is that if you just give the money creation power to the biggest thieves, somehow, they will fight over it amongst themselves and everything will work out all right for the rest of us. For whatever reason, Mises couldn't see this outcome from his point in history. So he clung to his gold like a religion, and tried to do his best at solving the problems within the impossible confines of the debt money system.

Anarcho-Capitalists

Of course, Mises was exactly right about unchecked money printing, but he was exactly wrong on the cure. He advocated an extreme policy of non-governmental interference. In fact, many in, and closely affiliated with the Ludwig von Mises Institute admit that anarchy is one of their core beliefs. Von Mises author, Professor Murray Rothbard referred to himself as an "anarcho-capitalist" and favored the elimination of the state in favor of individual sovereignty in a "free market." According to Wikipedia:

Anarchy symbol

Chapter 6: The False Solution

> In an anarcho-capitalist society, law enforcement, courts, and all other security services would be provided by voluntarily funded competitors such as private defense agencies rather than through taxation....[21]

Anarchist author Lew Rockwell, has frequently acknowledged Rothbard's anarchist sentiments:

> Rothbard is an anarchist, but others, such as Rand and Nozick, see a role for a limited government to protect individual rights.[22]

Lew Rockwell

Llewellyn Rockwell, (b. 1944), is the founder and chairman of the Ludwig von Mises Institute. He also served as Ron Paul's congressional chief of staff from 1978 to 1982.

Anarcho-capitalism symbol

> It was clear to me at the time that Murray Rothbard was Mises's successor, and I followed his writings carefully. I first met him in 1975, and knew immediately that he was a kindred spirit....
> I cannot remember the day that I finally came around to the position that the state is unnecessary and destructive by its nature – that it cannot improve on, and indeed only destroys, the social and economic system that grows out of property rights, exchange, and natural social authority – but I do know that it was Rothbard who finally convinced me to take this last step.[23]

Of course, it would be completely unfair to characterize Austrian economic thinking as monolithic, however it is fair to say that in general they pine for a world where, in the absence of a "coercive" government, a cooperative free market will somehow spontaneously evolve – and even more incredibly – survive without any form of collective protection (such as that which a democratically elected government might provide). One

---

[21] Wikipedia, *Anarcho-capitalism*, retrieved Feb. 3, 2011.
[22] Block, Walter and Rockwell, Llewellyn H., Jr. *Man, Economy and Liberty: Essays in Honor of Murray N. Rothbard* (Auburn, Alabama, The Ludwig on Mises Institute, 1988), p. 276.
[23] Doherty, Brian. "Libertarianism and the Old Right." LewRockwell.com. 1999. Orig. published by *SpintechMag.org*, 12 May 1999.

can applaud them for their utopian dreaming, but those of us who are serious about trying to create a system which has some chance of effectively holding the raging wolves of the Money Trust at bay from devouring what's left of national sovereignty and thereby freedom, have to point out the weaknesses of economists who build their solutions around myths and short-sighted understanding of human nature.

De-Centralization of Power

Unfortunately, the anarcho-capitalist theory is somewhat utopian and equally impossible. It would be just great if all people were well intentioned and when left to their own devices would always do the right thing, but history has shown otherwise, especially when it comes to the money question. If self-government retires from the battlefield, the Money Trust will not simply allow these "anarcho-capitalists" to go about their merry way unchecked and allow human freedom to flourish. Their "free market," absent self-governance is pure social science fiction.

The last thousand years of human history have been characterized by the march of humanity towards freedom – out of serfdom. Self-government has been the common man's only way to escape bondage to the Money Trust – the only way to de-centralize their power. Yes, government can be, and has often become too powerful – too centralized – too statist; but the Money Trust would love nothing better than to have the anarchists – and their gold money - succeed in completely eliminating the collective power of the people and the rule of law of their Constitution. That is the only possible force which can effectively oppose them, to effectively ensure freedom.

The key going forward should be "de-centralization of power." Neither governments, nor the Money Trust will ever be accused of too much de-centralization.

Support from the Rockefellers

But there appears to be still another side to the Mises story. Early in my career, I received an incredible 8-page handwritten letter from a brilliant 85-year-old lady from California which was subsequently misplaced. She

Chapter 6: The False Solution

explained that Mises was brought to America by the Rockefeller Foundation, to seed the false solution – gold money – into the fabric of American economic academia.

Could it be true? For years, I didn't want to touch that one. Not surprisingly, Ludwig von Mises does not bother to mention or acknowledge this association, but it increasingly appears to be true. Richard M. Ebeling, writing in *The Independent Review: A Journal of Political Economy* is just one of several authors who now recount a similar tale:

> Many readers may be surprised to learn the extent to which the Graduate Institute and then Mises himself in the years immediately after he came to United States were kept afloat financially through generous grants from the Rockefeller Foundation. In fact, for the first years of Mises's life in the United States, before his appointment as a visiting professor in the Graduate School of Business Administration at New York University (NYU) in 1945, he was almost totally dependent on annual research grants from the Rockefeller Foundation.[24]

This detail is something about which the Mises Institute fails to inform their readers and followers as well. Does it strike anyone that the Rockefeller Foundation is likely to fund something that is truly in the public interest, particularly when it comes to the topic of control of the greatest power of them all, the money power? As we will see, it was John D. Rockefeller, along with J.P. Morgan, who, in 1907, deliberately caused the Crash of 1907, to teach President Teddy Roosevelt a lesson for having come after them with his Money-Trust-busting prosecutions. In addition, the 1907 Panic was one of the primary justifications used by the Money Trust to justify the creation of the Federal Reserve System in 1913.

Is it reasonable to assume that these very folks – the Rockefeller Foundation – were so concerned about the public welfare a few decades later, that they would support Mises to help him plant the pro-gold, pro-

---

[24] Richard M. Ebeling, *The Life and Works of Ludwig von Mises*, Summer 2008 issue of *The Independent Review*; http://www.independent.org/publications/tir/default.asp?issueID=54

anarchy viewpoint, if they thought it would eventually bring down their money machine system? This strains credibility.

Mises, like many others who sport economic theories (ahem), was very dogmatic and unbending when it came to being challenged.

> Fritz Machlup was a student of Mises's, one of his most faithful disciples. At one of the Mont Pelerin meetings, Fritz gave a talk in which I think he questioned the idea of a gold standard; he came out in favor of floating exchange rates. Mises was so mad he wouldn't speak to him for three years. Some people had to come around and bring them together again.[25]

Milton Friedman considered Mises intolerant in his personal behavior:

> The story I remember best happened at the initial Mont Pelerin meeting when he got up and said, "You're all a bunch of socialists." We were discussing the distribution of income, and whether you should have progressive income taxes. Some of the people there were expressing the view that there could be a justification for it.[26]

Conclusion

Mises and the Austrians have done a wonderful job of sniffing out the problems inherent in the current debt money system supposedly controlled by the Fed. They have been great bloodhounds over the years. That said, bloodhounds don't solve crimes, they merely uncover them. To be a problem solver, a dose of open-mindedness and reality is needed.

1. A truly free market can never exist without some modicum of the collective power of a representative government. In the words of one of the primary authors of the U.S. Constitution, Gouverneur Morris, in a letter to James Madison written on July 2, 1787:

   > *The rich will strive to establish their dominion and enslave the rest. They always did. They always will.... They will have the same effect here as*

---

[25] "Best of Both Worlds (Interview with Milton Friedman. *Reason*. June 1995.
[26] "Best of Both Worlds" Interview with Milton Friedman. *Reason*. June 1995. http://reason.com/archives/1995/06/01/best-of-both-worlds

Chapter 6: The False Solution

elsewhere, if we do not, by [the power of] government, keep them in their proper spheres.[27]

2. A commodity-backed currency will not control the quantity, and therefore the quality or value of money, Commodity money can still be fractionalized – in fact it <u>must</u> be fractionalized – and to make matters worse, this commodity can itself be manipulated, cornered, monopolized, horded or counterfeited.
3. The real power behind the Money Trust is "fractional reserve lending". No serious economist trying to fix the current world economic instability can possibly omit this.
4. No More National Debt. Without the power to borrow, governments will become more dependent on the electorate and less dependent on the Money Trust. No More National Debt means more accountability in the public interest.

In the event of breaking news or updated information on the Austrian School's position on monetary reform, HyperScan here:

URL: 7.tv/19c6

---

[27] The Anti-Federalist Papers and the Constitutional Convention Debates, Ralph Ketcham, ed. (New York, NY, Penguin Group, Signet Classic, 2003), p. 107.

Chapter 7 - How Did I Get Into This?

I started out believing that gold backing for our money was the answer also.

In 1980, while editing a weekly newspaper in Northern Virginia, I got a phone call from a gentleman named Ed Durell, a wealthy manufacturer of farm implements originally from Ohio. He told me a wild and fantastic story; "There is no gold left in Fort Knox."

Mr. Durell was able to back up his claim, however, with hundreds of documents – letters from the Secretary of the Treasury, Director of the Mint, and many Congressional Representatives and Senators. He even caused the doors of Fort Knox to be cracked open in 1973 for a very brief and very controlled peek at some of the gold inside.

After reviewing Mr. Durell's information, it was clear to me that the U.S. government was hiding something. Not only was it hiding something, but also it was taking big risks to hide something. My experience is that government doesn't take big risks unless it is hiding something big.

Director of the U.S. Mint, Mary Brooks telling reporters, "It's all here" inside vault #13 at Fort Knox on September 23, 1974.

So much pressure had been brought to bear on Congress by Mr. Durell in 1973-74, that finally the Secretary of the Treasury, William Simon, ordered Director of the U.S. Mint, Mary Brooks, to take a group of Congressmen and the press on a limited tour of just one of the thirteen smaller vaults in Fort Knox. Unfortunately for Treasury, the peek show raised more questions than it answered.

On September 23, 1974, Mrs. Brooks led six congressmen and one senator

Chapter 7: How Did I Get Into This?

on the tour. It was the first time since Roosevelt visited the vault in April 1943 that anyone except Mint and Treasury employees had been allowed inside.

The visitors were shown only what the Treasury officials intended they should see. The entire atmosphere was carnival-like, and only one of the thirteen compartments supposed to contain gold was actually opened to the visitors. In addition, there was no visit to the vast central core vault, nor was there any mention of it.

Mrs. Brooks delighted in being photographed by both Associated Press and United Press International photographers standing in front of a wall of gold bars. But the visitors noticed that the bars they were allowed to look at were orangish in hue. This coloration was indicative of coin-gold bars, that is, bars that contained at least 10% copper.

Apparently, the group was not shown any .995 "good delivery" gold bars (99.5% pure, also known as .995 gold, the minimum requirement for use in international trade), the very thing critics had been concerned about. Ultimately, the peek inside Fort Knox put to rest few doubts, and aroused even more questions.

The Great Weight Controversy

One of the questions raised by the September 1974 Congressional tour of Fort Knox concerned the weight of one of the bars of gold. Associated Press ran a photo of one of the visiting congressmen of that day, Rep. John B. Conlan (R-AZ), weighing a bar of gold on a common postal scale. Unfortunately for Treasury, the U.S. Postal scale in the photo shows a weight of only 22 pounds for the gold bar, significantly less than expected. This touched off another storm of controversy.

During the 1953 physical audit of a portion of the gold in Fort Knox, approximately 9,000 bars of gold weighed in at about 130 tons, according to a Treasury press release. If Treasury was referring to "short tons" of 2,000 pounds — which is most likely — that would mean that the average bar should have weighed 28.9 pounds, or 31% more than the bar Congressman Conlan selected. If metric tons were being used, then the figure anticipated would be 10% higher.

Rep. Gene Snyder (R-KY), left, holds scale as Rep. John Conlan (R-AZ), places a gold bar on U.S. Postal scales during the September 23, 1974 Fort Knox Tour.

Chapter 7: How Did I Get Into This? 49

An enlargement of the U.S. Post Office scale shown in the previous picture showing that the gold bar weighs only 22.25 pounds.

Rep. Conlan wrote specifically about this discrepancy to the Treasury. Secretary of the Treasury William E. Simon responded on May 4, 1976. His response is typical of an unending government smoke screen that was to frustrate Ed Durell for the rest of his life. Simon excused the discrepancy in this way:

> "The 22-pound bar of gold ... was a coin gold bar weighed on a household scale during the Congressional inspection of the Fort Knox depository on September 23, 1974. Coin gold bars are lighter in weight than the standard fine gold bar because of their copper content. They are also subject to a 10% variation in weight as are all gold bars, due to the casting process. These factors can bring the weight of the coin gold bars to near the 22-pound level. Also, the only accurate way to weigh gold is on a balance beam scale, rather than the spring type household scale."

Even if you grant that during the 1953 audit, Treasury weighed only the .999 fine gold bars to get their 130-ton figure, which divided out, equals 28.9 pounds per bar, then the minimum weight of a coin-gold bar containing 10% copper would be 27.4 pounds, nearly 25% more than the bar Congressman Conlan selected.

What bad luck for the Treasury that Mr. Conlan just happened to pick a bar that weighed nearly 25% less than the minimum weight Sec. Simon describes above.

Even if the supposed 10% weight variation for gold bars were fact — which is doubtful — that would yield a minimum weight for a bar of coin gold of 24.66 pounds.

Secretary Simon then blames the only possible culprit left, the scale. The scale used is, as seen in the photo, apparently a standard, government-issue U.S. postal scale, not a "household scale." In other words, that would mean that the government's own postal scale mis-weighed a 22-pound bar of gold by 2.66 pounds.

The point is not to quibble over the arcane intricacies of gold assay, but to show that there are significant variations in the quantity and fineness of the gold left in Fort Knox. Possibly, there is a reasonable explanation for these discrepancies, but why then doesn't the Treasury openly pursue the questions and put them to rest? The government could have easily quelled the worst fears of the skeptics at any time with a simple, conventional audit, where all bars are counted, and weighed, and a large, random sample in which they are assayed by the standard drilling method as mentioned in Treasury's explanation of their 1953 audit.

Faced instead with the government's devious actions over the last twenty years, a reasonable judgment has to be that the Treasury has something to hide."

The Central Core Controversy

About a year after the Mary Brooks "peek" inside Fort Knox, the former commanding general of the facility came forward and asked why the media hadn't been shown the main storage room for the gold, something he called the "central core vault." From 1956 to 1959, the Commanding

Chapter 7: How Did I Get Into This?

General of Fort Knox was Lt. General John L. Ryan, Jr. In addition, Gen. Ryan had been stationed at the bullion depository twice earlier, initially, just shortly after its completion in 1937. On November 16, 1975, he wrote a letter confirming the existence of the central core vault, as he had earlier testified before the congressional committee of Representative Otis Pike. Here is a copy of the actual letter:

> LT. GEN. JOHN L. RYAN, JR., USA RET.
> 5200 BRITTANY SOUTH, APT. 707
> ST. PETERSBURG, FLORIDA 33715
>
> November 16, 1975
>
> Dear Dr. Graham:
>
> This is to confirm certain statements I have made to you, Dr. Peter D. Beter, Mr. Edward Durrell, and Congressman Otis Pike. This is a condensed version omitting many minor details but does, I believe, include all the salient points.
>
> I reported for duty at Fort Knox, Kentucky, during the latter part of April 1937. I was assigned to Troop "A", 13th Cavalry (Mechanized) but was placed on special duty as Military Assistant to a Mr. Edward Van Horn, Treasury Department Agent-in-Charge of the United States Bullion Depository, commonly referred to as The Gold Vault.
>
> Mr. Van Horn took me on a familiarization tour of the entire structure and explained the innovations and characteristics of the major components as rehearsals for receiving, checking, weighing and storing the gold bricks were to be held during the ensuing few days.
>
> When I use the word "vault" I am referring to the central core of the Depository where the bullion was stored. This vault was below ground level and could be entered only through a specially constructed bank-type door that opened onto a screw-lift. This door was in the receiving-shipping area of the Depository.
>
> The receiving-shipping room was above ground level; the vault was below ground level. Around the vault proper, or central core, below ground level, was a passageway. On this passageway were a number of cell-like compartments. There was no means of entering the vault from this passageway. An emergency escape hatch which could be opened only from inside the vault was at this level.

The second page of General Ryan's letter continued as follows:

> "On the vault door were two combination locks, two key-operated locks, and a timing mechanism that prevented opening the door except at preset days

Chapter 7: How Did I Get Into This?

and hours. The Agent-in-Charge knew one combination and had one key; his Deputy knew the other combination and held the other key. I was told that the key to the timing mechanism was kept in Washington....

"I departed Fort Knox in July 1942, and returned in January 1952 for duty as Chief of Staff. In the spring of 1953 I believe but it could have been later, Mr. Van Horn received secret instructions to conduct a 100% inventory of the bullion. Specialists to check serial numbers, take 'plug' samples for assay, weigh the bricks etcetera, would be sent in but hiring men to move the gold bricks from the vault up to the receiving room, then back into the vault was up to the Agent-in-Charge.

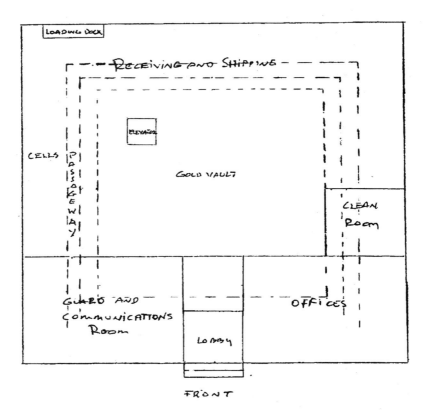

General Ryan's hand-drawn map of the ground floor of the Fort Knox Gold Repository, with the basement features, including the central core vault - which he called the "Gold Vault."

Chapter 7: How Did I Get Into This?   53

"Upon approval of the Commanding General, a number of selected non-commissioned officers were put on furlough status to become temporary Treasury Department employees to perform the labor involved in moving the gold bricks. I was in the Depository several times during this inventory and know that the bullion was stored in the vault.

"Mr. Van Horn told me that during WWII many irreplaceable documents such as the Declaration of Independence, the Constitution and amendments had been secured in the cell-like compartments surrounding the vault. At the moment, our war reserve of rare drugs were stored there in the compartments.

"I departed Fort Knox in November 1954 and returned in May 1956 as Commanding General. Mr. Van Horn had retired or died, I cannot recall which; his Deputy, Mr. Al Evans, was Agent-in-Charge. Although I was in the depository on a few occasions, I was not in the Depository when the vault was open. I departed Fort Knox in May 1959. It is my firm belief that until that time, May 1959, the bullion was stored in the vault."

Signed, John L. Ryan, Jr.

General Ryan then drew a rough map of the layout of the depository with its huge subterranean central core vault clearly indicated as "Gold Vault." As shown, the central core that takes up about 75% of the floor space of the basement level is surrounded by a passageway, and the thirteen smaller vaults.

Coming a full year after the 1974 tour of the depository, and subsequent Treasury denials of the existence of a central core vault, General Ryan's map constituted damning evidence which the government has failed to adequately address to this day. If such a central core vault existed, why wasn't it shown to congressmen and reporters, and why has Treasury subsequently denied its existence so steadfastly? Wild speculations abound, but the truth probably is that the government didn't know how they would explain why the huge central core vault, measuring about 65-by-80 feet, was completely empty.

Ian Fleming

Ian Fleming, the author of the popular James Bond novel, *Goldfinger*, was a well-known member of the British counterintelligence service, MI-5. Some in the intelligence community believe that he wrote much of his fiction as a forewarning, as many authors of fiction do.

If the removal of all the "good delivery" gold from Fort Knox can be viewed as a deliberate raid on the U.S. Treasury, then such an operation might well have been years in the planning — namely 40 years — certainly time enough for Fleming to get wind of it and try to reveal it fictionally.

The Von Mises Take

According to the Ludwig von Mises Institute, the Fed owns the entire US gold stock.

> Legally, there is no "United States" gold stock. There is only the Fed's gold stock. It is stored, not in Fort Knox, Kentucky, but at 33 Liberty Street, New York City, New York. The US government has always sold its gold to the Fed.... Where did the Fed get the money to buy the gold? It created it, of course. In short, it counterfeited it.[28]

So how did the Fed get the gold? Well, it all started during the Great Depression of the 1930s. At that time, the Fed had only been in operation since 1913 – some 17 years. The Fed had supposedly been formed to prevent depressions. Instead, they actually at least helped it along. According to Nobel-Prize-winning economist, Milton Friedman, the Depression was caused by the Fed refusing to halt a deflation of 33% of the nation's money between 1929 and 1933.

> The drastic decline in the stock of money and the occurrence of a banking panic of unprecedented severity did not reflect the absence of power on the part of the [Federal] Reserve System to prevent them.

---

[28] http://mises.org/daily/4649#note4

Chapter 7: How Did I Get Into This?

> ...In retrospect... the contraction could almost certainly have been prevented and the stock of money kept from declining or, indeed, increased to any desired extent.[29]

So, first an initial contraction of money, President Franklin Roosevelt ordered that all privately held gold (except "gold coins having a recognized special value") be surrendered to the government at $20.67 per ounce, claiming that it was necessary to stop the fall in the QUANTITY of money. Again, according to the von Mises Institute:

> ... In 1933, the US government outlawed the private ownership of gold. It bought all the gold it could forcibly collect from the public, paying the going price of $20.67 per ounce. Then it sold it to the Fed at $20.67 per ounce. The next year, the government raised the price of gold to $35.00 an ounce. Net profit to the Fed: 75 percent.

> This raised the legal reserves for banks, and the money supply (so-called M1) zipped upward by 30 percent, 1933 to 1935.

"No!" you say to yourself. "It couldn't be true. The government confiscated our gold in 1933 so that a private corporation owned by the member banks could buy it at a discount? Impossible!"

All right, my skeptical friend, pick up a copy of any Friday edition of The Wall Street Journal. Somewhere in the second section (they always shift it around) you will find a table called Federal Reserve Data. Check the listing under "Member Bank Reserve Changes." You will see a quotation for "Gold Stock." It never changes: $11,090,000,000. They don't sell it, and it's kept on the books at the meaningless arbitrary price of $42.22 per ounce.[30]

Facts About Gold Confiscation

Dealers of gold coins like to play up this 1933 confiscation order to sell people older gold coins which, they claim, would be immune from future confiscation. However, here are two pertinent facts to consider:

---

[29] Friedman, Milton & Schwartz, Anna. *A Monetary History of the United States, 1867-1960* (Princeton, NJ; Princeton University Press, 1963), p. 11
[30] http://mises.org/daily/4649#note4

In 1977 the power to regulate gold or silver coin or bullion was taken away from the President during peacetime emergencies under the International Emergency Economic Powers Act (IEEPA) (P.L. 95-223, 91 Stat. 1626).[31]

Now before you get too excited, CMI Gold & Silver reminds us that this is only a law – a law that can be changed.

> Even if a law did exempt certain coins from future confiscation, the government could change that law. Sadly, the government often simply ignores laws. Dealers who say they sell "non-confiscateable" gold have no basis for making such claims.[32]

Conclusions

So return to gold backing requires the following questions be answered:

1. If we were to go to gold backing for the U.S. dollar today, how would that work? What's the plan?
2. From whence would we get any gold to fire up the system? If there were no good deposit gold left in Fort Knox how would we get some?
3. With what would we buy the gold? More promises to pay? They wouldn't be worth much.
4. Would there be anyone trying to take advantage of the changeover as the bill moved slowly through Congress? What do you think would happen to gold futures markets? Do you think it's any secret to the wealthiest folks that the U.S. Treasury has virtually zero good delivery gold? We will look at the history of the United States to see if anyone has taken advantage of these changeovers in the past.

---

[31] *International Emergency Economic Powers Act* (1977), by Michael P. Malloy, Enotes.com
[32] http://www.cmi-gold-silver.com/gold-confiscation-1933.html

Chapter 7: How Did I Get Into This?

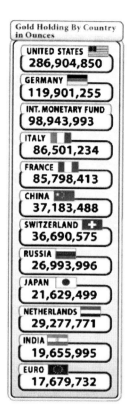

Gold Holdings by Country in Ounces

Source: USDebtClock.org

Chapter 8 – Ancient Greece

At the dawn of Greece, about 1194 B.C., oxen were largely used as money and a basis for currency, a cheap metal. That is why King Augeus of Elis so treasured his Augean stables which at one time were said to house 3,000 oxen.[33]

> Homer and Hesiod never speak of gold or silver money. They express the value of things by saying they were worth so many oxen. Homer values the golden armor of Glaucus at one hundred oxen, and the brazen armor of Democles at nine oxen.[34]

> Lycurgus, the lawgiver of Sparta, adopted a system of iron money, and that it might not be withdrawn from its legitimate purpose to be used in the arts (for iron was a scarce article in those days), he steeped it in vinegar to destroy its malleability.[35]

Very early on, a dual monetary system developed – cheap money for use within a sovereign state, and valuable money for use for international trade.

> Xenophon states that, "Most of the states of Greece have money which is not current except in their own territory."

> Plato recommended a double currency in every nation: "A coin," said he, "for the purpose of domestic exchange it must have a value among the members of the state, but no value to the rest of the world."

> For visiting and using in other states he proposed a coin of intrinsic value, which would pass current in foreign states."

> But the moneychangers have always fought a cheap money, and when they are successful, the people must suffer. In Attica in 595 B.C. they had destroyed cheap money, and interest was high. There was a mortgage stone at the corner of nearly every piece of land, the money loaning class had their grasp on everything, and they and their victims were about to clash

---

[33] Butler, Fabious Melton, *Lincoln Money Martyred* (Seattle, Washington, Lincoln Publishing Company, 1935), p. 16.
[34] Ibid.
[35] Ibid, p. 17.

and deluge the land with blood. But they finally agreed to arbitrate and consented to leave the matter to the philosopher Solon.[36]

About 594 B.C. the Athenian statesman, Solon, became the first effective advocate of democracy when he decentralized power, politically, in the judiciary, and most importantly, in the Athenian money system.

Greece was not really a nation at that time; it was controlled by independent city-states run in dictatorial fashion by tyrants for their economic benefit.

> ...There was conflict between the nobles and the common people for an extended period. For the constitution they were under was oligarchic in every respect and especially in that the poor, along with their wives and children, were in slavery to the rich.... All the land was in the hands of a few. And if men did not pay their rents, they themselves and their children were liable to be seized as slaves. The security for all loans was the debtor's person up to the time of Solon. He was the first champion of the people.[37]

To stabilize society, Solon decentralized power with a series of new laws. He repealed most of the previous harsh laws of Draco (as in Draconian) -- such as capital punishment for even minor offenses. Draconian law had not worked. Solon realized that for a society to be successful, the commoners had to have some power, some money, and the hope of success that an incentive-driven society provides. So established the first foundations of a true democracy by abolishing slavery, and allowing any citizen to serve in the legislature, the Ekklesia. He did the same with the judicial power by allowing commoners to sit on a jury.

On the monetary front, Solon ordered the mortgage stones taken up and debts forgiven once principal was repaid. There existed only a small amount of coined money. It was chiefly in the hands of the men of business and merchants. Solon called in all these coins of the realm and re-coined them. He doubled the money supply merely by cutting the amount of precious metal in the coins by one-half.[38] This invigorated

---

[36] Ibid.
[37] *Athenaion Politeia* 2.1 - 2.3
[38] Butler, p. 25

Athenian society with fresh money and helped it flower into what would be known as the Golden Age of Athens throughout the rest of the 500s B.C.

Just as in today's world, this devaluation made foreign goods more expensive and so imports were curtailed, but domestic production was boosted. Athenian black-figure pottery was exported in increasing quantities throughout the Aegean.[39] Only the plutocrats lost out, but they realized that this was a small price to pay compared to the entire nation falling into permanent chaos and lawlessness, so Solon remained popular with all classes of citizens.

As Nobel prizewinner Frederick Soddy would write in 1934:

> It was recognized in Athens and Sparta ... centuries before the birth of Christ that one of the most vital prerogatives of the State was the sole right to issue money.[40]

Solon's personal modesty and frugality served as a powerful example for the rich and powerful of Athens. Government was now being run in the public interest, not in the interest of powerful landowners only. This cut across the class structure – not entirely eliminating it, but reducing it. This fostered a heroic sense of civic duty can probably be compared to that which swept America and Britain during World War II. It was this public spiritedness long after Solon's death that helped Athens repel the Persian Army at the Battle of Marathon in 490 B.C., where 10,000 Athenians repelled an army of 500,000.

At the height of his power, Solon rejected calls to use his tremendous prestige to make himself a tyrant. This may have later served as the model for George Washington's rejection of calls to become King of America after winning the American Revolution.

Solon left Greece to travel for 10 years, after extracting a promise from the country to maintain his reforms in his absence. In 590 B.C., he sailed for Egypt. According to his descendent, Plato, Solon met with the Egyptian priests of Sais 300 years before the Ancient Library of

---

[39] Stanton G.R. *Athenian Politics c800-500BC: A Sourcebook*, Routledge, London (1990), page 76

[40] Soddy, Frederick: *The Role of Money* (London, George Routledge and Sons, Ltd., 1934), p. ix.

Alexandria was even founded. It was they who told him the ancient story of the lost continent of Atlantis, a story which would have been lost to antiquity had not Plato, retold it 200 years later, in 360 B.C. in his dialogues *Timaeus* and *Critias*.

At a later date, King Croesus, king of Lydia, asked Solon if the laws he had made could be improved upon after many years of observing their effects. But Solon saw no room for improvement. He still thought his laws were "the best they were capable of receiving."[41] Solon's formula for national financial success can be boiled down to two points:

1. Abolish debt by abolishing interest.
2. Provide a plentiful supply of government-issued, debt-free money.

Today's politicians would do well to consider Solon's wise counsel.

Within four years of Solon's departure, things started to fall apart. Eventually one of Solon's relatives, Pisistratus, took power by force. Upon Solon's return to Greece, he blamed the Athenians of stupidity and cowardice for allowing their freedoms to be lost.[42] He became a staunch opponent of Pisistratus until his death, but the freedom for the middle and lower classes that was lost was never regained.

---

[41] Butler, p. 25.
[42] Plutarch *Solon* 30: http://tinyurl.com/2f62e2m

Chapter 9 – Carthage

About 500 B.C., Carthage (present-day Tunisia) was the most prosperous nation on earth. The white sails of her merchant fleet dotted the waters of the known world. It is said that her silver mines produced 300 pounds of silver per day. Her mighty navy included a fleet of over 300 warships. This maritime might gave Carthage the ability to enforce a trade monopoly over tin-rich Britain and the Canary Islands. Tin was essential for the manufacture of bronze in the ancient world.

URL: 7.tv/23f1

Interestingly, none of the silver production of Carthage was used for money on the domestic front. Silver was used only in foreign trade. Carthage, too, had discovered the benefits of a plentiful form of cheap, debt-free money made of leather. To prevent counterfeiting, it contained a metal core, a secret amalgam of metals known only to the government.

The system worked very well in Carthage, and the nation continued to grow stronger. The city of Carthage had massive walls running 23 miles in length. The success of Carthage was due to fortunate geography and a relatively democratic political and monetary system. The government was an oligarchic republic, which relied on a system of checks and balances to ensure that power remained well distributed. Carthage was ruled by two Suffets, the equivalent of a dual presidency in the U.S. It also had elected legislators, a Constitution, trade unions and held town meetings. The legislature had an upper house, which Roman sources called the Carthaginian Senate composed of the national elite, and a lower house referred to as a popular assembly. Aristotle reported in his *Politics* that unless the Suffets and the Senate reached a unanimous decision, the Assembly had the decisive vote.

Chapter 9: Carthage

The Greek historian Polybius said that the Carthaginian public held more sway over their government than the people of Rome held over theirs.[43]

Carthage stood in the way of Roman expansion in the Mediterranean. The two fought a series of three wars known as the Punic Wars between 264 and 146 B.C. During the Second Punic War, Carthaginian general Hannibal attacked Rome through what is not Spain and crossed the Alps led by a cavalry of three-dozen attack elephants and overwhelmed the Roman Army. The Romans retreated within the walls of Rome itself which Hannibal was never able to penetrate.

With Hannibal's absence, the moneylenders who had been driven from Greece were finally able to get a foothold in Carthage.

> [Hannibal] had left an enemy in Carthage far worse than those he was fighting. The money power had destroyed cheap money and come to a money of precious metals. They had control of all government offices.... They considered only their immediate interests, so refused aid to Hannibal and recalled him. Hannibal withdrew from Rome; Scipio immediately followed him and was soon thundering at the gates of Carthage.
>
> With the destruction of cheap money of Carthage came an era of corruption, even the judges became so corrupt that Hannibal when made Preator was compelled to impeach the whole bench of judges, and he corrected other evils, and says Rollins the historian: "They exclaimed vehemently against these regulations as if their own property had been forced out of their hands and not the sums they had plundered from the people."[44]

After Hannibal's defeat in the Second Punic War, Carthage became a Roman client state. Rome demanded a war indemnity of 14,200 pounds of silver per year for 50 years from Carthage, and the Carthaginian Navy was limited to 10 ships to ward off pirates. Gone were the days where Carthage ruled the seas.

In 151 B.C., after 50 years of war reparations, Carthage declared the debt to be paid, but Rome decided it should be made permanent. On top of that, Rome's population was rising fast because they too had discovered

---

[43] Aristiotle, *Politics, Book 2*, part 11
[44] Butler, p. 18.

the value of a cheap money supply. Feeding the growing population of Rome was a major challenge and the bountiful soil surrounding Carthage was some of the most productive farmland not yet completely under Roman control.

In 146 B.C., the Roman Army, after a stiff battle, sacked Carthage and burned it to the ground. It's buildings and its magnificent harbor was utterly destroyed.

Chapter 10 - Rome

What made Rome great? There were many factors, but certainly the most overlooked was the money system of the Roman Republic.

About 300 BC, the Roman Republic took a lesson from Carthage and supplied the people with a plentiful form of cheap money – money made from copper and bronze. Then they spent this cheap money into the economy.

Today, opponents of this money system call it fiat money – money not backed by precious metals. But what the Roman Republicans had discovered from the Carthaginians was that it doesn't matter what backs the money; all that matters is who controls its quantity. If the money supply is created without the constant drain of interest payments by national borrowing, the nation had more money to spend in the public interest.

The results were spectacular. The common man had sufficient money that virtually all transactions were done on a cash basis. Power was spread out amongst the people via the Roman Republic and it's complex Constitution.

> Without the use of either gold or silver, Rome became mistress of the commerce of the world. Her people were the bravest, the most prosperous, the most happy, for they knew no grinding poverty. Her money was issued directly to the people, and was composed of a cheap material – copper and brass – based alone upon the faith and credit of the nation. With this abundant money supply she built her splendid Pantheon and her magnificent courts and temples. She fought her battles and extended her domains, improved her agriculture, distributed her lands among the people in small holdings, and wealth poured into the coffers of Rome from every busy mart of the world."

> This was all done on fiat money, that had no value except legal value, but which was full legal tender money.

> At the commencement of the Christian era the legal tender money of Rome amounted to about $2,000,000,000, and all of it was in the hands of the people, in the various avenues of trade and the industries, and was a per

capita sufficiently large to do all business on a cash basis. But here the money power commenced to get in its work. Copper and brass were demonetized and gold and silver substituted, and the volume of money reduced from $2,000,000,000 to $200,000,000.

During the process of contraction, population dwindled, the arts, learning, commerce and prosperity took flight. The once proud, free and prosperous people were reduced to a condition of abject serfdom. Because of a lack of a proper medium of exchange the price of labor, lands, and products fell; the lands were sold for taxes, and were soon concentrated in a few hands; the masses sank to the lowest depths of degradation, while the favored few amassed fabulous fortunes.

Prior to the fall of Rome 1,160 rich families, many of them with an income of a million and a half dollars yearly, owned practically all the wealth, while those whose industry and thrift had made it the proudest nation in the world were mere serfs. The consequences of this terrible crime could not long be averted, so when attacked by Alaric, in the year 410 after Christ, Italy could find none to resist, and Rome fell."[45]

Caesar's successful wars had netted $1,800,000,000 in gold and silver.[46] But as production in the Empire's mines declined, the supply became more stable and the moneychangers were able to corner the market on these precious metals, and then hoard them. One historian put it this way:

> The Imperial Democracy that held a world beneath its sway, from the Senators who have historic names, down to the humblest tiller of the soil, from Julius Caesar down to the smallest shopkeeper in a back street of Rome, was at the mercy of a small group of usurers.[47]

Taxes increased, as did corruption. Usury and the debased coin of the realm were everywhere. As a result, the common people lost their lands and homes. With this, the masses lost not only confidence in their government and refused to support it. The treasure of Rome was all too soon gone and the empire was plunged into the gloom of the Dark Ages,

---

[45] Milford, Howard, *The American Plutocracy*, 1895
[46] Butler, p. 21
[47] *Elliott on Usury,* p. 71; as quoted by Butler, Fabious Melton, *Lincoln Money Martyred* (Seattle, Washington, Lincoln Publishing Company, 1935), p. 27.

as was the rest of the world that had been part of the Roman Empire. The contraction of the volume of money was so great that it continued until civilization was nearly snuffed out.

Although many factors led to Rome's long death spiral, certainly this monetary contraction and runaway money lending was a contributing factor. As Lyman E Stowe put it in his book, *What Is Coming*:

> With the destruction of Commerce, which always comes if the shrinkage of the volume of money is great enough, came poverty, distress, and loss of patriotism, and the final downfall of Rome.[48]

In 1935, at the height of the Great Depression in the United States, Fabious Melton Butler, writing under the penname, Dr. R.E. Search, noted the similarity between the conditions preceding the fall of Rome, and those artificially created in America of his era.

> And now many of our unemployed millions are listening to the fake remedy. Of "Russian Communism," instead of informing themselves of the real reason for their distress — the manipulation and issuing ... of the nation's money by a private group of money changers.[49]

He goes on to comment on the power usury builds up:

> When usury is practiced, it soon builds up a powerful ring of money lenders who leave no stone unturned to keep and further their use of the practice of usury, and the power that they can attain by corrupting the government officials with the vast quantities of money that must inevitably accumulate by usury.
>
> They do not stop at wholesale murder, nor any degree of corruption, and generally end by the overthrow of free government and the establishment of a dictator or despot they can control by the use of money.
>
> If we wish to see what eventually happens to this kind of dictatorship, we may read what happened to Rome. In that time, oppression became worse and worse, and people who wanted liberty and freedom fled to other countries, and finally when the barbarians swept down in ever-increasing

---

[48] Butler, p. 21.
[49] Ibid, p. 17.

numbers, there was not enough patriotism left in the citizens for their own country to cause them to defend it, and it went down to destruction.[50]

With the decline of plentiful money in Rome, wealth was concentrated to a greater degree in fewer hands. This left the lower class impoverished and hopeless and without a stake in the success of society. The outcome was that no one was willing to work for the good of the whole. As a result, the highly organized civilization that was Rome came apart at the seams about 476 A.D.

With the breakup of Rome, Western Europe was plunged into a 500-year period of dissolution known as the Dark Ages. Without an organized society, starvation was rampant in cities. Eventually, urban life virtually disappeared. Knowledge survived only in a few monastery and palace schools. Many of the secrets of the arts and crafts handed down from the ancient world were lost.

Whether the immorality of Rome caused a corrupt financial system, or vice-versa, is debatable, but the dissolution of Rome's organized society is not. However, this dissolution was not worldwide. The Arabs spread a splendid civilization from Spain to the borders of China. Interestingly, the Roman Empire had a Christian branch in the east, which continued to flourish more or less throughout the Dark Ages, thanks, at least, in part to a monetary policy conducted in the public interest.

---

[50] Ibid.

Chapter 11 – The Biblical View

One of the main problems with our current banking system is that it is based on usury. But what is usury, anyway? In the broadest definition, usury is taking unjust, unfair, unethical, and even illegal interest on anything loaned -- usually money. What constitutes "unjust" interest, then? Well, that depends on your values.

It's important to remember that "the West" was civilized according to the Judeo-Christian values laid out in the Bible. The ethical codes found in this millennia-old guide to human behavior are the very bedrock of western civilization and the secret to its success. The Bible's Golden Rule of "do unto others as you would have them do unto you," makes nations strong. The "every man for himself" credo that promotes usury renders them weak. In other words, usury makes the rich richer, and the poor, poorer. And that's bad for any nation.

In the Old Testament portion of the Bible,

God gave specific instructions to Israel that money lent to a fellow Israelite had to be lent without interest.

> If you lend money to My people, to the poor among you, you are not to act as a creditor to him; you shall not charge him interest.   Ex. 22:25

Was it acceptable to charge interest to the more wealthy people of God? No, it was not! But as Moses explained, charging interest was acceptable in some cases:

> You shall not charge interest to your countrymen: interest on money, food, or anything that may be loaned at interest. You may charge interest to a foreigner, but to your countryman you shall not charge interest, so that the Lord your God may bless you in all that you undertake in the land which you are about to enter to possess.
>
> Deuteronomy 23:19-20

But how much is too much? Nehemiah explained when he urged his people to stop taking usury:

> Please let us leave off this usury. Please give back to them this very day their fields, their vineyards, their olive groves, and their houses, also the

hundredth part of the money and of the grain, the new wine, and the oil that you are exacting from them.   Neh. 5: 10-11

The Ryrie Study Bible explains that to Nehemiah, usury was a "hundredth part." — 1%. This was not 1% per year, but — according to Ryrie's note — 1% per month, or 12% per year. Under the New Testament (which means new agreement or covenant), the injunctions against usury extended to all people, just as salvation was offered to Jew and Gentile alike.

Money Changers in the Temple

Driving the moneychangers from the Temple of Solomon was the one and only time that Jesus used force or direct action during His ministry. Why? What was so important about their activities?

When the Jews came to Jerusalem to pay their Temple tax to support the priesthood, they could only pay it with "the half shekel of the sanctuary". This was a special coin, a half-ounce of pure silver. It was the only coin of assured weight and purity, and therefore the only coinage acceptable to God. But these Temple half shekels were not plentiful. The moneychangers, having most of the money anyway, were soon able to corner the market on these coins. Then, they raised the price of them — just like any other commodity — to whatever the market would bear.

When the Jews came to the Temple, they were also required to sacrifice an unblemished dove or other animal. Since it was inconvenient for many of the out-of-town visitors to carry their sacrifices with them on their journey to Jerusalem, they had to purchase them when they arrived at the Temple. Naturally, these sacrifices could only be purchased with the unblemished half shekels of the sanctuary, and once again, moneychangers artificially inflated the price.

So, what Jesus objected to was not the normal banking business of the day — namely exchanging foreign money for local money — but doubling the price of the coins above their normal, tax-paying value because moneychangers held a monopoly on a required form of precious metal coin. In other words, the moneychangers were stealing from the poorest Jews, on their holiest ground.

F.R. Burch, provided an interesting perspective on Christ's action in his book, *Money and Its True Function*:

> As long as Christ confined his teachings to the realm of morality and righteousness, He was undisturbed; it was not till He assailed the established economic system and 'cast out' the profiteers and 'overthrew the tables of the money changers,' that He was doomed. The following day He was questioned, betrayed on the second, tried on the third and on the fourth crucified.[51]

Early Christian Attitudes

After Christ's death, the Church maintained an anti-usury policy for hundreds of years. Usurers were not to be admitted to communion or receive a Christian burial, and, according to *Ashley's English Economic History*, members of the clergy taking alms from a usurer were automatically suspended until they had spoken to their Bishop. Also, the wills of usurers who did not make restitution were considered invalid, and any government official who did not make them return their ill-gotten gain would be excommunicated.

Martin Luther said usurers should be "hanging from the gallows." John Calvin agreed:

> For we altogether condemn usuries, we shall impose severer restrictions upon the consciences than the Lord Himself desired....[52]

Why did Calvin go even further than the Lord, himself, in condemning usury? Because he saw the consequences as they played out in his world:

> While if we make the least concession, many will use it as a pretext and will snatch at a bridleless license, which can never afterward be checked by any moderation or exception.[53]

---

[51] *The American Mercury*, 1964, vol. 96-101, p. 18
[52] Canada Parliament, House of Commons, 1939, *Debates: Official Report*: Volume 2, p. 459. And, Loux, Du Bois Henry, *Science of Theocratic Democracy*, 1920, p. 45.
[53] Ashley, Sir William James, *1893 An Introduction to English Economic History and Theory*; Volume 1, p. 459.

English Prohibitions on Usury

In early England, taking any interest on loaned money was universally considered a sin. In 900 A.D., King Alfred implemented a law that moneylenders who took usury would forfeit all their possessions to the King. By 1050 A.D., King Edward the Confessor added that the usurer would be declared an outlaw and banished from England. And in the fourteenth century, Edward III made usury a capital crime. But he didn't practice what he preached. He borrowed heavily from the moneychangers. In fact, one of the reasons he made it a capital crime was so that he wouldn't have to repay them if he got into a financial squeeze. By the sixteenth century, Henry VIII began relaxing the laws against usury. Yet it took another 300 years, until 1854, to completely repeal all legal prohibitions against usury.

Suffice it to say that usury has been considered a criminal act throughout most of human history, until the last 200-300 years. Why? Because the people who are forced to pay interest on borrowed money are the very ones who can least afford it. Usury is like taxing the poor; they don't have enough to begin with.

Usury Today

What constitutes usury in today's secular (non-Christian) world? Since nowhere else does the Bible define it, 12% per year must certainly be considered usury — as would credit card interest, which usually runs around 18% per annum.

But our problems today are caused by a form of usury far beyond debates over 6% or 12% or 18% interest rates. You see, no matter what the rate of interest, before the dawn of the 18th century, men risked their own money in making loans. Justifiably or not, they felt they deserved a return for their risk.

In today's system, however, risk has been eliminated for the moneychanger class. The U.S. government has gotten into the business of bailing out banks, savings and loans, and now even entire nations? If bankers make risky loans for which they gain a larger percentage of interest then usual, they profit handsomely if the debts are repaid. If they are not repaid, the taxpayers are asked to "bail them out" and pay the bills. This is usury of the worst kind, and should be considered a criminal act, not one deserving of corporate charity.

Unfortunately, that is still not the worst of it. As we will see, when it comes to the system of the Federal Reserve, by law, usurers create money OUT OF NOTHING! Then they charge a fee for it. That's an infinite rate of interest. If I loan you $100 and charge you a fee of $10 for the loan, then the interest rate is 10/100, or 10%. If you go out and steal $100, then charge a $10 fee to loan it out, that's 10/0, because zero is what you really put into it. Your interest rate is infinitely large.

You can debate all you want about whether 6% or 10% or 12% interest constitutes usury. That's not the point. The worst abuse, by far, in our money system is the rate of interest charged by our central bank, the Federal Reserve, when it loans our government money at far greater than 12%, or even 18% interest. It loans us money it creates out of thin air — out of nothing. Now, that's usury!

All taxpayers, no matter how poor, are forced to pay for this system, even though we have no control over it. Certainly this central bank system, perfected over the last two centuries, is the most outrageous form of usury ever devised by the mind of man.

Chapter 12 – England

Flash forward 7 centuries to 1100 A.D. in England. There were no banks like we think of them today. What served as banks were the goldsmiths – those who made their gold into gold coins. Although most people didn't understand it, these goldsmiths controlled the economy of the nation and thereby even the politics – even in a monarchy.

By acting in concert, goldsmiths could either make money plentiful or scarce. When they made their gold money plentiful, the economy of the nation flourished. When they made their gold coins scarce, a depression set in and they could buy up assets for pennies on the dollar. To prevent being lynched, goldsmiths had learned early on, how to blame the king for any economic hardship that they caused by manipulating the quantity of their gold money.

Tally Sticks

About 1100 A.D., King Henry 1, the son of England's first Norman king, William the Conqueror, was low on gold money. A series of costly wars had depleted the royal treasury. So just as colonial Pennsylvania would do hundreds of years later. Henry created a unique form of government-issued money called tally sticks.

Tally sticks did not represent any quantity of gold, or any other commodity. They were simply polished sticks of wood issued by the King that he declared to be good for the payment of taxes. That made tally sticks just as good as any other form of money.

According to Bank of England Museum curator John Keyworth, Tally Sticks were one of oldest forms of British money.

> The idea with the tally stick was that you cut notches in a piece of wood -- usually it was Hazel --and these notches were of a prescribed size to represent the amount the stick represented
>
> One side is called the stock. This was kept by the person who made the loan, or paid the money in, and the other was called the foil. So the foil would be spent into existence and the idea was that splitting the stick down

Chapter 12: England

the middle was to prevent counterfeiting, because of course, a stick splits uniquely down the middle. When the debt was repaid the two pieces were put together, and if they didn't tally something was awry.[54]

The longer half of a tally stick was called the stock, the root word for "stocks" and bonds or "stockholders". For centuries, the supporters of gold backed money have belittled tally sticks as an unimportant form of "fiat" money -- one not backed by gold or silver. Some authors, anxious to paint a picture that only gold has worked as money down through the ages, have claimed that tallies weren't a real money system because they were only used for very large transactions. But that's just not the case.

> In the Middle Ages, the average size was reckoned to be the length from the tip of a man's thumb to the tip of his forefinger, quite short. So the wider the spacing, the larger the amount. But it was a prescribed distance. It was an inch, and then one half an inch for hundreds, and a quarter of an inch for 10s, and then it became a little lines drawn across with a saw.[55]

For more about Tally sticks from Bank of England Museum John Keyworth:

URL: 7.tv/26a6

So it is clear that tally sticks were used for smaller denominations too, and worked well as an effective, debt-free money system for 726 years. Without the crushing weight of debt-based money, England flourished into the greatest power on earth for many centuries. At their peak, it has been estimated that 95% of English money was in the form of Tally Sticks. Compare that to today, where the only debt-free, government issued money is in the form of coin – about 3% of the money supply in the UK, and far less in the U.S.

---

[54] Videotaped interview with the author, October, 2008.
[55] Videotaped interview with the author, October, 2008.

After he democratized the money power of the nation with tally sticks, King Henry then began decentralizing political power as well. King Henry granted something called the *Charter of Liberties*, voluntarily stating what his powers were under law. Before that, kings had assumed unlimited power. This was followed in 1215 by the Magna Carta, the basis of the U.S. Constitution.

A new class began to develop – the merchant class. Trade routes grew and new towns sprang up along them. This mercantile class needed stability and so they supported the King, his strong central government, and the rule of law.

In 1265 the first Parliamentary elections were held. Government by the people – in England -- was born. As money poured into the middle class – the small businesspersons of the day – feudalism began to break down and the English Renaissance was born.

By the 1600s, serfdom in England was legally banned. Humanity – at least in England – was finally set free. As a result, literature flourished. Now there was money to support artistic endeavors like the plays of William Shakespeare. The nation was at ease due to a debt-free money.

Although life in the Late Middle Ages was certainly not easy by today's standards, once tally sticks were killed and the nation became indebted to bankers, it got worse.

The Birth of Fractional Reserve Lending

Tally Sticks did not kill the use of gold coins. Gold circulated as a complimentary currency. But just because your money is valuable, doesn't insure its safety or its honesty.

In the early 1600s, there were no banks as we think of them today. Merchants with gold they wanted to protect stored it in the king's mint for safekeeping. However, in 1638, when Charles I needed gold he just confiscated the merchants' gold, calling it a "loan". So the merchants started depositing their gold in the safes of local goldsmiths.

By the end of the civil war, in the late 1660s, the goldsmiths fell prey to the temptation to print pseudo-warehouse receipts not covered by gold and lend them out; in this way fractional reserve banking came to England.[56]

Bank of England

After 600 years, the moneychangers were finally able to begin to reassert their control over English money when they convinced the Parliament to create the Bank of England in 1694. This put the banking community back in control of manipulating the quantity of English money. Now England had to borrow its money supply from banks and pay interest on it, instead of the government simply issuing it's own money without such debt.

The tally stick system was killed in 1694 with the founding of the Bank of England. England was now borrowing all its money from private banks, instead of just creating it debt free.

---

[56] Rothbard, Murray, *A History of Money and Banking in the United States Before the Twentieth Century*, (Auburn, Alabama; Ludwig von Mises Institute, 2005), p. 57.

Chapter 13 – Colonial America

Within 75 years of the founding of the Bank of England, just the interest payments on England's debts consumed 75% of its budget. As a result, England needed to squeeze more and more money from all her colonies to pay the interest on this new growing debt. America was no exception.

Pre-Revolutionary America was still relatively poor. There was a severe shortage of precious metal coins to trade for goods, so the early colonists had successfully printed their own homegrown paper money. This paper money was called Colonial Scrip.

Gold-money advocates like Professor Murray Rothbard acknowledge that England did forbid the minting of gold and silver coin in the colonies, and even prohibited the export of English coin to America, but then stubbornly insists:

> In reality, there was no such shortage.... Americans were able to import Spanish and other foreign coin, including English.[57]

It is also possible to get a drink of water from your neighbor's home across town, but if that was your only source of water, it certainly would make life more difficult, but the problem is that Rothbard is just flat wrong in this assertion. Harvard Law Professor Robert G. Natelson, sets the record straight:

> Throughout the seventeenth and eighteenth centuries, British America enjoyed what was probably the fastest-growing economy in the world. A surging rate of economic exchange required a circulating medium that would keep pace. Yet British America had no gold or silver mines, and the authorities in London decided against flooding their colonies with specie. With one temporary exception, the authorities also forestalled efforts to establish mints in America.
>
> Most of the limited specie available was Dutch, Portuguese, or Spanish, with the most common coin being the Spanish dollar, or "piece of eight." The British accepted these foreign tokens as the primary colonial circulating medium, and set their values by royal proclamation. But even with foreign

---

[57] Rothbard, Murray, *A History* ...., p. 50.

issues available, the quantity of specie proved woefully inadequate for American needs. Americans also resorted to sophisticated forms of barter, which proved to be clumsy and therefore unsatisfactory.

It was in this context that the colonists embarked upon an extraordinary voyage of financial creativity. "One would be hard pressed," observed Professor Richard Sylla, "to find a place and time in which there was more monetary innovation than in the British North American colonies in the century and a half before the American Revolution."

During the seventeenth century, New Englanders made wampum their principal measure of ordinary retail trade. Virginians and Marylanders paid their bills in tobacco. South Carolinians remitted quit rents and public charges with skins, cheese, tar, whale oil, butter, tallow, corn, wheat, tobacco, pork, and beeswax. At various places and times other colonists resorted to sugar, rum, molasses, beads, bullets, rice, indigo, and other products as currency.

The colonists were familiar with bills of exchange in foreign transactions, promissory notes in domestic transactions, and letters of credit. These instruments may have planted the idea of using paper as material for currency. Whatever the inspiration, some kind of informal paper medium--its exact nature is uncertain--was circulating in New England well before 1684. In 1690, Massachusetts issued the first government-sponsored American paper money in the form of £7000 in bills of credit. That colony emitted another £33,000 the following year, of which £10,000 was eventually redeemed and burned. More Massachusetts paper appeared in 1702 and later. The colony of South Carolina issued paper money in 1703; New Hampshire, New York, and Connecticut did so in 1709; Rhode Island in 1710; North Carolina in 1712; Pennsylvania in 1723; and Maryland in 1733. By 1760, every colony had followed suit.[58]

In the colonies, America was learning about money the hard way. In 1690, the Massachusetts Colony raided the French colony in Quebec. It was not the first time they had done so. But this time, the mission was a dismal failure and without sufficient plunder to pay the troops, the

---

[58] Natelson, Robert G.: *Paper Money and the Original Understanding of the Coinage Clause*, Harvard Journal of Law & Public Policy, Summer, 2008, 31Harv. J.L. & Pub. Pol'y 1017.

government was in trouble. Its coffers were empty and additional taxes were politically unpopular.

So, the government of Massachusetts decided to print money and promise the soldiers that the new currency would be redeemable in gold or silver coin as soon as there was sufficient tax revenue to do so. They also promised that they would print no new money until after the first batch of notes had been redeemed in coin. The citizens of Massachusetts, knowing their elected officials were reliable, trusted their government. They accepted the notes, and exchanged them for goods.

Now, everything would have been all right had the government not violated the second promise — not to print any additional notes — but such was not the case. Within six months, they created six times as many notes and put them into circulation.[59]

It was a mixed record. In general, the New England colonies performed poorly. Rhode Island notes lost more than 80% of their value. Maryland and the Carolinas suffered significant inflation, but Virginia did not, neither did New York, New Jersey or Pennsylvania.[60]

Benjamin Franklin was a supporter of colonial governments printing their own money in times of shortages of coin. In 1736, at age 30, he apologized for his Pennsylvania Gazette being late from the printers, and explained that the printer was:

> ...with the Press, labouring for the publick Good, to make Money more plentiful.[61]

During this period, the colonies thrived. America was quite literally inventing a new way to do business. Naturally there would be failures. Despite these problems, America was growing more prosperous with each passing year. To say that all fiat currency is an inflationary disaster is to totally ignore a fair reading of American monetary history.

---

[59] Griffin, G. Edward. *The Creature from Jekyll Island* (Westlake Village, CA, American Media, 2010), p. 157.
[60] Natelson, Robert G.: *Paper Money and the Original Understanding of the Coinage Clause*, Harvard Journal of Law & Public Policy, Summer, 2008, 31Harv. J.L. & Pub. Pol'y 1017.
[61] *Register of Pennsylvania*: Vol. 6, (Philadelphia, July, 1830), p. 137.

Chapter 13: Colonial America

One thing is for sure; colonial paper money was a very dangerous concept indeed -- for British bankers. It broke the colonies free of the privately owned central bank system where money had to be created by banks and then loaned to governments and the general populace.

Throughout his career, Franklin was an advocate for paper money, publishing *A Modest Enquiry into the Nature and Necessity of a Paper Currency* in 1729, and his printer printed money. He was influential in the more restrained and thus successful monetary experiments in the Middle Colonies, which stopped deflation without causing excessive inflation. In 1766 he made a case for paper money to the British House of Commons.[62] Franklin explained the ingenious system employed in Pennsylvania in more detail to a friend in England, David Hume:

> You mention several kinds of money, sheep, oxen, fish, employed as measures of exchange, or as money, in different parts of the world. You have overlooked that, in our colony of Pennsylvania, the land itself, which is the chief commodity, **is coined**, and passes in circulation. The manner of conducting this affair is as follows: A planter, immediately after he purchases any land, can go to a public office and receive notes to the amount of half the value of his land; which notes he employs in all payments, and they circulate through the whole colony, by convention.
>
> To prevent the public from being overwhelmed by this fictitious money, there are two means employed first, the notes issued to any one planter, must not exceed a certain sum, whatever may be the value of his land: secondly, every planter is obliged to pay back into the public office every year one-tenth part of his notes; the whole, of course, is annihilated in ten years; after which, it is again allowed him to take out new notes to half the value of his land.[63]

The emphasis above on "is coined" is added because it will come in handy later on during the discussion of that term's controversial appearance in the U.S. Constitution. As a result of this system, Dr. Franklin said:

---

[62] http://en.wikipedia.org/wiki/Benjamin_Franklin
[63] *Life and correspondence of David Hume:* from the papers bequeathed by his nephew to the Royal Society of Edinburgh, and other original sources, by John Hill Burton, 1846

> Between the years 1740 and 1775, while abundance reigned in Pennsylvania and there was peace in all her borders, a more happy and prosperous population could not perhaps be found on this globe. In every home there was comfort. The people generally were highly moral, and knowledge was extensively diffused.[64]

Franklin asked his English friends how England, with all its wealth, could have so much poverty among its working classes. His friends replied:

> ... that England was prey to a terrible condition; it had too many workers! The rich said they were already overburdened with taxes, and could not pay more to relieve the needs and poverty of this great mass of workers. Several rich Englishmen of that time actually believed what economist Thomas Malthus later wrote, that wars and epidemic disease were necessary to rid the country from "manpower surpluses".[65]

Such is the result of the worst of all worlds – a gold-money system combined with a national debt.

The Currency Act of 1764

In 1764 the Bank of England, realizing that Colonial Scrip was cutting into their profits – not to mention their control -- pressed the British Parliament for the passage of the Currency Act. It was duly passed on September 1, 1764. This ordered all Americans to pay their taxes only in gold or silver coin.

> [Dr. Franklin] went before a committee of Parliament to answer a report of the Board of Trade, dated February 9, 1764, containing reasons for restricting the issue of paper bills of credit in America 'as a legal tender,' and, in his unanswerable argument against the restriction, he said:
>
> If carrying out all the gold and silver ruins the country, every colony was ruined before it made paper money. But far from being ruined by it, the colonies that have made use of paper money have been and are all in a thriving condition. Pennsylvania, before it made paper money, was totally

---

[64] Leavitt, Samuel: *Our Money Wars*; 1894

[65] Radio address given by the late Congressman Charles G. Binderup, of Nebraska in the 1950s, and compiled by Mrs. Lucie Boulrice, 1133 Liberty, Springfield, MA 01104. *How America created its own money in 1750.*

Chapter 13: Colonial America

stripped of its gold and silver ... The difficulties for want of cash were accordingly very great, the chief part of trade being carried on by the extremely inconvenient method of barter; when, in 1723, paper money was first made there, which gave new life to business, promoted greatly the settlement of new lands (by lending small sums to beginners on easy interest, to be paid in installments), whereby the province has so greatly increased in inhabitants that the export from hence thither is now more than tenfold what it then was, and by their trade with foreign colonies they have been able to obtain great quantities of gold and silver to remit hither in return for the manufactures of this country.[66]

Professor Natelson of Harvard explained:

This measure extended the ban on issuance of legal tender paper currency from New England to all American colonies. The immediate effect was significant deflation that eventually fostered considerable colonial resentment. Feelings had been deteriorating for some time, and continued to erode as older currencies were retired and the British rejected several substitutes for maintaining liquidity.[67]

For those who believe that a return to a gold-backed money is the answer for America's current monetary problems, look what happened to America after the Currency Act of 1764 was passed. According to Franklin:

That on a frivolous complaint of a few Virginia Merchants, nine Colonies were restrained from making paper money, they thought [it had] become absolutely necessary to their internal commerce, from the constant remittance of their gold and silver to Britain.[68]

But modern-day goldbugs ignore Franklin's explanations. The ever-determined Austrian, Murray Rothbard postulates that this "cheap" form of money – as opposed to "value" money – drove out gold and silver coin:

---

[66] Franklin, William Temple, *The Life and Writings of Benjamin Franklin.* (Philadelphia, McCarty & Davis, 1834), Vol. 2, p. 441

[67] Natelson, Robert G.: *Paper Money and the Original Understanding of the Coinage Clause*, Harvard Journal of Law & Public Policy, Summer, 2008, 31Harv. J.L. & Pub. Pol'y 1017.

[68] Benjamin Franklin; January 7, 1768; reprinted in The London Chronicle, August 30 and September 1, 1774

> ...it was precisely paper money issues that led, by Gresham's Law, to outflows and disappearance of specie from the colonies.[69]

Interestingly, this is one of the arguments the British used in support of passage of the Currency Act of 1764. According to Franklin:

> In the Report of the board of trade, dated February 9, 1764, the following reasons are given for *restraining the emission* of paper-bills of credit in America, as *a legal tender.*
>
> 1. "That it *carries the gold and silver out* of the province, and so ruins the country...."[70]

In other words, Rothbard's "Gresham's Law" argument that "cheap" paper money drives out value money. Today this theory is considered settled "fact" amongst the Austrian economists and goes unchallenged. Here is Franklin's response:

> That paper-money carries the gold and silver out of the province, and so ruins the country; as experience has shown, in every colony where it has been practiced in any great degree." -- The opinion, of its ruining the country, seems to be merely speculative, or not otherwise founded than upon misinformation in the matter of fact. The truth is, that the balance of their trade with Britain being greatly against them, the gold and silver are drawn out to pay that balance; and then the necessity of some medium of trade has induced the making of paper-money, which could not be carried away. Thus, if carrying out all the gold and silver ruins a country, every colony was ruined before it made paper-money.
>
> But, far from being ruined by it .... New England, particularly in 1696 (about the time they began the use of paper-money) had in all its provinces but 130 churches ... in 1750 they were 530.... the goods exported to them from England in 1750, before the restraint took place, were near five times as much as before they had paper-money.
>
> Pennsylvania, before it made any paper-money, was totally stript of its gold and silver.... The balance of trade carried out the gold and silver as fast as they were brought in.... The difficulties for want of cash were accordingly

---

[69] Rothbard, *A History*...., p. 50.
[70] Franklin, William Temple, *The Life and Writings of Benjamin Franklin.* (Philadelphia, McCarty & Davis, 1834), Vol. 2, p. 441

Chapter 13: Colonial America

> very great, the chief part of the trade being carried on by the extremely inconvenient method of barter; when in 1723 paper-money was first made there, which gave new life to business .... the province has so greatly increased in inhabitants, that the export from hence thither is now more than tenfold what it then was....
>
> New York and New Jersey have also increased greatly during the same period, with the use of paper-money; so that it does not appear to be of the ruinous nature ascribed to it.[71]

Franklin's rebuttal to the report of the British Board of Trade is very interesting reading. It is currently available online at Google Books:

URL: 7.tv/27d0

Thomas Jefferson felt that:

> Before the 19th of April, 1775 [the day succeeding the Battle of Lexington,] I never had heard a whisper of a disposition to separate from Great Britain. The Colonies had not yet cut asunder the ties of allegiance to the Crown. The Continental Congress had sent a petition to the King denying any intention of separation from England.[72]

In 1899, the respected monetary historian, Alexander Del Mar, explained that America's paper money was so beloved that forbidding it was the pivotal act that sent the colonies onto the unstoppable course of revolution.

> Although the Colonies were as yet uncertain of their course with respect to separation, there was no uncertainty with regard to their monetary system. This they had determined should be independent of the Crown and

---

[71] Franklin, William Temple, *The Life and Writings of Benjamin Franklin*. (Philadelphia, McCarty & Davis, 1834), Vol. 2, p. 442
[72] Del Mar, Alexander, *The History of Money in America: From the Earliest Times to the Present*, 1899, p. 96.

> this determination the had expressed in overt acts that had long marked them as disaffected rebels and were now to mark them as outlaws.
>
> Lexington and Concord were trivial acts of resistance which chiefly concerned those who took part in them and which might have been forgiven; but the creation and circulation of bills by revolutionary assemblies in Massachusetts and Philadelphia, were the acts of a whole people and coming as they did upon the heels of the strenuous efforts made by the Crown to suppress paper money in America, they constituted acts of defiance so contemptuous and insulting to the Crown that forgiveness was thereafter impossible.
>
> After these acts there was but one course for the Colonies; to stand by their monetary system. Thus the bills of credit of this era, which ignorance and prejudice have attempted to belittle into the mere instruments of a reckless financial policy, were really the standards of the revolution. They were more than this: they were the Revolution itself![73]

The bottom line was that goldbugs love to highlight the failings of paper money, but one fact remains unchallenged: paper money was popular. Professors Paul Studenski and Herman E. Krooss have summed up the colonial experience with paper money in this way:

> The depreciation of colonial paper money has usually been exaggerated. Where the bills were used in moderation and not as substitutes for taxes to pay current expenses, and where the bank notes were is sued cautiously and subject to rigid redemption, they did not have a bad history. Indeed, in seven colonies the experience was favorable while in the six others it was unfavorable.
>
> People were willing to accept the risks of inflation and the inconveniences of the lack of monetary uniformity over the economic consequences of deflation. As historian Mary M. Schweitzer observed of Pennsylvania, "paper money was virtually an 'apple pie and motherhood' issue throughout the colonial period."
>
> Nor were the advocates of paper money all--or even mostly--radical redistributionists and demagogues. Many responsible Americans believed that paper money, when properly secured, was a sensible approach to the colonies' need for liquidity. They believed that the colonies needed paper

---

[73] Ibid.

money to prevent the deflation that results when the supply of circulating media does not keep pace with a quickening economy.[74]

Inflation Financed the Revolution

Once the fighting broke out in the spring of 1775, the Continental Congress, having few alternatives, started its long march down the road to hyperinflation. According to Harvard's Professor Natelson:

> The Continental Congress decided to issue bills of credit worth two million Spanish-milled dollars to finance the cause. There were several reasons for this decision. First, Congress had the power to issue bills of credit but no authority to raise money through taxation. Second, the states did not pay the full amount of congressional requisitions but rather competed with Congress for European loans. Third, as noted above, paper money was popular. Congress soon issued more bills of credit. By 1778, continental issues had grown to $30 million; by 1779 to $150 million; and by 1780 to $240 million....
>
> It is easy to condemn the Continental Congress's venture into hyperinflation, but difficult to see how Congress could have financed the Revolution otherwise. At the time, many people did not see the episode as a failure at all. The liquidity was received favorably (at least at first), and the depreciation was seen as an informal tax for financing the war. And, of course, the war had been won.[75]

Here we have the absolute nub of the debt-free money issue, which goldbugs call "inflation" money. In a debt free system where the commonwealth's resources are being used for the common good, people understand that suffering inflation is sometimes necessary to affect a common goal. People understand – as they do even today in Guernsey – that at least all citizens are enduring the effects of the inflation equally, and they also understand that if it becomes intolerable, they can halt it at any time. This type of informed citizenry is the only kind that can possibly withstand the constant attacks and obfuscation of the money changers in order to reinstitute either a gold-backed deflationary money, or a completely debt-based so-called "elastic" currency, the gyrations of which

---

[74] Natelson, p. 7
[75] Ibid.

they and only they control. Neither helps the cause of freedom, nor furthers humankind's escape from serfdom.

Professor Rothbard completely ignores these arguments and their implications. Goldbugs today try to claim that because paper money didn't work during the Revolutionary War, it shouldn't be used today, but first of all, it did work, and secondly, it doesn't matter what backs your money, all that matters is who controls its QUANTITY? Will it be your elected officials? Or will it be some unelectable banker? Colonial paper money before the Revolution had worked so well that the Bank of England had Parliament outlaw it and forced America to use gold money which they could control.

British Counterfeiting of Continental Currency

On top of the inflation generated by Congress, there is the little-understood counterfeiting of American money as an act of economic warfare by the British.

British counterfeits were so good that:

> ...in April 1777 the king's counterfeiters ran an ad in a New York newspaper offering to sell their false currency to loyal subjects of the Crown at a rock-bottom price – the cost of the paper it was printed on.[76]

In 1777, Governor Josiah Bartlett of New Hampshire complained:

> We have lately discovered a most diabolical scheme to ruin the paper currency by counterfeiting it, vast quantities of the Massachusetts bill & ours, that are now passing are counterfeit, and so neatly done that it is extremely difficult to discover the difference... by what appears at present, it is a Tory plan and one of the most infernal that was ever hatched.[77]

The British had an elaborate distribution network throughout the colonies as well. These were called "shovers":

---

[76] Craughwell, Thomas: *Stealing Lincoln's Body*. (Cambridge, Mass., Belknap Press of Harvard University Press, 2007), p. 33.
[77] Josiah Bartlett to William Whipple, 1777, Gilder Lehrman Document Number: GLC 193 at Digital History Website, University of Houston.

Two of the British shovers, David Farnsworth and John Blair, were arrested in Danbury, Conn., with $10,000 in counterfeit currency on them. One of their excuses to try and avoid prison was that they were petty criminals compared to other shovers who were circulating $40,000 - $50,000.[78]

Needless to say, the QUANTITY of money was out of control.

The victory of the Americans in 1781 was a terrible defeat for moneychangers. It came as a complete shock that the new nation had been able to throw off its shackles from the richest nation in the world. With an entire continent from which to draw natural resources, America was destined to grow rich as it expanded westward. If America grew wealthy and printed her own debt free currency, other nations would surely follow her lead. Something had to be done.

---

[78] Glaser, Lynn: *Counterfeiting in America: The History of an American Way to Wealth*, (Philadelphia: Clarkson Potter, 1960), p. 37-39.

Chapter 14 – American Central Banking

In 1781, towards the end of the War, the Continental Congress met in Philadelphia. They pondered what to do about their grave financial situation. The money was so worthless that people papered their walls with it. Congress finally agreed to give a group of bankers a monopoly on creating U.S. money – by loaning it to the government. It was the first American privately owned central bank. The plan, of course, was modeled on the Bank of England.

Bank of North America

The new bank would be called the Bank of North America. Headed by Robert Morris, it would be the first of a string of controversial privately owned central banks that Congress would charter, then in the face of public outrage un-charter, over the years.

Morris was the man who handled the banking business for the Continental Congress. A Tory at heart, he refused to sign the Declaration of Independence until several weeks after its adoption in the hopes that reconciliation with Great Britain could still be achieved.[79] According to *Encyclopedia Britannica*:

> As Financial Superintendent of the Continental Congress, Morris was able to reduce the United States Treasury to a state of indigence by the end of seven years of war.[80]

So after a stiff battle, Congress killed this, the first privately owned central bank in America.

1787 – U.S. Constitution

Two years later, when it came time to write the Constitution In 1787, many of the delegates did not remember how well America's government-issued paper money had worked in Pennsylvania. They were still stung

---

[79] Lewis Paul Todd and Merle Curti, *Rise of the American Nation*; (New York: Harcourt, Brace & World, Inc, second edition), p. 131 .
[80] *Encyclopedia Britannica*, 15th edition (1980), s.v. "Morris, Robert."

by the inflation of the Bank of North America and the hyperinflation during the Revolution, primarily caused by British counterfeiting.

Strangely, the Constitution allows the federal government to borrow money, but until 2008 with the publication of Dr. Natelson's paper, this broader definition of "to coin Money" was highly debatable, and so some argued that the Constitution was silent on the federal role in Federal government's issuance of paper money.

Bills of Credit

Although Congress had approved the Articles of Confederation in 1777, just two years into the Revolution, it did not become effective until the thirteenth state, Maryland, ratified it in 1781. The Articles gave the Congress the express right to "emit bills on the credit of the United States."

There is so much confusion on the definition of a "bill of credit" let's try to unravel this centuries-old mystery. Strangely, emitting "bills of credit" was specifically forbidden by the U.S. Constitution of 1787 as a power for the States (Article 1, Section 10), but there is no mention of the federal role. A bill of credit was government I.O.U. – either state or federal – that circulated as money.

> ... The phrase "bill of credit" was, technically, only one kind of paper money – a circulating instrument representing a government debt.[81]

In other words, the specific intent of the U.S. Constitution may well have been to allow federal government borrowing, but to forbid States from borrowing by issuing debt-based paper money. In any case, as a result, the issuance of debt-based money fell to private banks.

Article 1, Section 8

> The Congress shall have Power ...
>
> [Clause 2] To borrow Money on the credit of the United States ...

---

[81] Natelson, p. 11.

> [Clause 5] To coin Money, regulate the Value thereof ....

To Thomas Jefferson, clause 2 was the biggest – if not the only – defect he saw in the Constitution:

> I wish it were possible to obtain a single amendment to our Constitution. I would be willing to depend on that alone for the reduction of the administration of our government; I mean an additional article taking from the Federal Government the power of borrowing.[82]

Notice how Jefferson had successfully thought through the consequences of no more national debt: it would automatically reduce the size of government spending. This question needs to be asked again and again; why would a sovereign nation borrow when it has the power to create?

This defect in the Constitution is at the root of all our economic problems today.

To "coin" Money

Another contentious phrase in the Constitution is in Article 1, Section 8:

> Congress shall have the power ... To coin Money, regulate the Value thereof....

First of all, the term "coin" is in lower-case, indicating a verb. If the term "coin" implies the use of metallic coins only, then why would its "Value" need regulating? G. Edward Griffin's "Natural Law No. 1" proclaimed that gold is stable in value – and should need no government regulation:

> LAW: Long-term price stability is possible only when the money supply is based upon the gold (or silver) supply without government interference.[83]

So then, why did King Henry feel compelled to issue tally sticks in 1100 A.D. in England to break the power of the goldsmiths? Why did England force the American colonies to use gold money instead of their new, cheap paper money? As Harvard's Robert G. Natelson points out:

---

[82] Randall, Henry Stephens, *The Life of Thomas Jefferson*: 1858, vol. 2, p. 453. Also cited as a letter to John Taylor of Caroline, November 26, 1798; reproduced in *The Writings of Thomas Jefferson* v. 10, edited by Lipscomb and Bergh.
[83] Griffin, p. 146

Chapter 14: American Central Banking 93

... coin ... even in monetarist Britain [meant] Payment of any kind" and "all Manner of the several Stamps and Species in any Nation. The verb "to coin" could mean "to make or forge anything" (represented today by the common expression, "to coin a phrase"); so, pursuant to this usage, paper money could be "coined."

To the modern speaker of English, the metallic meaning seems the more natural one, but this was less so in the eighteenth century.

In 1700, the anonymous author of a pamphlet on trade reflected on how other nations might compete with the English woolen trade by "Coining Paper Money."

In 1720, economist John Law proposed "Coining Notes of one Pound" and otherwise "coining" paper money.

A few years later, Daniel Defoe related how tradesmen "coined bills payable from one to another."

When the American colonies declared their independence, John Shebbeare attacked them for "coining paper money."

The debates in the Irish Parliament of 1784 include a reference to "coining paper into money."

Thomas Paine argued that "[o]f all the various sorts of base coin, paper-money is the basest."

When Benjamin Franklin urged issuance of Pennsylvania paper money secured by land, he characterized it as "Coined Land."

In the 1742 case of Charitable Corporation v. Sutton, Chancellor Hardwicke referred to "notes coined" by private parties, and to "coining notes."[84]

The U.S. Supreme Court has also found that America can issue money other than metallic coin.

To once again view Julliard v. Greenman, 1884:

---

[84] Griffin, p. 156.

Chapter 14: American Central Banking

URL: 7.tv/26bc

Over a century ago, the Supreme Court decided the Legal Tender Cases, holding that Congress could authorize legal tender paper money in addition to metallic coin. ... On the other hand, those who argue that the original Constitution authorized paper currency observe that the Constitution's specific bans on bills of credit and tender laws apply only to the states, and therefore (expressio unius est exclusio alterius) those prohibitions do not apply to the federal government...[85]

Professor Natelson goes on:

In April 1601, an Irish merchant, Brett of Drogheda, purchased some goods from a London merchant named Gilbert, for which Brett promised to pay £200, half of which was to be remitted at a certain locale in Dublin shortly thereafter, payable in "sterling, current and lawful money of England."

On May 24, 1601, however -- before Brett was to tender the first £ 100 -- Elizabeth issued for Ireland, then under English control, a coinage made of an alloy of silver and base metal. The Queen ordered that this "mixed money" was to replace the more nearly silver "sterling" coins that before had circulated in Ireland. She further ordered that the new coinage was to be legal tender, for she expressly commanded that this money should be so used, accepted and reputed by all her subjects others, using any traffick, or commerce within this kingdom; and that if any person or persons should refuse to receive this *mixed money* according to the denomination or valuation thereof, *viz.* shillings for shillings, sixpenny pieces for sixpenny pieces, &c. being tendered for any payment of any wages, fees, stipends, debts, &c. they should be punished . . . .

---

[85] Natelson, Robert G.: *Paper Money and the Original Understanding of the Coinage Clause,* Harvard Journal of Law & Public Policy, Summer, 2008, 31 Harv. J.L. & Pub. Pol'y 1017.

Chapter 14: American Central Banking 95

At the appropriate time and place, therefore, Brett offered Gilbert £ 100 in the new, less valuable currency, which, of course, Gilbert did not want to accept. The question before the Privy Council was whether Brett had made a good tender.

The Council decided that he had. First, it declared that every country needed a common standard of money for purposes of exchange. Citing civil law scholar Jean Bodin, the Council characterized money as a "public measure," for "[m]oney is the proper medium and measure of the exchange of things."

Next, the Council ruled that it was the Crown's exclusive prerogative to make or coin money and that "it appertaineth to the King only to put a value upon coin, and make the price of the quantity, and to put a print to it; which being done the coin is current."

Thirdly, the Privy Council ruled "that as the King by his prerogative may make money of what matter and form he pleaseth, and establish the standard of it, so may he change his money in substance and impression, and enhance or debase the value of it, or entirely decry and annul it" and that he could "set the value of money" at his own discretion, without the consent of others. In the Council's view, the power to strike coin and to regulate its value went together as a matter of law: "*Monetae aestimationem dat qui cudendi potestatem habet.*" In other words, the Crown had full right to claim *seigniorage*, the profit generated from pegging the currency at a legal tender value greater than the sum of the minting and material costs. The Council added that the power of the sovereign to alter the form of money *included the power to use any material he or she chose.* The sovereign could even fabricate money out of leather if he or she so pleased. (Indeed, later in the century, the deposed James II, then in possession of Ireland, actually did coin leather money.

The sovereign was always free to set the legal tender value well above intrinsic value, as Queen Elizabeth had done for Ireland. Queen Anne's proclamation for the colonies mandated legal tender values higher than intrinsic values for all coins listed. In Britain, gold passed by weight, but the legal tender value of silver or copper coin was set at its "tale," or face amount, which was generally above intrinsic value.

To summarize: The royal prerogative included authority to regulate British domestic commerce, and regulation by prerogative sometimes was extended to the colonies. As the Framers recognized, this commercial authority included governance of weights and measures, of which the medium of payment was considered one branch. The royal power over the medium of payment included authority to strike "coin" of any denomination and from any material, and to regulate the value of that coin and of foreign money. Regulating the value of money encompassed designating what items were legal tender and at what rates (and for what debts) they had to be accepted. The Crown took any profit derived from setting legal tender value higher than minting costs.

So it is clear that the term "To coin Money" gives Congress the power to make anything become money. Interestingly, Griffin avoids examining the Constitutional meaning of these terms so central to his pro-gold money thesis. In fact, he does not mention "Constitution" or "U.S. Constitution" – a single time -- at least in the Index -- in his 600-page defense of gold money.

Article 1, Section 10

Legal Tender

You frequently hear Goldbugs lambast "legal tender laws." What's this all about? As Griffin explains it:

> The two characteristics of fiat money ... are (1) it does not represent anything of intrinsic value and (2) it is decreed legal tender. Legal tender simply means that there is a law requiring everyone to accept the currency in commerce. The two always go together because, since the money really is worthless, it soon would be rejected by the public in favor of a more reliable medium of exchange, such as gold or silver coin.[86]

Another author published by the Ludwig von Mises Institute, puts it this way:

> ... The question arises why legal-tender laws have been tried so frequently in the history of monetary institutions. There are two possible answers: ignorance of the political leadership or shameless iniquity.[87]

---

[86] Griffin, p. 155.
[87] Hulsmann, Jorg Guido, *The Ethics of Money Production*. (Auburn, Alabama, Ludwig von Mises Instutite, 2008), p. 128

Chapter 14: American Central Banking

However, there are other reasonable opinions. Pelatiah Webster of Philadelphia explained the common understanding of the period when in 1780 he wrote:

> The nature of a Tender-Act is no more or less than establishing by law the standard value of money, and has the same use with respect to the currency, that the legal standard pound, bushel, yard, or gallon has to these goods, the quantities of which are usually ascertained by those weights and measures....[88]

There were many examples of items of value -- not made of gold or silver -- being used as money and defined by legal tender laws:

> In 1637, the government of Massachusetts declared white wampum legal tender for debts under twelve pence at the rate of four white beads per penny, and in 1640 it declared "blueu" wampum legal tender at 2 beads per penny. Wampum retained this legal tender status for another twenty-one years. Massachusetts also designated musket balls legal tender at four per penny. Wool became legal tender for some purposes in Rhode Island, as did rice in South Carolina.

> Not surprisingly, this experimentation gave Americans expansive ideas about the materials proper for money. One Boston essayist writing in 1740 defined "Money" as "*any Matter*, whether Metal, Wood, Leather, Glass, Horn, Paper, Fruits, Shells, Kernels &c. which hath Course as a Medium of Commerce" -- a formulation in sharp contrast to the metal-oriented definitions current in Britain. It was during the course of this experimentation that the British colonists created "the first fiat paper moneys in the western world."[89]

As we saw earlier in British history, someone has to decide what form, what material and what purity.

> ... For only by deciding issues of legal tender could Congress fully "regulate the Value" of money. If Congress were denied the power to determine questions of legal tender, then it would be missing an important tool that governments traditionally employed for monetary regulation.

> The historical record does not seem to contain anything that suggests the ratifiers' understanding of the phrase "regulate the Value [of Money]" differed from the public meaning at the time.[90]

---

[88] Natelson, p. 12.
[89] Natelson, p. 6.
[90] Natelson, p. 12

In summary, the U.S. Constitution grants Congress full authority to issue any form of money, not just metallic money. According to Harvard's Professor Natelson:

> According to the original understanding, the Constitution's Coinage Clause granted to Congress the express power to coin money and bestow legal tender quality upon that money....
>
> In addition, the money thus "coined" did not need to be metallic. Paper or any other material that Congress selected would suffice.[91]

1st Bank of the United States

The lack of defining who <u>could</u> issue bills of credit under the new Constitution left the door wide open for Alexander Hamilton and his banker friends to ram a bill through Congress in 1791, 4 years after the Constitution had been signed, to turn over creation of the nation's money to private bankers once again.

Like all the privately owned central banks that would follow, the new bank was given a name that would deceive people into thinking it was part of the U.S. government. But it was not!

It was called the 1st Bank of the United States (1st BUS). After a contentious debate, Congress granted the new bank a 20-year charter – a private monopoly. Again, the nation's money would be created out of thin air by the new bank and loaned to the government and to private individuals – all at interest – just as our money supply is created today.

For a picture of the 1st BUS:

URL: 7.tv/28cf

---

[91] Natelson, p. 16

So if there was $100 million worth of money in the economy, there would be $100 million of national debt – debt the citizens and their children would have to pay interest on by taxation. And so it is today, the national debt is roughly the same as the national money supply.

The Bank was given a monopoly on the printing of U.S. currency, even though 80% of its stock would be held privately. The U.S. government would hold the other 20%. As with the Bank of North America, however, this was merely a device to help the private stockholders come up with their initial subscription amounts. When the U.S. put up $2,000,000 in cash, Hamilton and Thomas Willing multiplied that through the magic of fractional reserve banking to lend their friends sufficient amounts to enable them to come up with the additional $8,000,000 in capital needed for this risk-free investment.

The 1st BUS immediately got down to the business of loaning the Federal government money, instead of the government simply creating it without debt and being restrained in its spending by having to raise taxes <u>immediately</u> to cover any potential deficit spending. Now, with a central bank in place, the effects of excessive government spending could be hidden behind a curtain of borrowing, pushing off repayment until the current members of Congress had passed from the scene and any retribution.

As Thomas J. DiLorenzo, professor of economics at Loyola College put it:

> Hamilton... wanted to create a large national debt, period. If the states were permitted to pay off their own war debts, this would not be possible. Hamilton called the public debt "a public blessing" because of his belief that it would tie the wealthy (who would own the government's bonds) of the country to the government, and they would in turn provide political support for higher and higher taxes, to make sure that there was enough money in the treasury to pay off their principal and interest.[92]

Gouverneur Morris, an assistant to Robert Morris (though no relation) and one of the primary authors of large sections of the U.S. Constitution,

---

[92] *Hamiltonian Hagiography,* a monograph by Thomas J. DiLorenzo, July 14, 2008, LewRockwell.com. http://www.lewrockwell.com/dilorenzo/dilorenzo145.html

described the motivations of the owners of the Bank of North America in a letter to James Madison written on July 2, 1787:

> The rich will strive to establish their dominion and enslave the rest. They always did. They always will.... They will have the same effect here as elsewhere, if we do not, by [the power of] government, keep them in their proper spheres.[93]

Gouverneur Morris was exactly right, and you see this same theme being replayed in today's political discourse. It is popular to chastise government in general, and Congress in particular as being too corrupt to handle the money power. As Gouverneur Morris correctly points out, government is all we have to keep the powers of financial capitalism from devouring the rest. Government is all we've got – the only power strong enough to keep a return to serfdom at bay.

With the creation of the 1st BUS, the financial system had been given over completely into the hands of financial capitalism once again; Alexander Hamilton, Robert Morris, and the other proponents of the privately owned central bank. And the result, according to Professor DiLorenzo:

> Hamilton succeeded in turning many wealthy people into lobbyists for statism. As Douglas Adair an editor of *The Federalist Papers*, explained: "With devious brilliance, Hamilton set out, by a program of class legislation, to unite the propertied interests of the eastern seaboard into a cohesive administration party, while at the same time he attempted to make the executive dominant over the Congress by a lavish use of the spoils system. In carrying out this scheme ... Hamilton transformed every financial transaction of the Treasury Department into an orgy of speculation and graft in which selected senators, congressmen, and certain of their richer constituents throughout the nation participated."[94]

Four years after the founding of the 1st BUS, in 1785, the value of the new currency had plummeted. Inflation was rampant. Prices had risen by 72%.

> Hamilton's "system of public credit for the national government," which is praised by Bordewich and all other Hamiltonian hagiographers, was in reality a recipe for financial irresponsibility and corruption. As John C. Miller

---

[93] *The Anti-Federalist Papers and the Constitutional Convention Debates*, Ralph Ketcham, ed. (New York, NY, Penguin Group, Signet Classic, 2003), p. 107.
[94] *Hamiltonian Hagiography*

wrote in *The Federalist Era*, after Hamilton's "system" was put into place, "the national debt soared to a total of over $80 million. To service this debt, almost 80 percent of the annual expenditures of the government were required. During the period 1790-1800, payment of the interest alone of the national debt consumed 40 percent of the national tax revenue.... a staggering burden of debt."[95]

Within a single year, Jefferson, as the first Secretary of State blasted the notion of perpetual national debt.

> As the doctrine is that a public debt is a public blessing, so they think a perpetual one is a perpetual blessing, and therefore wish to make it so large that we can never pay it off.[96]

Within 5 years, the federal government owed $6.2 million to the 1st BUS.[97] The entire U.S. budget for that year, 1796, was only $5.9 million![98] During the same 5-year period, wholesale prices jumped by 72%. Remember, the 1st BUS endured for 20 years.

State Banks

But just as today, government borrowing wasn't the only problem. The money creation power was now left to the "free market," and a new series of State banks sprung up to meet the money needs of the expanding nation.

Before the 1st BUS was founded, there were only 4 commercial banks in the entire United States. In the first years, 1791-92, eight new commercial State banks were founded, and 10 more by 1796.[99] All of them were printing their own paper money as well as lending out much more bank

---

[95] *Hamiltonian Hagiography*
[96] *The Jeffersonian Cyclopedia*. Edited by John p. Foley, (New York & London, Funk & Wagnalls Company, 1900), p. 236; citing "To Nicholas Lewis. iii, 348. Ford ED, v. 505. (Pa., April 1792)
[97] Rothbard, Murray, *A History of Money and Banking in the United States Before the Twentieth Century*, (Auburn, Alabama; Ludwig von Mises Institute, 2005), p. 69.
[98] http://tinyurl.com/2badc96
[99] Rothbard, Murray, A History ...., p. 70.

credit money then they actually had gold in the vaults -- between 4 and 5 times as much.[100] So much for "honest" "gold-backed" money.

The 1st BUS, itself was lending out 2.5 times as much as it had gold on deposit.[101]

In July of 1797, just 4 months after George Washington retired from being the nation's first president, he spoke out on debt as well in a letter to his nephew, Samuel Washington:

> For you may be assured, that there is no practice more dangerous than that of borrowing money (instance as proof the case of your father and uncles), for when money can be had in this way, repayment is seldom thought of in time; the interest becomes a moth; exertions to raise it by dent of industry cease; it comes easy and is spent freely, and many things indulged in that would never be thought of if [they were] purchased by the sweat of the brow; in the mean time the debt is accumulating like a snow ball in rolling.[102]

1792: The Coinage Act Myth

Goldbugs have frequently challenged me during speeches or radio interviews that the Coinage Act of 1792 specifically mandates that a U.S. dollar must be made of gold or silver. Well, that's not exactly true, so let's set the record straight once and for all.

The official name of the Coinage Act of April 2, 1792 is:

> An Act establishing a Mint, and regulating the Coins of the United States.

Interestingly, it does not mention paper money (bills of credit). It does not forbid paper money. It does not say that only gold and silver may be used as money. It merely established how much pure gold and silver will be in each coin and established the existence of a Mint to create these coins. In Sec. 16 it states only that "... all gold and silver coins ... struck at ... the mint, shall be a lawful tender in all payments....

---

[100] Ibid, p. 71.
[101] Ibid
[102] George Washington in a letter to his nephew, Samuel Washington, Mount Vernon, 12 July, 1797, as cited by Edward Everett Hale, *The Life of George Washington: Studied Anew*, 1887, p. 356

Chapter 14: American Central Banking

It says "a" lawful tender, not "the" lawful tender. It doesn't say that these coins are the only money in the realm. In fact, apparently the purity and weight of the coins was set to conform to the Spanish coins of that day so they could be used as well, though it does not specifically spell that out.

Despite things I have been told for decades, this document certainly does NOT say that the U.S. Dollar is defined EXCLUSIVELY as a certain weight of gold or silver and therefore nothing else should be considered as official U.S. money.

Feel free to read the Coinage Act for yourself at the U.S. Mint's website:

URL: 7.tv/12b9

The relevant passages begin at Section 9 where it defines how what purity and weight of gold shall be in gold and silver coins:

> That there shall be from time to time struck and coined at the said mint, coins of gold, silver, and copper, of the following denominations, values and descriptions, viz. Eagles—each to be of the value of ten dollars or units, and to contain two hundred fort-seven grains and four eighths of a grain of pure, or two hundred and seventy grains of standard gold. Half eagles—each to be of the value of five dollars, and to contain one hundred and twenty three grains and six eights of a grain of pure, or one hundred and thirty five grains of standard gold. Quarter Eagles—each to be of the value of two dollars and a half dollar, and to contain sixty one grains and seven eighths of a grain of pure, or sixty seven grains and four eights of a grain of standard gold. Dollars or the same is now current, and to contain three hundred and seventy-one grains and four sixteenth parts of a grain of pure, or four hundred and sixteen grains of standard silver, Half Dollars—each to be of half the value of the dollar or unit, and to contain one hundred and eighty-five grains and ten sixteenth parts of a grain of pure, or two hundred and eights of a grain of standard silver. Quarter Dollars—each to be of one fourth the value of the dollar or unit, and to contain ninety-two grains and thirteen sixteenth parts of a grain of pure, or one hundred and four grains of

standard silver. Dismes—each to be of the value of one tenth of a dollar or unit, and to contain thirty seven grains and two sixteenth parts of a grain of pure, or forty one grains and three fifth parts of a grain of standard silver. Half Dismes—each to be of the value of one twentieth of a dollar, and to contain eighteen grains and nine sixteenth parts of a grain of pure, or twenty grains and four fifth parts of a grain of standard silver. Cents—each to be of the value of the one hundredth part of a dollar, and to contain eleven pennyweights of copper. Half Cents—each to be of the value of half a cent, and to contain five penny-weights and half a penny-weight of copper.

Section 10 spells out what legends and emblems should be on the coins. Section 11 says that the ratio of gold to silver in U.S. coinage shall remain 15 to 1, etc., etc.

War of 1812

Although Jefferson served two terms as President from 1801 to 1809, nothing was done until the Bank's charter came up for renewal in 1811. Jefferson probably knew that Congress was sharply divided with the new State banks having plenty of money to spend to insure that the 1st BUS system continue their guaranteed income. The press openly attacked the Bank calling it "a great swindle".

After another contentious debate, the Bank's renewal bill was defeated by a single vote in both the House and Senate. The disbanding of the 1st BUS did not take the money power away from the new State banks, however. They kept printing and lending money just like before.

Certainly the printing of paper money by these state banks was a DIRECT violation of Article 1, Section 10 of the Constitution authored only a generation earlier:

> No state shall ... coin Money; emit Bills of Credit; make any Thing but gold and silver Coin a Tender in Payment of Debts....

And yet Austrian economist Prof. Murray Rothbard – whose book is otherwise very useful in the details of banking of the period -- never mentions this in, *A History of Money and Banking in the United States Before the Twentieth Century*. Within five months, the War of 1812 was on. In 1813, Jefferson wrote to his son-in-law, John Eppes:

Chapter 14: American Central Banking

> Although we have so foolishly allowed the [power of issuing our own debt free money] to be taken from us by private individuals, I think we may recover it . . . . The states should be asked to transfer the right of issuing paper money to Congress, in perpetuity.[103]

Jefferson had it exactly right. Congress and only Congress should have the right to issue America's paper money – and at no interest to no one. By January 1814, however, Jefferson saw things differently:

> I see that this infatuation of banks must take its course, until actual ruin shall awaken us from its delusions. Until the gigantic banking propositions of this winter had made their appearance in the different Legislatures, I had hoped that the evil might still be checked; but I see now that it is desperate, and that we must fold our arms and go to the bottom with the ship.[104]

In 1814, the British successfully attacked Washington and burned the White House and the Capitol. Shortly thereafter, a series of bank failures were triggered by too much fractional reserve lending by the burgeoning number of State banks. The southern states had no banks before the creation of the 1st BUS. The south, being newer economies, had less gold, so the southern banks were inflating about 5 times as much the New England banks. Here are the reserve ratios of outstanding notes and credit money compared to gold reserves as reported by Rothbard:

> Massachusetts – 1.96 to 1
> New Hampshire – 2.7 to 1
> South Carolina – 18.46 to 1
> Virginia – 18.73 to 1

The bubble burst in the summer of 1814 when the New England banks demanded that the southern banks redeem all their paper money for gold. The British navy had successfully blockaded much of the coastline and the British Army was trying to cut off New England from the rest of the nation. In August of 1814, the U.S. government, with the concurrence of the southern state governments, allowed the southern banks to suspend these specie payments:

---

[103] Jefferson, Thomas: *Memoir, Correspondence, and Miscellanies: From the Papers of Thomas Jefferson*, 1829, p. 199.
[104] *The Jeffersonian Cyclopedia*. p. 75; citing "To President Madison. Ford ed., ix, 453. (M., Feb. 1815)"

...That is, to stop all redemption of notes and deposits in gold or silver – and yet continue in operation.... While they themselves could expand their loans and operations and force their own debtors to repay their loans as usual.[105]

Jefferson wrote to Thomas Cooper:

> The paper interest is now defunct. Their gossamer castles are dissolved, and they can no longer impede and overawe the salutary measures of the government. Their paper was received on a belief that it was cash on demand. Themselves have declared it was nothing....[106]

Jefferson termed this unbridled private money creation "insanity itself" when "abandoned to the discretion of avarice and of swindlers."[107]

> It is impossible not to deplore our past follies, and their present consequences, but let them at least be warnings against like follies in future.[108]

Jefferson then compared this privately issued money to debt-free government issued money:

> The crush will be tremendous; very different from that brought on by our paper money. That rose and fell so gradually that it kept all on their guard, and affected severely only early or long-winded contracts. Here the contract of yesterday crushes in an instant the one or the other party. The banks stopping payment suddenly, all their mercantile and city debtors do the same....[109]

> Providence seems, indeed, by a special dispensation, to have put down for us, without a struggle, that very paper enemy which the interest of our citizens long since required ourselves to put down, at whatever risk. The work is done. The moment is pregnant with futurity, and if not seized at once by Congress, I know not on what shoal our bark is next to be stranded.[110]

Then Jefferson lays out a simple plan:

> The banks have now discontinued themselves. We are now without any medium [of exchange]; and necessity, as well as patriotism, and confidence, will make us all eager to receive treasury notes, if founded on specific taxes. Congress may now borrow of the public, and without interest, all the money they may want, to

---

[105] Rothbard, Murray, A History ...., p. 74.
[106] *The Jeffersonian Cyclopedia*. p. 76; citing "To Thomas Cooper. vi,382 (M., Sep. 1814)
[107] *The Jeffersonian Cyclopedia*. p. 76; citing "To Thomas Cooper. vi,382 (M., Sep. 1814)
[108] Ibid
[109] Ibid
[110] Idib

Chapter 14: American Central Banking

the amount of a competent circulation, by merely issuing their own promissory notes, of proper denominations for the larger purposes of circulation, but not for the small. Leave that door open for the entrance of metallic money.[111]

Shortly thereafter, Jefferson wrote to President Madison:

> The failure of our banks ... restores to us a fund which ought never to have been surrendered by the nation, and which now, prudently used, will carry us through all the fiscal difficulties of war.[112]

Jefferson made a number of pro-hard money quotes as well and goldbugs always use those, and ignore those above. This can lead them astray. For example, Prof. Mark Skousen holds the Benjamin Franklin Chair of Management at Grantham University. He is an Austrian economist and a frequent contributor on CNBC's *Kudlow & Company*. In a review of Murray Rothbard's *The Panic of 1819*, Skousen said:

> Jefferson believed that only specie should be allowed to circulate.

The above Jefferson quotes indicate that at least Jefferson was unsure of that.

The War of 1812 ended with the Treaty of Ghent on Christmas Eve, 1814, but news of the peace treaty took two months to reach the U.S., during which time, fighting continued. In January 1815, Jefferson wrote to President Monroe again:

> The dominion of the banks must be broken, or it will break us.[113]

In February 1815, Jefferson wrote to W.H. Crawford:

> The fatal possession of the whole circulating medium of our banks, the excess of those institutions, and their present discredit, cause all our difficulties.[114]

A further study of Jefferson's feelings about monetary policy is warranted. Although he produced many quotes talking about metal coinage, at least,

---

[111] Ibid

[112] *The Jeffersonian Cyclopedia*. p. 76; citing "To President Madison. vi,386 (M., Sep. 1814)".

[113] *The Jeffersonian Cyclopedia*. p. 75; citing "To James Monroe. vi, 409 Ford ed., ix, 498. (M., Jan. 1815)".

[114] *The Jeffersonian Cyclopedia*. p. 75; citing "To W.H. Crawford. vi, 419 Ford ed., ix, 503. (M., Feb. 1815)".

he produced many that were obviously right on target for monetary reformers.

Chapter 15 – 2nd BUS

After the conclusion of the war of 1812, the very next year, the bankers were back trying to get Congress to reinstate their precious privately owned central bank.

By the end of the War of 1812, the nation's money supply had tripled. The U.S. government had encouraged new startup banks in the southern states to buy government war bonds to help finance the war, and in return, let them be used as a basis for currency formation. Now that bill was coming due. Prices tripled. Banking was in a state of chaos.

If Congress would have had the political will, as Jefferson said, this was the perfect time to take back the money power, but such was not the case. The privately owned central bank had done great things for bankers, and they were determined to get it back. In October 1815, Jefferson lashed out in a letter to then Treasury Secretary Gallatin:

> The treasury, lacking confidence in the country, delivered itself bound hand and foot to bold and bankrupt ... bankers pretending to have money, whom it could have crushed at any moment.[115]

The 2nd BUS bill was pushed through Congress by the Secretary of Treasury, Alexander J. Dallas, a wealthy Philadelphia lawyer who was a close friend and counsel to one of the two wealthiest men in America, Stephen Girard. Girard had been the largest stockholder in the 1st BUS, and was a heavy investor in the war debt of the U.S. during the War of 1812.[116] Senator William H. Wells from Delaware was a vocal opponent of the 2nd BUS bill, saying that it was:

> ...ostensibly for the purpose of correcting the diseased state of our paper currency by restraining and curtailing the overissue of bank paper [-- State bank notes --], and yet it came prepared to inflict upon us the same evil, being itself nothing more than simply a paper-making machine.[117]

---

[115] Thomas Jefferson, October 1815 letter to Gallatin. *Letters and Addresses*, edit. William Parker, (New York: 1905).
[116] Rothbard, Murray, *A History* ...,, p. 84.
[117] Rothbard, Murray, *A History* ...., p. 85.

Chapter 15: 2nd BUS

Jefferson, writing to Samuel Kerchival in 1816, noted the sad state of the debt-burdened English people:

> If we run into such debts... as the people of England are, our people, like them, must come to labor sixteen hours in the twenty-four, give the earnings of fifteen of these to the government for their debts and daily expenses; and the sixteenth being insufficient to afford us bread, we must live, as they now do, on oatmeal and potatoes; have no time to think, no means of calling the mismanagers to account; but be glad to obtain subsistence by hiring ourselves out to rivet their chains on the necks of our fellow-sufferers.[118]

Think about it. Does this sound like conditions today?

Despite the protests of Jefferson and others, in 1816, Congress passed the 2nd BUS bill. The bank's 20-year charter was a carbon copy of that of the 1st BUS in every main respect. Again the U.S. Government owned 20% of the shares of the bank, and again, this was done primarily to secure immediate cash from government coffers which could, through the magic of fractional reserve lending, be multiplied to provide the required startup capital. The bank failed to raise the minimum amount of gold necessary for legal startup operations -- $7 million. In fact, no more than $2.5 million in gold was ever held by the 2nd BUS.[119]

Within a year, the nation was awash in money. The estimate for the total amount of money rose from $67.3 million in 1816, to $94.7 million by the end of 1818 – 40.7% in two years.

> Most of this increase was supplied by the Bank of the United States.[120]

Banks sprang up at every bend in the road as America surged westward. The total number of U.S. banks grew by 46% in the first two years following the Bank's charter. Each new bank multiplied it's capital by whatever they could get away with – sometimes by the complete fraud of infinity.

---

[118] *The Jeffersonian Cyclopedia*. p. 235; citing "To Samuel Kerchival. Ford ed., vii, 14. Ford ED., x, 41. (M., 1816)"
[119] Rothbard, Murray, *A History* ...., p. 86.
[120] Rothbard, Murray, *A History* ...., p. 87.

Chapter 15: 2nd BUS

To Murray Rothbard, the precedent for this unchecked money creation by private banks started with the suspension of specie redemption in August of 1814:

> Historians dedicated to the notion that central banks restrain state or private bank inflation have placed the blame for the multiplicity of banks and bank credit inflation during the War of 1812 on the absence of a central bank. But... both the number of banks and bank credit grew apace during the period of the First Bank of the United States ... and would continue to do so under the Second Bank.... And the federal government, not the state banks themselves, [was] largely to blame for encouraging new, inflated banks to monetize the war debt. Then... it allowed them to suspend specie payment ... for two and a half years after the war was over, until February 1817. Thus... banks were permitted to operate and expand while issuing what was tantamount to fiat paper and bank deposits.[121]

In other words, with the suspension of specie payment in 1814 to prevent the collapse of the new State banks, bankers got used to the idea that they could inflate as much as they wanted without fear of retribution from Washington. This inflation was extreme. Wholesale prices increased 35% per year on average:

> ...[In] different cities ... inflation [ranged] from 28 percent to 55 percent. Since foreign trade was cut off by the war, prices of imported commodities rose far more, averaging 70%.
>
> But more important than this inflation was the precedent set ... for the banking system for the future. From then on, every time there was a banking crisis brought on by inflationary expansion... state and federal governments looked the other way.... It thus became clear to the banks that in a general crisis they would not be required to meet the ordinary obligations of contract law or of ... property rights, so their inflationary expansion was permanently encouraged....[122]

Just three years into the new central bank that was supposed to control such matters, the 2nd BUS decided to exercise its control by severely reducing the money supply lest the nation suffer continued inflation. The 2nd BUS contracted its money supply alone by 47.2% in the first year.

---

[121] Rothbard, Murray, *A History* .... p. 75.
[122] Rothbard, Murray, *A History* .... p.76.

Compare that to the deliberate contraction of the money supply by the Fed in the 1930s which was the admitted cause of the Great Depression – only 33% over a period of 3 years.

As a result the nation under control of the 2nd BUS was a massive rash of defaults:

> There was a vast drop in real estate values and rents.... Public land sales dropped ... from $13.6 million in 1818 to $1.7 million in 1820.[123]

The economy came to a screeching halt. Money of any kind became scarce. Murray Rothbard paints a picture of benign ignorance on the part of the 2nd Bank in regard to the contraction and subsequent depression. His idea is this was just the natural outgrowth of inflation and even refers to it as the "first nationwide 'boom-bust' cycle"[124] as though it is as immutable and unmanageable as the transits of Uranus. Other authors saw it differently, however:

> Why wait for the apples to fall when the harvest can be hastened simply by shaking the tree?[125]

It wasn't the first contraction of the American currency. Certainly Parliament's banning of Continental currency before the Revolution, then offering only half its face value, was equally disastrous – a 50% deflation – and hardly accidental. But this was just the first of a series of booms and busts that has plagued our nation ever since.

By 1819, the entire nation had fallen into a deep financial depression. Naturally, this didn't sit too well with the American people, and it didn't take much encouragement by up-and-coming politicians to finger the Bank as the culprit.

For more info on the 2nd BUS:

---

[123] Rothbard, Murray, *A History* .... p.90.
[124] Rothbard, Murray, *A History* .... p.89.
[125] Griffin, p. 344.

URL: 7.tv/10bf

Andrew Jackson

After Andrew Jackson beat the British at the Battle of New Orleans — the last battle of the War of 1812 — there was a growing movement determined to undo the abuses of power perpetrated by the Bank of the U.S. Since the Republican Party had fallen away from its opposition to central banking, this populist movement sprang up as a third party in the 1820's. Calling itself the "Democratic Republican" Party, Andrew Jackson ran for president under its banner in the election of 1828, and the Bank was one of the main campaign issues.

To the surprise and dismay of the moneychangers, Jackson was swept into office by a landslide (56%-44%). He was determined to kill the Bank at the first opportunity and he wasted no time in trying to do so. But he was also determined to keep the Union together. During his inauguration speech, he proclaimed that:

> The Federal Constitution must be obeyed, States rights preserved, our national debt must be paid, direct taxes and loans avoided, and the Federal union preserved. These are the objects I have in view, and regardless of all consequences, will carry into effect.[126]

After his speech, hundreds of cheering farmers and frontiersmen rushed up to shake Jackson's hand. So great was his popularity that thousands of carriages, wagons and people on foot followed him as he made his way on horseback along an unpaved Pennsylvania Avenue to the White House.

---

[126] *The Life of Andrew Jackson*, Robert V. Remini, (New York, Penguin Books, 1990), p. 210.

Former *Washington Post* Managing Editor, William Greider, wrote in his 800-page tome on the Federal Reserve System:

> The popular resentments ... were not the misinformed fears of a backward citizenry. Opposition to the Bank reflected real economic complaints, real questions about the practical dimensions of who held power in a democracy.[127]

The Bank's 20-year charter didn't come up for renewal until 1836, so Jackson had to content himself with routing out the minions of the Bank from government. He and his closest advisor, Secretary of State Martin Van Buren, fired 2,000 of the government's 11,000 employees and introduced the "spoils system," rewarding his supporters with government jobs.

The Bank's supporters counterattacked by wrongly accusing Jackson of having an affair with the most beautiful woman in Washington, Peggy Eaton, the wife of his Secretary of War, John Eaton. Jackson discovered that the rumors were coming from his own Vice-President, John Calhoun, a known supporter of the Bank. Jackson also discovered that Calhoun was planning to oppose him in the next election and had been promised the financial support of the Bank. Jackson knew that since the Bank's charter came up for renewal in 1836, at the end of the next term, whoever was President at that time would get to veto (or pass) the charter renewal bill for the Bank.

Jackson explained the ongoing battle for the hearts and minds – and votes – of Congress.

> I have no hesitation to say if they can re-charter the bank, with this hydra of corruption they will rule the nation and its charter will be perpetual and its corrupting influence destroy the liberty of our country. When I came into this administration...I had a majority of 75. Since then it is now believed it has bought [votes in Congress] by loans, discounts, etc. until...there were 2/3 for re-chartering it.[128]

In 1828, Jackson and Calhoun butted heads again. Congress passed a law increasing tariff rates on foreign manufactured goods. Calhoun

---

[127] Grider, William. *Secrets of the Temple* (New York, Simon & Schuster, 1989), p. 258.
[128] President Andrew Jackson, April 7, 1833 letter to R. H. M. Cryer. Ralph Catterall, The 2nd Bank of the U.S., (Univ. of Chicago Press, 1902).

complained that the law hurt his native state of South Carolina. Incidentally, Jackson was a native South Carolinian as well, but had moved to Nashville as a young attorney at age 21. He was a delegate to the state constitutional convention and was later elected to the U.S. House of Representatives in 1796, at age 33.

Despite Jackson's well-known feelings on the importance of maintaining the union, Calhoun secretly wrote to legislators in his native state of South Carolina voicing the opinion that any law passed by Congress could be rejected or nullified if they considered it to be unconstitutional.

This dispute eventually led to Calhoun's resignation, but not before the Bank – the 2nd BUS -- applied still more pressure on Jackson. In 1832, Jackson was visited by the president of the Bank, a wealthy, arrogant man by the name of Nicholas Biddle. Biddle asked Jackson not to block a law allowing the Bank to open branches all around the country. Biddle explained that once established, the branches would be better able to control the entire nation.[129]

Of course, this didn't sit well with Old Hickory, the populist. He saw the principle of power sharing as the most basic tenet of the Constitution. Jackson lashed out at Biddle, saying that his proposal was a menace to the nation, and that:

> Instead of helping him get permission to establish branches, that he, Jackson, would do all in his power to keep him from doing so; and not only that, but he would also do all in his power to have the bank charter extension bill beaten when it came up.
>
> Mr. Biddle replied that if Jackson was going to act that way about the matter, he (Biddle) and other bankers would finance a campaign to prevent Jackson's reelection to the presidency.
>
> President Jackson replied to that with one of the most bitter presidential campaigns ever held; in which he fought the bankers to a finish and won his reelection by a handsome majority.[130]

---

[129] Butler, Fabious Melton, *Lincoln Money Martyred* (Seattle, Washington, Lincoln Publishing Company, 1935), p. 43.
[130] Butler, p. 43.

Chapter 15: 2nd BUS

Seeing that Jackson's opposition to the Bank was unshakable, Biddle came up with a brilliant plan. He decided to try to catch Jackson off guard by asking Congress to pass the renewal bill as soon as possible, hoping Jackson wouldn't risk controversy in a reelection year. Naturally, Congress was, for the most part, in Biddle's pocket. In the summer of 1832, the Congress complied. They renewed the Bank's charter and sent it to the President for his signature. Jackson promptly accepted the challenge by vetoing the charter bill. Biddle branded Jackson's veto a "manifesto of anarchy." But on July 13, 1832, Congress was not able to override Jackson's veto.

Jackson denounced the bank in his veto message, especially the issue of foreign ownership of the nonvoting shares.

> It is not our own citizens only who are to receive the bounty of our Government. More than eight millions of the stock of this bank are held by foreigners. By this act, the American Republic proposes virtually to make them a present of millions of dollars.... It appears that more than a fourth part of the stock is held by foreigners and the residue is held by a few hundred of our own citizens, chiefly of the richest class. For their benefit does this act exclude the whole American people from competition in the purchase of this monopoly and dispose of it for many millions less than it is worth.
>
> Is there no danger to our liberty and independence in a bank that in its nature has so little to bind it to our country?.... Controlling our currency, receiving our public monies, and holding thousands of our citizens in dependence.... would be more formidable and dangerous than a naval and military power of the enemy.
>
> It is to be regretted that the rich and powerful too often bent the acts of government to their selfish purposes. Distinctions in society will always exist under every just government. Equality of talents, of education, or of wealth cannot be produced by human institutions. In the full enjoyment of the gifts of Heaven and the fruits of superior industry, economy, and virtue, every man is equally entitled to protection by law; but when the laws undertake to add to these natural and just advantages artificial distinctions, to grant titles, gratuities, and exclusive privileges, to make the rich richer and the potent more powerful, the humble members of society — the farmers, mechanics, and laborers — who have nether the time nor the means of securing like favors to themselves, have a right to complain of the injustice of their Government. There are no necessary evils in government. Its evils exist only in its abuses. If it would confine itself to equal protection, and, as Heaven does its rains, shower its favor alike on the high and the low, the rich and the poor, it would be an unqualified blessing. In

Chapter 15: 2nd BUS

the act before me there seems to be a wide and unnecessary departure from these just principles.[131]

Earlier in May of that year, Jackson had been re-nominated to run for president by the Democratic Republicans, but this time, with Martin Van Buren as his Vice-Presidential running mate. Van Buren was a worthy colleague of Jackson. After President Jackson vetoed Congress' re-charter the 2nd Bank of the US and paid-off the national debt, President Van Buren was confident the goal of defending the US from a privately-owned central bank was won:

> The practice of funding the public debt...has long been discontinued...A National Bank has become a completely 'obsolete idea' among us, as thoroughly condemned in public opinion as a national debt.[132]

The "National" Republicans nominated Senator Henry Clay as their candidate, with John Sergeant, head of the legal staff of the Bank of the United States, as Vice-President.

For the first time in history, Jackson took his presidential campaign on the road, speaking directly to the people. This was unprecedented. Presidential candidates stayed at home during the campaign and looked presidential, while others did the campaigning. But Jackson had a message he wanted to take directly to the people.

> If Congress has the right under the Constitution to issue paper money, it was given them to be used by themselves, not to be delegated to individuals or corporations.[133]

Notice how Jackson himself alluded to the imprecision in the Constitution regarding the ability of Congress to issue government money -- U.S. Notes. His thesis -- if Congress has the right, then it cannot be delegated to a private bank. The Supreme Court would validate his supposition 40 years later.

---

[131] Williams, Edwin, *Presidents' Messages*, (New York, Edward Walker, 1846) vol. 2, p. 768.
[132] Catterall, Ralph Charles Henry, *The Second Bank of the United States*. (Chicago, The University of Chicago Press, 1903), p. 385.
[133] Congressional Record: Proceedings and Debates of Sixtieth Congress, First Session, (1908), p. 465

With the campaign in full swing, and the Bank as the central issue, Calhoun tried to divert attention and make Jackson look badly again. South Carolina declared null and void the tariff laws passed by Congress with which it did not agree. They even threatened to secede from the Union if the government tried to collect the duties at the port of Charleston.

Jackson wasted no time responding. He ordered troops and warships concentrated near Charleston and proclaimed:

> The laws of the United States must be executed. I have no discretionary power on the subject.... Disunion by armed force is treason.[134]

Apparently Calhoun and his friends at the Bank wanted to split the fledgling nation. Their plan would not succeed for another generation.

Senator Robert Hayne (D-SC) resigned over the matter and won election as governor of the state. Calhoun resigned the vice-presidency and took over Hayne's seat in the Senate. But the Congress supported Jackson and passed a law authorizing him to use force to collect the taxes. As Jackson was about to move, his opponent in the presidential race, Senator Clay, pushed a compromise bill through Congress that temporarily defused the situation. Less than 30 years later, South Carolina was the first state to secede from the Union, and thereby ignite the Civil War.

Despite the fact that the Bank spent $3,000,000 financing Clay's campaign, Jackson crushed him in the election, beating Clay by a 55-to-37 percent margin (with a third candidate getting 8%), and winning the Electoral College vote by 219-49.

But Jackson knew the battle was not over.

> The hydra of corruption is only scotched, not dead.[135]

Jackson wasted no time in ordering his new Secretary of the Treasury, Louis McLane to start removing the government's deposits from the Second Bank of the United States and place them in state banks. But both McLane and his successor, William J. Duane, refused to do so.

---

[134] *World Book Encyclopedia*; (1980), s.v. "Jackson, Andrew."
[135] Remini, Robert. *Andrew Jackson* (New York, Harper Perennial, 1999), p. 373.

Chapter 15: 2nd BUS

Duane sincerely thought that such a move could send the economy into a tailspin, and he was essentially right, but right for the wrong reasons.

The economy would not plummet as a result of some natural force of economics, but as a result of the machinations of the moneychangers. They contracted the amount of currency in circulation to punish the American people for supporting Jackson and his policies.

After Duane refused to act, Jackson fired him and named Roger B. Taney to the office. Taney finally carried out the President's orders. On October 1, 1833, government funds began to move out of the Second Bank of the United States. Jackson proclaimed:

> I have it chained. I am ready with screws to draw every tooth and then the stumps.[136]

But the Bank was not so easily subdued. As a result of Taney's action, the Senate rejected his nomination as Treasury Secretary. This was the first time a Cabinet officer nominee had been rejected. Biddle countered with typical arrogance.

> This worthy President thinks that because he has scalped Indians and imprisoned Judges, he is to have his way with the Bank. He is mistaken.[137]

Biddle was referring to the fact that Jackson had once put on Black Hawk's Indian headdress before meeting a pro-Bank delegation.

> I don't think these fellows would like to see me in this.[138]

But Nicholas Biddle had an even broader and more desperate counterattack planned.

> Nothing but widespread suffering will produce any effect on Congress.... Our only safety is in pursuing a steady course of firm restriction — and I have no doubt that such a course will ultimately lead to restoration of the currency and the recharter of the Bank.[139]

---

[136] Rogin, Michael Paul, Fathers & Children: Andrew Jackson and the Subjugation of the American Indian (New York, Knopf, 1991), p. 373.
[137] Ibid, p. 281.
[138] Ibid
[139] Remini, p. 373.

What a stunning revelation! Here was the pure truth, revealed with shocking clarity. The intentions of the moneychangers exposed naked, for all to see. Biddle intended to use the money contraction power of the central bank to cause a fast-moving depression in America in order to sway Congress to re-charter the Bank. Hundreds of years of the economic manipulations of the central bankers were now on the line. If the United States escaped their grasp, undoubtedly other nations would follow.

Biddle sharply contracted the money supply by refusing to extend new loans and calling in old ones, and a panic and subsequent sharp depression ensued. Naturally, Biddle blamed the panic on Jackson's withdrawal of federal funds from the Bank. And Biddle's plan worked well. By the time Congress could reconvene in December, the nation was in an uproar. Newspapers attacked Jackson as the culprit for the nation's woes. By March 28, 1834, Jackson was officially censured by a resolution that passed in the Senate by a vote of 26 to 20. It was the first time a President had been censured by Congress. Sadly, in this year, Jackson's home near Nashville, The Hermitage, was destroyed by fire. The fire, however, seems to have been an accident.

Jackson raged to a delegation of the Bank's supporters:

> You are a den of vipers. I intend to rout you out and by the Eternal God I will rout you out.[140]

With the entire future of humankind's economic freedom teetering on a knife-edge, the popular sentiment gradually started to swing back towards Jackson. Suddenly, a miracle occurred. The Governor of Pennsylvania came out in support of the President's position and strongly criticized both the Bank and its president, Mr. Biddle. Within days Congress shifted in the breeze of public opinion and on April 4, 1834, the House of Representatives voted 134 to 82 against rechartering the Bank. Furthermore, by an overwhelming vote of 175 to 42, the House established a special committee to see if the Bank had instigated the crash.[141]

---

[140] Herman J. Viola, *Andrew Jackson* (New York: Chelsea House, 1986), p. 86.
[141] Griffin, p. 356.

> When the investigating committee arrived at the Bank's door in Philadelphia armed with a subpoena to examine the books, Biddle flatly refused. Nor would he allow inspection of correspondence with Congressmen relating to their personal loans and advances. And he steadfastly refused to testify before the committee back in Washington.[142]

Back in Washington, the committee demanded a contempt citation, but Southern Democrats were able to block it. Biddle bragged that there was no way he would go to prison:

> ...By the votes of members of Congress because I would not give up to their enemies their confidential letters.[143]

On January 8, 1835, Jackson paid off the final installment on the national debt. He was the only President to ever do so and has been a hero in conservative financial circles ever since. A few months later, on January 30, 1835, an assassin by the name of Richard Lawrence tried to shoot President Jackson. He stuck two flintlock pistols in Jackson's midsection, but by the grace of God, both pistols misfired. Lawrence was later found not guilty by reason of insanity. After his release, he boasted to friends that powerful people in Europe had put him up to the task and promised to protect him if he were caught.[144]

The following year, when its charter ran out, the Second Bank of the United States quietly expired. Biddle was later arrested and charged with fraud. He was tried and acquitted, but died shortly thereafter while still tied up in civil suits.

Without the restraining effect of the Bank, America quickly grew rich thanks to the expansion in the West. Congress and the President agreed to share the wealth with the States and more than $35 million was distributed for public works projects. But that sudden growth spurt produced growing pains as well. Without the controlling influence of the central bank, the independent State banks proliferated. With the sudden influx of cash, many of these State banks went wild with speculation,

---

[142] Griffin, p. 356.
[143] Remini, p. 274.
[144] Donavan, Robert J., *The Assassins*, (New York, Harper & Brothers, 1952), p. 83.

greedily and recklessly using the fractional reserve system that 20 years of Biddle's central bank had taught them so well.

The government was not prepared to fill the regulatory vacuum that the Bank's disappearance had created. Certainly overly centralized control was bad, but no control had many problems, too. The flood of cheap paper money allowed speculators to inflate the price of public land wildly. In an attempt to control the situation, in July of 1836, Jackson directed all government agents to accept only gold or silver in payment for public lands in the west. Banks could no longer make loans for land purchases without security in gold or silver. The order helped to curb speculation in land, but prices, interest rates, and wages continued to rise in a chaotic fashion.

In 1837, Jackson, having saved his country from the greatest evil that had threatened it, went into retirement at his restored home, the Hermitage, near Nashville, Tennessee. On June 8, 1845, Jackson suddenly fell into unconsciousness and died.

Just 67 days into the administration of Jackson's successor, Martin Van Buren, the inflationary bubble burst. Banks in Philadelphia suffered runs and were forced to close. Those in New York followed, and soon every bank in the country did likewise. Though the depression raged for two years, and led to Van Buren's certain defeat in the next presidential election, the basic strength of the American economy had been restored. In other words, left on its own, the financial ship of state had righted itself, found its direction, and taken off on a new course after decades of central bank control.

William Greider described the period after Jackson closed the Bank, saying:

> Without the Bank's overarching control of money and credit, a vast boom developed — followed by a surge of inflation and eventually economic contraction.... Bray Hammond, the Federal Reserve's own historian, disparaged the results — 'a promising monetary system was destroyed, state banks were freed from federal control, rampant speculation was encouraged. The consequences', Hammond lamented, was a 'reckless, booming anarchy.'
>
> A wild economic boom developed, fed by dizzyingly generous creation of money and credit (created by banks 'more or less out of nothing,' as one economic

Chapter 15: 2nd BUS

historian complained). Without Biddle's Bank to inhibit them, frontier dreamers and land speculators plunged forward hopefully with new schemes, some sound and some outlandish.

The decade of the 1830s, even with its excesses, became a time of extraordinary development — gambles that mostly paid off and permanently advanced the economic structure of the nation. More than three thousand miles of canals were built between 1816 and 1840 — about two-thirds during the thirties. The decade produced roughly the same mileage in new railroads. The transportation systems linked markets and, thus, allowed the division of labor to progress to a higher plane, the specialization of production that was the keystone of an efficient capitalist economy. The developing economic markets fueled a spectacular urban boom as towns and cities grew twice as fast as the overall population. In a single decade, the North Central states doubled in population. In 1830, Chicago was a mere dream of land speculators; thirty years later, it was a bustling reality.[145]

All of this prosperity was fueled not by a gold-backed money, but a totally inflationary paper money system, all issued at debt mostly by wildcat State banks. Even with an out-of-control money system, the nation somehow survived the inflation and started exploring its 3.7 million square miles. Although Jackson could not eliminate the moneychangers' influence entirely, they wielded much less power during America's westward expansion. The genie of American prosperity was now unleashed and no matter how hard the money changers tried, it took them 77 years to undo the great good Old Hickory had done for the emerging nation.

President Jackson's Farewell address in 1837 explained the conflict with the 2nd BUS and is still completely relevant to every nation:

> But when the charter for the Bank of the United States was obtained from Congress it perfected the schemes of the paper system and gave to its advocates the position they have struggled to obtain from the commencement of the Federal Government to the present hour. The immense capital and peculiar privileges bestowed upon it enabled it to exercise despotic sway over the other banks in every part of the country. From its superior strength it could seriously injure, if not destroy, the business of any one of them which might incur its resentment; and it openly claimed for itself the power of regulating the currency

---

[145] Greider, p. 258-9.

throughout the United States. In other words, it asserted (and it undoubtedly possessed) the power to make money plenty or scarce at its pleasure, at any time and in any quarter of the Union, by controlling the issues of other banks and permitting an expansion or compelling a general contraction of the circulating medium, according to its own will. The other banking institutions were sensible of its strength, and they soon generally became its obedient instruments, ready at all times to execute its mandates; and with the banks necessarily went also that numerous class of persons in our commercial cities who depend altogether on bank credits for their solvency and means of business, and who are therefore obliged, for their own safety, to propitiate the favor of the money power by distinguished zeal and devotion in its service. The result of the ill- advised legislation which established this great monopoly was to concentrate the whole moneyed power of the Union, with its boundless means of corruption and its numerous dependents, under the direction and command of one acknowledged head, thus organizing this particular interest as one body and securing to it unity and concert of action throughout the United States, and enabling it to bring forward upon any occasion its entire and undivided strength to support or defeat any measure of the Government. In the hands of this formidable power, thus perfectly organized, was also placed unlimited dominion over the amount of the circulating medium, giving it the power to regulate the value of property and the fruits of labor in every quarter of the Union, and to bestow prosperity or bring ruin upon any city or section of the country as might best comport with its own interest or policy.

We are not left to conjecture how the moneyed power, thus organized and with such a weapon in its hands, would be likely to use it. The distress and alarm which pervaded and agitated the whole country when the Bank of the United States waged war upon the people in order to compel them to submit to its demands can not yet be forgotten. The ruthless and unsparing temper with which whole cities and communities were oppressed, individuals impoverished and ruined, and a scene of cheerful prosperity suddenly changed into one of gloom and despondency ought to be indelibly impressed on the memory of the people of the United States. If such was its power in a time of peace, what would it not have been in a season of war, with an enemy at your doors? No nation but the freemen of the United States could have come out victorious from such a contest; yet, if you had not conquered, the Government would have passed from the hands of the many to the hands of the few, and this organized money power from its secret conclave would have dictated the choice of your highest officers and compelled you to make peace or war, as best suited their own wishes. The forms of your Government might for a time have remained, but its living spirit would have departed from it.[146]

Every American should read Jackson's speech. The complete document is on the San Diego State University website at:

URL: 7.tv/18b5

---

[146] San Diego State University, Dept. of Political Science, http://tinyurl.com/24oa5qo

Chapter 16 – Abe Lincoln

Twenty-five years later, the central bankers were still angry with the results of Jackson killing the 2nd Bank of the United. Since then, America's economy had boomed – a bad example for the rest of the world. America had to be stopped, so they devised a plan to split the rich, new nation -- divide and conquer America by war.

President Jackson saw this coming. In his Farewell Address back on March 4, 1837 he warned the nation:

> Has the warning voice of Washington been forgotten, or have designs already been formed to sever the Union?

> ... This great and glorious Republic would soon be broken into a multitude of petty States, without commerce, without credit, jealous of one another, armed for mutual aggression, loaded with taxes to pay armies and leaders, seeking aid against each other from foreign powers, insulted and trampled upon by the nations of Europe, until, harassed with conflicts and humbled and debased in spirit, they would be ready to submit to the absolute dominion of any military adventurer and to surrender their liberty for the sake of repose. [147]

The bankers figured that no matter what the outcome, a war between North and South would leave America so financially strapped that the entire Western Hemisphere would once again be opened to colonization.

Standing directly in the way was newly elected President Abraham Lincoln.

Lincoln evaded assassins in Baltimore in February of 1861 on his way to his inauguration in Washington on March 4. The very next month, the first shots were fired at Fort Sumter, South Carolina after seven southern states succeeded from the Union.

Lincoln was in a classic double bind. No matter what he did, he was being forced into a war by the hidden hands behind the financial curtain.

---

[147] Blau, Joseph L., edited by, *Social Theories of Jacksonian* Democracy, (Indianapolis, IN, USA, Hackett Publishing Company, Inc., 1954), p. 5. Also a .pdf of his speech: http://tinyurl.com/24oa5qo

Chapter 16: Abe Lincoln

He agonized over the fate of the Union, sensing that it was only through the strength of union that the financial powerhouses of Europe – primarily England -- could be held at bay.

In 1861, Lincoln went to New York to apply for the necessary war loans from what he hoped were patriotic American bankers. But the bankers – many with ties to the British banking houses - saw him coming and knew that the plan was to split the country in two and so there was a high probability that Lincoln's government would default on any loans.

Consequently, they demanded an interest rate of as much as 36%.[148] Lincoln returned to Washington depressed.

Then Lincoln came up with his the most brilliant idea of his presidency. He decided to return to America's colonial monetary roots – have the government issue their own money. As Congressman E.G. Spaulding from Buffalo, New York, the Chairman of the House Ways & Means Committee explained it:

> Why then should we go into Wall Street, State Street, Chestnut Street, or any other street, begging for money? Their [private bank] money is not as secure as Government money... I am unwilling that this government should be left in the hands of any class of men, bankers or moneylenders, however respectable or patriotic they may be. The Government is much stronger than any of them. All the gold they possess would not carry on the Government for ninety days. They issue promises to pay, which, if Congress does its duty, are not half as secure as United States Treasury notes based on adequate taxation upon all the property of the country.
>
> I prefer to assert the power and dignity of the Government, by the issue of its own notes, pledging the faith, the honor, and property of the whole loyal people of the country to maintain their circulation and provide for their redemption....
>
> In this way the Government will be able to get along with its immediate and pressing necessities without being obliged to force its bonds on the market at ruinous rates of discount; the people, under heavy taxation, will be

---

[148] *General Revenue Revision: Hearings Before the Committee on Ways and Means*, House of Representatives, 85th Congress, Second Session, (Washington, D.C., U.S. Government Printing Office, 1958), Vol. 1, p. 246.

> shielded against high rates of interest; and the capitalists will be afforded a fair compensation for the use of their money during the pending struggle of the country for national existence.[149]

So, that is exactly what Lincoln did. From 1862 to 1865, Congress authorized the printing of $450,000,000 of the new bills that he called "U.S. Notes". To distinguish them from debt-based money, he had them printed in green ink on the back and a red seal on the front. That is why the notes were called "Greenbacks."

Since Congress had declared Greenbacks to be "legal tender" for all debts, Lincoln was able to pay his troops and buy their supplies with this new money – all created at no interest to the federal government. As Congressman Spaulding explained it:

> The United States, at the breaking out of the rebellion, had no national bank currency, and no gold or available means in the Treasury, or Sub-Treasury, to carry on the war for the Union, and consequently the means to prosecute the war had to be obtained upon the *credit* of the government, and by taxation. The fundable legal tender currency was the most available form of credit which the government could use in crushing the rebellion. It was at once a *loan* to the government without interest, and a *national currency*, which was so much needed for disbursement in small sums during the pressing exigencies of the war. It was indispensably necessary, and a most powerful instrumentality in saving the government and maintaining the national unity.[150]

Modern-day critics take issue with Lincoln's Greenback money plan as ignoring – or being ignorant of – the risks involved with government issued, debt-free money. According to Congressman Spaulding, the temptation of the government printing too much money was well known by he and the Secretary of Treasury:

> ... The risk of a depreciated, and depreciating, and finally worthless paper money; the immeasurable evils of dishonored public faith and national bankruptcy; ... are possible consequences of the adoption of a system of

---

[149] Congressman E. G. Spaulding, 1862 speech to Congress, *History of the Legal Tender Paper Money Issued During the Great Rebellion Being a Loan Without Interest and a National Currency* (Buffalo, New York, Express Printing Company, 1869), p. 37.

[150] Ibid, p. 1.

Government circulation. It may be said, and perhaps truly, that they are less deplorable than those of an irredeemable bank circulation. Without entering into that comparison, the Secretary contents himself with observing that, in his judgment, those possible disasters so far outweigh the probable benefits of the plan, that he feels himself constrained to forbear recommending its adoption.[151]

And this argument is still relevant today. Yes, Congress might print too much, but at least that's better than having the banks print too much because bank money is ALL at interest!

Henry C. Carey, Civil War Economist

Economist Henry C. Carey was Lincoln's chief economic advisor. Carey co-founded the Franklin Fire Insurance Company of Philadelphia in 1835. He published his most famous book, *Principles of Political Economy* in 1837. Carey founded what would be known as the American school of economics that dominated American economics thought for over a century. He was the Milton Friedman of his century, and is equally despised by the gold money "Austrian" economists of this era. Libertarian economist Murray Rothbard referred to Carey's American school of economics as a "cheap-money, inflationist policy".[152]

Rothbard's characterization is more than just an ungenerous assessment of the leading economist of that day; it presumes that the quantity of money would not be controlled.

In February 1865, Carey wrote a series of letters to Speaker of the U.S. House of Representatives, Schuyler Colfax entitled, *The Way to Outdo England Without Fighting Her* to help prevent the destruction of the Greenbacks by the National Banking Act and its subsequent modifications.

Carey believed Greenbacks were a way to create a circulating medium of exchange without the perpetual drain of interest of borrowing the national

---

[151] Ibid, p. 5.
[152] Rothbard, Murray, *A History* .... p. 148.

money supply from banks. He also suggested raising reserve requirements on commercial banks up to 50%.

In his *Letter Fifteenth* of Feb. 15, 1865 Carey ridiculed the *London Times* criticism of Lincoln's Emancipation Proclamation.

> The lugubrious predictions of the *London Times* have, thus far, not been verified. The war is now, to all appearance, coming rapidly to a close, and not only are we not yet ruined, but there prevails throughout the country a prosperity such as, until recently, had never before been known. To what causes may this properly be attributed? How has it been possible that a community should have furnished so many hundreds of thousands of men, and so many thousands of millions of the material of war, without becoming even poorer than before?....
>
> That the development of our mineral resources has been great beyond all former example:
>
> That diversification in the pursuits of our people now exhibits itself in the naturalization of many of the minor branches of industry in regard to which we had before been wholly dependent upon Europe:
>
> That the demand for labor has been so great as to cause large increase of wages:
>
> That the high price of labor has caused great increase of immigration:
>
> That demand for the farmer's products has so largely increased as to have almost altogether freed him from dependence on the uncertain markets of Europe:
>
> That the internal commerce has so largely grown as to have doubled in its money value the many hundreds of millions of railroad stock:
>
> That the prosperity of existing railroads has caused large increase in the number and the extent of roads:
>
> That here, for the first time in the history of the world, has been exhibited a community in which every man who had labor to sell could sell it if he would, while every man who had coal, iron, food, or cloth to sell could find at once a person able and willing to buy and pay for it:
>
> That, for the first time, too, in the history of the world, there has been presented a community in which nearly all business was done for cash, and in which debt had scarcely an existence:

> That, as a necessary consequence of this, there has been a large and general diminution of the rate of interest:
>
> That farmers, laborers, miners, and traders have therefore become more independent of the capitalist, while the country at large has become more independent of the "wealthy capitalists" of Europe:
>
> That, so great have been the economies of labor and its products, resulting from great rapidity of the societary circulation, that, while building more houses and mills, constructing more roads, erecting more machinery, and living better than ever before, our people have been enabled to contribute, in the form of taxes and loans, no less a sum than three thousand millions of dollars to the support of government.[153]

Having cited the benefits of the Greenback system, he then attacked the system rapidly destroying these beneficial effects after passage of the National Banking Act – an Act seemingly benefiting only the "English capitalists".

> The most serious move in the retrograde direction is that one we find in the determination to prohibit the further issue of that circulation to which we have been so much indebted. Why is it made? .... Because men who depend on fixed incomes fancy that they should live better were the gold standard once again adopted! Because every free-trader in the land charges the high price of gold to the use of "greenbacks," and sees therein the causes why he cannot, with profit to himself, fill our markets with British cloth and British iron!

Carey chastised the Treasury for not issuing the full amount of Greenbacks authorized in 1862:

> What is the present effect of the hesitation of the Treasury to use the power that yet remains at its command? It is paralyzing the societary movement, to the great loss of both the people and the Government. Labor is less in demand. Cloth, iron, and a thousand other commodities move more slowly. Why all these things? Because the Treasury does not fulfill its contracts. The unpaid requisitions amount to $125,000,000, and the Treasury is empty....

---

[153] Carey, Henry C., *The Way to Outdo England Without Fighting Her*, (Philadelphia, Industrial Publisher, 1865), p. 150.

Carey refers to Greenbacks as the "machinery of circulation":

> Anxious for a reduction in the price of gold, journalists are almost everywhere calling upon Congress to increase the taxes, to give up *selling* machinery of circulation that costs it nothing, and to take to *buying* such machinery at the market price....
>
> This is certainly a high price to pay for the use of a little money, and the reason why it is so high is that the supply of the commodity needed is diminishing in the proportion borne by it to public and private needs....

Already Carey sees interest payable by Lincoln's government mounting. Notice the eerie similarities to our situation today, nearly 150 years later:

> The gold interest now payable requires $60,000,000. Adding these new loans, and making their interest payable in gold, we shall, three years hence, need $108,000,000, most of which is likely to have to go to Europe. Add now to this, first, the $30,000,000 required for payment of interest on the old foreign free trade debt; second, only an equal amount for absentees, temporary and permanent; and we obtain a demand amounting to $168,000,000, that *must* be met before we can purchase a piece of cloth or a ton of iron. Where is all this gold to come from?
>
> Tax the people is the answer. Give us an income tax of 25 per cent! Tax sales! Tax manufactures! All this is being done, and so thoroughly that important branches of manufacture are likely to be taxed entirely out of existence. Paying his taxes in paper, and obtaining cash for his products, the ironmaster can scarcely even to-day make head against those "wealthy capitalists" of England who have already placed themselves on such a footing, as regards freight and duty, that it is *they* who, under a gold system, will be protected, and not their American competitors.
>
> ... We are killing the goose that has already laid the many golden eggs so well described in the following paragraph, from this day's *Tribune:* —
>
> The internal revenue for the month of January just past amounted to the enormous sum of $31,076,902 89—over a million of dollars a day, including Sunday! And yet confessedly the machinery for collecting this branch of the nation's income is imperfect and undergoing change. Vast as is that sum of internal revenue, daily and monthly, how light a burden is it to the business of this rich and vigorous nation! And with what patriotic cheerfulness and

Chapter 16: Abe Lincoln

acquiescence the people pay this tax to preserve their nation and to maintain democracy.

Carey refers to the speed and convenience with which Greenback circulate – today known as the "velocity of money" as the "rapidity of the societary circulation."

> To what do we owe these wonderful results of a state of civil war? To rapidity of the societary circulation, and to nothing else! To what have we been indebted for that rapidity to [protective tariffs] and the "greenbacks"! What is it that we are now laboring to destroy? [Protective tariffs] and the Greenback!
>
> Let us continue on in the direction in which we now are moving, and we shall ere long see, not resumption but repudiation; not a contradiction but a confirmation of the predictions of the *Times*; not a re-establishment of the Union, but a complete and final disruption of it.

As MIT Professor Dr. Davis Rich Dewey would write 40 years after Lincoln's issuance of Greenbacks in his *Financial History of the United States*:

> The underlying idea in the greenback philosophy... is that the issue of currency is a function of the government, a sovereign right which ought not to be delegated to corporations.[154]

For more information on the Greenbacks (U.S. Notes):

URL: 7.tv/13e1

---

[154] Dewey, Davis Rich; *Financial History of the United States*; (New York, Longmans, Green, and Co., 1903), p. 379.

Chapter 16: Abe Lincoln

The Hazard Circular

Within four days of the passage of the law authorizing Greenbacks, bankers met in convention in Washington, D.C. to discuss the situation. It was agreed that Greenbacks would surely be their ruination. Something had to be done. They circulated a private letter, known as the *Hazard Circular*, amongst themselves and their wealthiest stockholders, which was later placed into the historical record by Congressman Charles A. Lindbergh, the father of famed aviator "Lucky" Lindbergh. The *Hazard Circular* proclaimed that the great debt that would result after the war:

> ...Must be used as a means to control the volume of money. To accomplish this the [United States] bonds must be used as a banking basis.[155]

In other words, YIKES! America had broken free of their debt money system and this had to be fixed immediately, if not sooner.

> We are now waiting for the Secretary of the Treasury to make this recommendation to Congress. It will not do to allow the greenback, as it is called, to circulate as money any length of time, as we cannot control that. But we can control the bonds and through them the bank issues.[156]

By "bank issues", they meant the amount of money banks could issue into circulation – incidentally, all of it – every dollar – as a debt, with interest attached.

But Lincoln was not to be so easily deterred. So the moneychangers formulated a clever plan. They would urge Congress to pass an addition to the new law, called the "Exception Clause." This law began a gradual process of undermining the acceptability of the Greenback. As Thoren and Warner explained in *The Truth In Money Book*:

> The intent of the clause was to strip the Greenbacks of their full legal tender status by adding a statement that the notes would be accepted in payment of all debts, public and private except duties on imports and interest on the

---

[155] Lindbergh, Charles A, *Banking and Currency and the Money Trust* (Washington, D.C.: National Capital Press, 1913), p. 102.
[156] Ibid.

public debt. Duties on imports and interest on the public debt would henceforth be payable only in gold.[157]

And guess who had control of the gold? Authors Thoren and Warner explained how the undermining of the Greenback took place:

> Under this new rule, importers had to go to the banks and purchase the gold required to pay duty on the goods they imported. The banks took advantage of the situation and slapped a surcharge of $185 on the price of gold. People had to pay $285 in Greenbacks for every $100 of gold they bought from banks.[158]

Senator Thaddeus Stevens railed against the Exception Clause from the floor of the Senate on February 20, 1862:

> I have a melancholy foreboding that we are about to consummate a cunningly devised scheme, which will carry great injury to all classes of people throughout the Union."[159]

But the big banks won this round and the bill was passed. After passing the Exception Clause, Senator Stevens is reported to have explained why he felt reluctantly compelled to vote for it:

> We did not yield, however, until we found that the country must be lost or the bankers gratified, and we have sought to save the country, in spite of the cupidity of its wealthier citizens.[160]

The National Bank Act

This legislation was followed by the passage of the National Bank Act in February 1863, which was designed to further undermine the quality of the Greenback.

> The act established a system of nationally chartered banks. The structure was similar to the Bank of the United States with the exception that, instead

---

[157] Thoren, Theodore R. and Warner, Richard F. *The Truth in Money Book* (1989), p. 122-3.
[158] Ibid.
[159] *The Encyclopedia of Social Reform*: edited by William Dwight Porter Bliss (New York and London, Funk & Wagnalls Company, 1897), p. 441.
[160] *The Arena*, edited by B.O. Flower. (Boston, The Arena Publishing Company, vol. 17, #1, Dec. 1896) p. 220.

of one central bank with power to influence the activities of the others, there were now to be many national banks with control over all of them coming from Washington.[161]

The new National Banks were given virtually tax-free status. In fact, these national banks remain today and are denoted by the suffix, N.A. (National Banking Association). For example, Bank of America, N.A., or Citibank, N.A. means their origin was as the result of this 1863 National Bank Act.[162] National Banking Association Banks would be mentioned in the introduction to the Federal Reserve Act of 1913:

The terms "national bank" and "national banking association" used in this Act shall be held to be synonymous and interchangeable.

For a PDF of the original (1913) version of the Federal Reserve Act:

URL: 7.tv/04c4

(Note: PDF's are not optimized for mobile phone displays; you may elect to forward the resulting link to your desktop email address for subsequent viewing).

These new National Banks would buy government bonds at a discount with depreciated Greenbacks,[163] then turn the bonds back to the Treasury and receive permission to print an equal amount of their own money, "United States Bank Notes." This mechanism was supposed to keep the quantity somewhat controlled. So, *U.S. Bank Notes* were a debt-based currency that was issued to make the banks rich; as compared to Lincoln's Greenbacks, called *U.S. Notes*, which were issued debt-free

---

[161] Griffin, p. 386.
[162] http://en.wikipedia.org/wiki/National_bank
[163] W. Cleon Skousen, Behind the Scenes (Salt Lake City, UT: The Freemen Institute, 1980), p. 5.

Chapter 16: Abe Lincoln

and in the public interest. Today the equivalent of *U.S. Bank Notes* are called *Federal Reserve Notes*.

By the end of the Civil War, so many of these *U.S. Bank Notes* had been issued that *U.S. Notes* were only 20% of the money supply.

But despite these assaults on the new currency, Greenbacks hung on. Although *U.S. Bank Notes* circulated as money and were counted as part of the American money supply; Congress did not give them the status of "lawful money".

> They were not legal tender for all debts, just for taxes and duties. Precious-metal coins and greenbacks were still the country's official money. It was not until the arrival of the Federal Reserve System fifty years later that government debt in the form of bank notes would be mandated as the nation's official money for all transactions....[164]

Despite that flimsy restriction, private banks now had the money power, and Congress would never again be able to wrest it from them.

> Another consequence of the national banking system was to make it impossible from that date forward for the federal government ever to get out of debt.[165]

As historian John Kenneth Galbraith put it:

> In numerous years following the war the Federal government ran a heavy surplus. It could not [however] pay off its debt, retire its securities, because to do so meant there would be no bonds to back the national bank notes. To pay off the debt was to destroy the money supply.[166]

Of course, that wasn't entirely true, because, as we will see, by 1886, virtually all that was left of the American money supply were Greenbacks. Had Congress at that point had the wisdom to repeal the National Bank Act, and double the quantity of Greenbacks in circulation, they may have broken the backs of the big bank, gold-only-money crowd once and for all.

---

[164] Griffin, p. 387.
[165] Griffin, p. 387.
[166] Galbraith, John Kenneth, *Money: Whence It Came, Where It Went* (Boston, Houghton Mifflin, 1975), p. 90.

In February 1863, Lincoln reluctantly signed the National Bank Act into law. He was well aware of the consequences and was privately opposed to the legislation, but with the Civil War at a critical stage, he felt compelled to withhold his veto.

Lincoln did not have the votes in Congress to issue more Greenbacks, but conversely, his opponents did not have the votes to kill them either. Despite the restricted quantity of Greenback, and the vast quantity of debt being created by *U.S. Bank Notes*, the solidity of one good source of debt-free national money went a long way towards helping Lincoln win the Civil War.

Emancipation Proclamation

The Emancipation Proclamation was not only Lincoln's greatest humanitarian achievement, but also an astute strategic move which helped end the Civil War and for that reason brought waves of protest from the British elite. The Emancipation Proclamation took effect by executive order on Jan. 1, 1863. It gave freedom to the slaves, the majority of whom worked Southern plantations. As the Union Army advanced into the South, thousand of slaves were freed each day, severely undercutting the morale of the Confederate Army, especially its officers.

Sensing that the Emancipation Proclamation might secure victory for Lincoln and his Greenback money, the *London Times* howled its disapproval:

> It must also be remembered that this act of the PRESIDENT, if it purposed to strike off the fetters of one race, is a flagrant attack on the liberties of another. The attempt to free the blacks is a flagrant attack on the liberties of the whites. Nothing can be more unconstitutional, more illegal, and more entirely subversive....

> ... The Negro can only exist apart from his master by a return to the savage state.... He cannot hope for a better situation than that of his race in the North – a situation of degradation, humiliation, and destitution which leaves the slave very little to envy.

... Mankind will be slow to believe that an act avowedly the result of military considerations has been dictated by a sincere desire for the benefit of those who, under the semblance of emancipation, are thus marked out for destruction....[167]

Lincoln's Assassination

In 1864, Lincoln was re-elected easily on a platform that contained a plank calling for a national currency. Had he lived out his second term, he would have certainly issued additional Greenbacks to help aid southern reconstruction.

Shortly before Lincoln was murdered, his former Secretary of the Treasury, Salmon P. Chase, who had recently resigned because of a policy dispute with Lincoln – namely trying to further undermine Greenbacks -- bemoaned his role in helping secure the passage of the National Banking Act only one year earlier.

> My agency in promoting the passage of the National Banking Act was the greatest financial mistake in my life. It has built up a monopoly that affects every interest in the country. It should be repealed, but before that can be accomplished the people will be arrayed on one side, and the banks on the other, in a contest such as we have never seen before in this country.[168]

Chase was ambitious. He had run against Lincoln for the 1860 Republican presidential nomination. He repeatedly tried to curry sufficient political favors to unseat him for the 1864 nomination. In the hopes of quenching Chase's ambitions, Lincoln appointed him to the Supreme Court just 4 months before his assassination.

On April 14, 1865, 41 days after his second inauguration, and five days after the end of the Civil War, Lincoln was shot by John Wilkes Booth, at Ford's theater.

---

[167] Herbert Mitgang, editor, *Abraham Lincoln: A Press Portrait*, p. 332-333 (*London Times*, January 15, 1863).
[168] Owen, Robert Latham, *National Economy and the Banking System of the United States*, (Washington, D.C., U.S. Government Printing Office, 1939), p. 22.

After the death of President Lincoln, the bankers continued to reassert their control over America's money. This was no easy task. Lincoln's Greenbacks – just like Rome's plentiful debt free coins, and England's debt-free tally sticks were generally popular and their existence had let the genie out of the bottle - the public was becoming accustomed to government issued, debt-free money. Popular songs sang the Greenback's praises, as this sheet music cover depicts:

URL: 7.tv/9c21

On April 12, 1866, nearly one year to the day of Lincoln's assassination, Congress passed the Contraction Act, authorizing the Secretary of the Treasury to begin to retire the Greenbacks in circulation and to contract the money supply.

Authors Theodore R. Thoren and Richard F. Warner explained the results of the money contraction in their book on the subject, *The Truth in Money Book*:

> The hard times which occurred after the Civil War could have been avoided if the Greenback legislation had continued as President Lincoln had intended. Instead, there were a series of 'money panics'— what we call 'recessions' — which put pressure on Congress to enact legislation to place the banking system under centralized control.[169]

In 1866, there was $1,800,000,000 in currency in circulation in the United States — about $50.46 per capita. In 1867 alone, $500,000,000 was removed from the U.S. money supply.

---

[169] Thoren, and Warner, p. 122-3.

Ten years later, in 1876, America's money supply was reduced to only $600,000,000. In other words, two-thirds of America's money had been called in by the bankers. Incredibly, only $13.33 per capita remained in circulation.

What's so important about how money was withdrawn from the U.S. money supply? Because this is the REAL cause of depressions – deliberate manipulations of the money supply by big bankers to get what they want politically – the very thing King Henry of Englandwas trying to put a stop to when he created Tally Sticks in 1100 AD.

Ten years later, the money supply had been further reduced to only $400,000,000, a 78% decline in just 20 years even though the population had boomed. The result was that only $7.02 per capita remained in circulation.

U.S. Money Supply per capita, 1866-1886				
Date	Amount in Dollars	Population	Amount per capita	% Greenbacks
1866	1,800,000,000	36,000,000	$50.46	19.8
1867	1,300,000,000	36,700,000	$35.42	26.6
1876	600,000,000	45,000,000	$13.33	57.7
1886	400,000,000	57,000,000	$7.02	86.5

Remember, by 1886 the $346 million worth of Lincoln's old Greenbacks now comprised 87% of the American money supply. Is it any surprise that Congress had not killed them off?

The people suffered terribly in a protracted, severe depression, but to the owners of gold that meant cheap labor and huge profits. This period was known as the "Gilded Age", the greatest period of economic growth in American history. America was expanding westward and discovering vast quantities of silver and gold. Nothing could stop the American rocket ship, not even a golden throttle siphoning off the riches of the robust new nation into the hands of a few wealthy monopoly capitalists – the very ones who had engineered the demise of Lincoln's debt-free Greenbacks.

Comparing the Money Supply Declines

Now, let's put these percentage figures into perspective. On Jan. 28, 2009, the world's business and government leaders met in Davos, Switzerland at the annual World Economic Forum which they optimistically titled "Shaping the Post-Crisis World" as though someone had already fixed the problem. According to Stephen Schwarzman, co-founder of Blackstone Group, one of the world's largest asset management firms specializing in leveraged buyouts – the world's money supply had nearly been cut in half in the previous 15 months:

> Between 40 and 45 percent of the world's wealth has been destroyed in little less than a year and a half. This is absolutely unprecedented in our lifetime.[170]

And how does that compare to the Great Depression of the 1930s?

According to Nobel-Prize-winning economist, Milton Friedman, the Depression was caused by the Fed refusing to halt a deflation of 33% of the nation's money between 1929 and 1933.

> The drastic decline in the stock of money and the occurrence of a banking panic of unprecedented severity did not reflect the absence of power on the part of the [Federal] Reserve System to prevent them.
>
> ... In retrospect... the contraction could almost certainly have been prevented and the stock of money kept from declining or, indeed, increased to any desired extent.[171]

In other words, by January of 2009, the world's money had been contracted more than that which caused the Great Depression in America in the 1930s. The difference is that today, the Fed can – and has – injected trillions of dollars into the American money supply. This may –

---

[170] Schwarzman, Stephen, Reuters, March 10, 2009. www.reuters.com/article/idUSTRE52966Z20090310
[171] Friedman, Milton & Schwartz, Anna. *A Monetary History of the United States, 1867-1960* (Princeton, NJ; Princeton University Press, 1963), p. 11

and I emphasize MAY – have worked in the short term, but it is only slowing the rate of deflation of the bubble economy and at a tremendous cost in additional government borrowing and the consequent interest. In other words, the Fed has just delayed the inevitable somewhat. Those in charge of the money supply are only hoping they can get out of town with their winnings safely in Swiss bank accounts before the collapse.

Court Challenges to the Greenbacks

After the Lincoln's death, the Greenback came under legal attack in the U.S. Supreme Court.

1870: Hepburn v. Griswold involved a lender who had made a loan in gold dollars before the issuance of the Greenbacks during the Civil War. The lender went to court when the borrower attempted to make repayment in Greenbacks. The high court ruled 4-3 that the borrower had to repay in gold – not surprising, and perfectly fair.

1871: Knox vs. Lee: Another case where one party refused to take U.S. Notes – Greenbacks. The Court ruled that Greenbacks were legal tender, thereby overturning the Hepburn v. Griswold case.

This case was upheld in subsequent Supreme Court challenges in 1872 and 1884.

Even gold money supporter Professor Murray Rothbard admitted defeat in his tomb published by the Ludwig von Mises Institute, *A History of Money and Banking in the United States Before the Twentieth Century*:

> From then on, paper money would be held consonant with the U.S. Constitution.[172]

So like it or not, debt-free, government-issued money IS Constitutional. It is now known as "settled law" and will likely never be challenged again on Constitutional grounds.

---

[172] Rothbard, Murray, *A History* .... p. 153.

Chapter 17 – The Crime of '73

The post-Civil-War era is one of the most important periods in the development of the monopolistic system of the central bankers in America. It shows why reliance on a "hard currency" plays right into the hands of those who profit from manipulating the American economy. Today, supporters of a return to a gold money system sincerely believe that only metal money can bring stability to the economic system. I must admit, that when I first started into this topic in 1980, I believed that too; but not today.

A return to gold is exactly what the central bankers want. Why? Because they directly or indirectly own or control most of the gold, and if gold is the basis of money they can thereby manipulate the quantity of money in circulation by either lending out their gold money liberally, or calling in those loans.

In an important respect, metalists are really our friends. They have correctly identified the problem – that the QUANTITY is out of control. They believe that gold will do provide that control – and they are right – the problem is control for whom? Unfortunately, under gold-based systems, the banks end up owning most of the gold, then the quantity of money can be manipulated very easily merely by loaning out either more or less gold. It's very simple!

Coinage Act of 1873 – The Crime of '73

In 1872, Congress passed the Coinage Act and on Feb. 12, 1873, President U.S. Grant signed it into law. Immediately, the minting of silver dollars stopped. It put the U.S. onto a gold-only money system. The effect was the same as it has always been in American history – a depression with falling prices, skyrocketing unemployment and major bank failures.

Of course, then, like today, the government came to the rescue of the biggest banks. Many of the nation's largest banks had over-speculated in the burgeoning railroad industry. On September 13, the largest bank in the nation, Jay Cooke & Company, stopped making any sort of payments.

Chapter 17: The Crime of '73

A panic ensued. On Sept. 20, the New York Stock Exchange was shut down for 10 days.

To stop the panic, Secretary of the Treasury William A. Richardson announced Treasury would buy back U.S. Bonds and pay for them with a new issue of $26 million of guess what? Greenbacks! Yes, good old unbacked paper money. The injection of this hot money saved the big banks and they reopened their doors. The New York Stock Exchange re-opened, and the financial sector recovered quickly.

But what about the rest of the nation? Not so lucky. No additional money for them. The depression lasted an additional 5 years and ruined thousands of businesses. Of course the depression could have been halted in its tracks for the rest of us had the government continued to issue additional Greenbacks, but that wasn't the plan. The plan was to prevent the big banks from going bankrupt.

Economist Murray Rothbard -- who called himself an "anarcho-capitalist" -- applauded the Crime of '73:

> In 1872, it became apparent to a few knowledgeable men at the U.S. Treasury that silver... was about to suffer a huge decline in value. The major reason was the realization that European nations were shifting from a silver to a gold standard....
>
> Working rapidly, these Treasury men, along with Senator Sherman, slipped through Congress in February 1873 a seemingly innocuous bill which in effect discontinued the minting of any further silver dollars....
>
> The furtive method of demonetizing silver, the "crime against silver," was in part responsible for the vehemence of the silver agitation for the remainder of the century.[173]

Even if the Crime of '73 was just a clever move by "these Treasury men" so what? It didn't do anything to relieve the ongoing depression for the average American. Wages dropped by 25% from 1873 to 1876.

---

[173] Rothbard, Murray, *A History* .... p. 158.

Chapter 17: The Crime of '73

Unemployment soared to 14%, and 25% of American railroads went bankrupt.[174]

Newspapers derided the Crime of '73 as the cause of the depression. Everybody knew about it. The average American hated it. Demonetizing silver made money even scarcer – it put the bankers, who were the primary holders of gold -- in even greater control of America. Ironically, after the Greenbacks bailed them out they spent the next decade trying to kill them.

According to Dr. Quentin Taylor, an Asst. Professor of History and Political Science at Rogers State University:

> It's been a puzzle to a lot of economic historians this obsession with keeping the amount of currency so strictly limited. It didn't seem to comport with the expanding economy at the time. You had this rapidly expanding economy. You have immigration that is in part fueling in it. You have westward expansion. You have no industries, new technologies, and yet you have a restricted money supply which makes it increasingly difficult for people to engage in consumption and purchases and other types of economic activity.[175]

Author Fabious Melton Butler, not a fan of a gold-based money, writing from the midst of the Great Depression of the early 1930s, compared the post-Civil War depression and the Crime of '73 in the United States to the Temple half-shekel scam 1850 years earlier in the time of Christ.

> Now, we will just step down through the pages of history to 1873 in the good old U.S.A., when silver was demonetized and gold was made the standard money. If you think that the price of MONEY can't be changed, just get your BUSINESS GRAPH and see what happened to the prices of 'things' in the longest 'depression' the U.S. had ever experienced up to that time. As it worked with the 'half-shekel of the sanctuary,' so also it worked with the Gold Standard.[176]

---

[174] McFeely, William S., *Grant: A Biography*. (New York: Norton, 1981), p. 371. ISBN 0-393-01372-3.
[175] Interview in the documentary "The Secret of Oz", 2010, www.secretofoz.com
[176] Butler, p. 33.

Chapter 17: The Crime of '73

The Greenback Party

As the result of the Crime of '73, mid-western farmers, who had been severely ravaged by the lack of sufficient money in circulation, formed the Greenback Party. People wanted more Greenbacks too. The Greenback Party was active between 1874 and 1884. It had:

> ... An anti-monopoly ideology.... The party opposed the shift from paper money back to a bullion coin-based monetary system because it believed that privately owned banks and corporations would then reacquire the power to define the value of products and labor.... they believed that government control of the monetary system would allow it to keep more currency in circulation, as it had in the war. This would better foster business and assist farmers by raising prices and making debts easier to pay....[177]

Powered by the outrage of the Crime of '73, the Greenbackers ran candidates for Congress and President. In the 1878 elections, 21 independents were swept into Congress, mostly Greenbackers.

The Greenbackers ran presidential candidates in 1876, scoring less than 1% of the vote; 1880, scoring 3.3%; and 1884, scoring a mere 1.7% of the popular vote.

Year	Convention City	Presidential Candidate	Popular Votes	Percent
1876	Indianapolis	Peter Cooper *(New York)*	75,973	0.9%
1880	Chicago	James Baird Weaver *(Iowa)*	305,997	3.3%
1884	Indianapolis	Benjamin F. Butler *(Mass)*	175,096	1.7%

The Resumption Act

Having failed in their Constitutional challenges of 1871 and '72, the moneychangers tried a different tact. Congress was in no mood to kill Greenbacks. By 1875, Greenbacks were fully half of the American money supply, and the nation was in the midst of a deep deflationary depression – in other words, there wasn't ENOUGH money!

---

[177] http://en.wikipedia.org/wiki/Greenback_Party

On Jan. 14, 1875, Congress passed the Resumption Act. This act allowed the Treasury to buy back 25% of the Greenbacks in circulation from the general public and pay for them in gold at the going rate. It was an audacious plan and would test the faith of the average American in the Greenback dollar. Would the public fall for the goldbug's plan to further monopolize the American money supply? Did they have faith in banker money, or did they have more faith in government money?

The act did not go into effect for 4 years, 1879. This gave the Treasury time to gradually accumulate a sufficient quantity of gold to redeem the Greenbacks. When 1879 rolled around, an unintended consequence appeared. The offer of gold redemption had actually strengthened the people's faith in Greenbacks. Almost no one gave up their Greenbacks for gold. Only $130,000 out of $347 million outstanding Greenbacks were turned in for redemption. The plan was a titanic flop. Of course the goldbugs of that day tried to salvage a public relations victory from the unmitigated disaster by hailing the redemption plan as a great success in that it strengthened the national currency.

From that point on, Greenbacks were never seriously challenged again until 1994 when the "Riegle Act" retired them gracefully:

> "The Secretary shall not be required to reissue United States currency notes upon redemption."

The official website of the United States Bureau of Engraving and Printing has a further explanation of the law that is interesting in its respectful tone for the old Greenback:

> This does not change the legal tender status of United States Notes nor does it require a recall of those notes already in circulation. This provision means that United States Notes are to be cancelled and destroyed but not reissued. This will eventually result in a decrease in the amount of these notes outstanding. United States Notes are an obsolete form of currency last printed by the Bureau of Engraving and Printing in 1968. The Riegle Community Development and Regulatory Improvement Act, Public Law 103-325, codified at 31 U.S.C. 5119(b)(2), enacted in September 1994, amended 31 U.S.C. by canceling the requirement to reissue these notes when they are redeemed. Some numismatic groups have expressed interest in selling selected notes to the public. The Bureau of Engraving and

Printing consulted with Treasury's Financial Management Service and the Bureau of the Public Debt, and the following determination was made:

> Releasing the notes to the public will violate the spirit of the act, which authorized the Secretary to "not be required to reissue United States Notes upon redemption."
>
> The Bureau of Engraving and Printing lacks the legal statutory authority to sell these notes to the public.
>
> The Bureau of Engraving and Printing lacks any mechanism by which it could release the notes to the public now that the requirement to reissue them when redeemed is no longer in effect.[178]

So in the end, the moneychangers never were able to kill the Greenback. They simply let it fade away respectfully as collectors snapped up the remaining U.S. Notes in circulation and they have never been replaced -- but there is absolutely nothing in the Constitution that prohibits their triumphant re-entry into the U.S. economy at any time and on very short notice.

The Silver Commission

In 1876, Congress created the United States Silver Commission to study the Crime of '73 situation. What had caused the depression of 1873?

Their report blamed the monetary contraction on removing silver from the money supply and compared it to the deflation of the Roman era. Their report, issued on March 2, 1876 read in part;

> History records no such disastrous transition as that from the Roman Empire to the Dark Ages. Various explanations have been given of this entire breaking down of the framework of society, but it was certainly coincident with a shrinkage in the volume [quantity] of money, which was also without historical parallel. The crumbling of institutions kept even step ... with the shrinkage in the stock of money and the falling of prices.

---

[178] http://www.moneyfactory.gov/historicallegislation.html

Chapter 17: The Crime of '73

> The disaster of the Dark Ages was caused by decreasing money and falling prices.... Without money, civilization could not have had a beginning, and with a diminishing supply it must languish and unless relieved, finally perish.
>
> Falling prices and misery and destitution are inseparable companions. It is universally conceded that falling prices result from the contraction of the money volume.[179]

Interestingly, the Silver Commission suggests that paper money was what finally brought the Dark Ages to an end:

> It is suggestive coincidence that the first glimmer of light only came with the invention of bills of exchange, and paper substitutes....[180]

They also discovered -- and duly reported -- a remarkable parallel between the collapse of the Roman monetary system, and that of the post-Civil War American money supply.

> At the Christian era the metallic money of the Roman Empire amounted to $1,800,000,000, by the end of the fifteenth century it had shrunk to less than $200,000,000....
>
> William Jacob. F.R.S., gives the following table of the amount of metallic money:[181]

Decline in Roman Money Supply: 14 to 806 A.D.	
A.D. 14	$1,790,000,000
A.D. 230	909,000.000
A.D. 410	537,000,000
A.D. 662	256,000,000
A.D. 806	168,000,000

---

[179] Jones, John P. on the Free Coinage of Silver; In the United States Senate, May 12 and 13, 1890: (Washington, D.C., Geo. R. Gray, Printer, 1890), p. 37
[180] Jones, John P., p. 37
[181] *The New Encyclopedia of Social Reform*: edited by William Dwight Porter Bliss and Rudolph Michael Binder (New York and London, Funk & Wagnalls Company, 1908), p. 778

Chapter 17: The Crime of '73

This was a decline of 90.6% over 800 years, as compared with the post-Civil War decline of 78% in a mere 20 years. What the committee failed to point out was that the population of Rome declined over that period – from 1,000,000 to not more than 100,000 people by 550 A.D.[182], whereas, the U.S. population increased from 36 million to 57 million in 20 years shown below. A direct per capita comparison is not useful due to the unreliability of the Roman census data.

Despite the ongoing U.S. population boom, within the next ten years, another $200,000,000 would be removed from the money supply of the United States.

	U.S. Money Supply per capita, 1866-1886			
Date	Amount in Dollars	Population	Amount per capita	% Greenbacks
1866	1,800,000,000	36,000,000	50.46	19.8
1867	1,300,000,000	36,700,000	35.42	27.4
1876	600,000,000	45,000,000	13.33	63.7
1886	400,000,000	57,000,000	7.02	86.5

NOTE: Today, the U.S. money supply is approx. $45,161 per capita – most of it with interest attached.

By 1876, with 1/3rd of the workforce unemployed, and having endured a decade of depression and starvation, the population was growing restless. People were clamoring for a return to the Greenback money system of President Lincoln, or a return to silver dollars — anything to make money more readily available. By 1877 the nation was in an uproar over the hated "Crime of '73". Riots broke out from Pittsburgh to Chicago. The torches of starving vandals lit up the sky.

The bankers huddled to decide on their next move. They decided to hang tough. At the 1877 meeting of the American Bankers Association – the

---

[182] http://www.unrv.com/empire/roman-population.php

ABA -- they urged their membership to do everything in their power to put down the notion of a return to Greenbacks. The ABA Secretary, James Buel, authored a letter dated Oct. 9, 1877 to the members that blatantly called on the banks to subvert not only Congress, but also the press:

> It is advisable to do all in your power to sustain such prominent daily and weekly newspapers, especially the Agricultural and Religious Press, as will oppose the greenback issue of paper money....
>
> To repeal the Act creating bank notes, or to restore to circulation the government issue of money will be to provide the people with money and will therefore seriously affect our individual profits as bankers and lenders.
>
> See your Congressman at once and engage him to support our interests that we may control legislation.[183]

By 1878, Congressmen and Senators were making angry protestations about the deception on the floors of Congress. Senator Voorhees of Indiana complained that he'd had no idea the bill demonetized silver:

> I do not think there were three members in the House that knew it.[184]

Senator Beck of Kentucky said on Jan. 10, 1878 that the Coinage Act:

> ... Never was understood by either House of Congress. I say that with full knowledge of the facts. No newspaper reporter — and they are the most vigilant men I ever saw in obtaining information — discovered that it had been done.
>
> I know that the bondholders and the monopolists of this country are seeking to destroy all the industries of this people, in their greed to enhance the value of their gold. I know the act of 1873 did more than all else to accomplish that result.[185]

Senator William B. Allison of Iowa put it this way:

---

[183] *The Encyclopedia of Social Reform*, p. 1248-49

[184] Congressional Record, 45th Congress, 2nd session, vol. 7, part 2, page 1605; as quoted by Butler, Fabious Melton, *Lincoln Money Martyred* (Seattle, Washington, Lincoln Publishing Company, 1935), p. 68-69.

[185] Ibid, p. 69.

> When the secret history of this bill of 1873 comes to be told, it will disclose the fact that the House of Representatives intended to coin both gold and silver... but that the bill afterward was doctored. It was changed after the discussion....[186]

> Senator Bogy of Missouri put it this way: Why the act of 1873, which forbids the coinage of the silver dollar, was passed no one at this day can give a good reason.[187]

Silver Certificates – The Bland-Allison Act of 1878

As a result of the ongoing uproar, Congress passed the Bland-Allison Act, but President Rutherford B. Hayes vetoed it. Hayes was from Cincinnati, Ohio and was strongly influenced by banking interests. Hayes explained his veto by saying:

> .... [E]xpediency and justice both demand an honest currency.[188]

Congress quickly overrode his veto on February 28, 1878. It was the only veto override that President Hayes suffered. Three years earlier, Hayes had unsuccessfully attacked the $382 million in Greenbacks outstanding. He encouraged Congress to pass the "Specie Payment Resumption Act" of 1875.

The bill did not provide for the "free and unlimited coinage of silver" demanded by Western miners, but it did require the United States Treasury to purchase between $2 million and $4 million of silver bullion each month from mining companies in the West and mint them into silver dollars. These are the famous "Morgan" silver dollars, named after their designer. Morgan silver dollars were legal tender and some did immediately circulate as money, but as Milton Friedman explained:

> ... Most of the coins were stockpiled in the Treasury as reserves for pieces of paper called silver certificates, or, after 1890, treasury notes of 1890 [U.S. Notes].[189]

---

[186] Gillmore, Jesse, *Disastrous Financial Panics: Cause and Remedy*, (San Diego, CA, Frye & Smith, 1908), p. 52.
[187] Gillmore, Jesse, *Disastrous Financial Panics: Cause and Remedy*, (San Diego, CA, Frye & Smith, 1908), p. 52.
[188] Hoogenboom, Ari. *Rutherford Hayes: Warrior and President.* (Lawrence, Kansas: University Press of Kansas, 1995), p. 358-60. ISBN 9780700606412.

The new silver certificates were printed in small denominations and were specifically designed to help relieve the lack of money in the economy. However, although silver certificates did increase the money stock, pegging a quantity of precious metal to the value of a dollar was – and will forever be a mistake. Almost immediately one silver certificate would buy less silver if redeemed to the government than could it would buy on the open market. As Friedman confirmed:

> ... It was cheaper to get silver by using paper money to buy it on the market, rather than convert the paper money into silver at the fictional legal price. In effect, the silver certificates were fiat money....[190]

President James Garfield

Two years later, in 1880, the American people elected General James Garfield President. Garfield understood how the economy was being manipulated. As a Congressman, he had been chairman of the Appropriations Committee, and was a member of the Banking and Currency Committee.

---

[189] Friedman, Milton. *Money Mischief.* (New York, Harcourt Brace & Company, 1994), p. 69.
[190] Ibid

Chapter 17: The Crime of '73

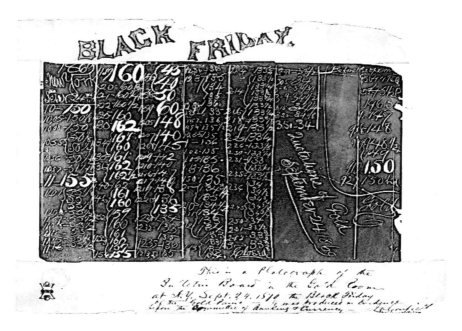

The above photograph is from the actual quote board from the New York Gold Trading Room, which Garfield introduced as evidence during a Congressional investigation the following year. Garfield's handwriting is at the bottom.

Garfield understood the ability of the very wealthy to manipulate gold money. He investigated the cause of the Black Friday gold market scandal of 1869 when financier Jay Gould and others cornered the gold market, causing wild fluctuations in the price.

After his inauguration, he slammed the moneychangers publicly in 1881:

> Whoever controls the volume of money in any country is absolute master of all industry and commerce. . . and when you realize that the entire system is very easily controlled, one way or another, by a few powerful men at the

top, you will not have to be told how periods of inflation and depression originate.[191]

Perhaps coincidentally, within a few weeks of making this statement, on July 2 of 1881, President Garfield was assassinated. For more on Garfield's assassination:

URL: 7.tv/9e3a

After Garfield's assassination, the "depression deepened, leaving [the] unemployed to face poverty and starvation....

Produce was left to rot in the fields.... The country was facing poverty amidst plenty, because there was insufficient money in circulation to keep the wheels of trade turning.

The country sorely needed the sort of liquidity urged by Lincoln ... and the Greenbackers; but the bankers insisted that allowing the government to print its own money would be dangerously inflationary. That was their argument, but critics called it 'humbuggery' ...."[192]

The big bankers finally had complete control of the money supply again by killing off the last competitor to their gold-only money system. Now, they had to hold on against the rising anger of the average American.

By 1891, the bankers were ready to unleash additional monetary restrictions. Their methods and motives were laid out with shocking clarity in a memo sent out by the American Bankers' Association (ABA) in 1891. Notice that this memo called for bankers to create a depression on a certain date three years in the future. Here is how it read in part (note the telling reference to England, home of the Mother Bank):

---

[191] Howard, Milford Wriarson, *The American Plutocracy*, (New York, Holland Publishing Co. 1895), p. 158. Also quoted by Flower, B. O. (editor), *The Arena*, (Boston, Arena Publishing Co., 1895), p. 82 from the Harry Houdini Collection (Library of Congress).

[192] Brown, Ellen, p. 94.

Chapter 17: The Crime of '73

On Sept. 1, 1894, we will not renew our loans under any consideration. On Sept. 1st we will demand our money. We will foreclose and become mortgagees in possession. We can take two-thirds of the farms west of the Mississippi, and thousands of them east of the Mississippi as well, at our own price.... Then the farmers will become tenants as in England....[193]

Why this massive, engineered crash? In 1892, Democrats campaigned against high tariffs and put Grover Cleveland back into the White House on March 4, 1893. Cleveland was the first Democrat elected after the Civil War (1885-1889), and the only President to leave the White House and return for a second term (1893-1897). But Cleveland was hardly a populist. Although he opposed the Republicans on the tariff issue, he also opposed free silver and firmly supported the gold standard.

Cleveland was not all bad, however. Some Constitutional scholars say that Cleveland was the most pro-Constitution president in history, vetoing more legislation on the basis lack of Constitutional authority than any other president. How he justified the gold standard on the basis of the Constitution remains a mystery.

The Panic Circular

Only 7 days after Cleveland's inauguration, on March 11, 1893, another foreboding leaflet appeared. Known as the "Panic Circular", it was issued by The American Bankers' Association and was subsequently published in many newspapers. Senator Robert Owen (D-OK) also testified before Congressional committee that he had received this circular in his role as President of the First National Bank of Muskogee, Oklahoma.

Interestingly, Owen would later go on to sponsor the Federal Reserve Act of 1913, but then later criticized the Fed for deliberately reducing the money supply during the late 1920s and early 1930s, which he claimed contributed to the onset of the Great Depression. The strange twists and turns of the American political system....

---

[193] 1891, American Bankers' Association, as printed in The Congressional Record, April 29, 1913.

The "Panic Circular" urged all national banks throughout the United States to help deepen the money panic:

> Silver, silver certificates, and Treasury bonds (that is to say, all the Government's money) must be retired, and [interest bearing] National Bank Notes made the only money.
>
> You will at once retire one-third of your circulation (your paper money) and call in one-half of your loans. Be careful to make a monetary [emergency] among your patrons, especially among influential businessmen.
>
> The future [of our debt-based money system] depends upon immediate action, as there is an increasing sentiment in favor of Government legal-tender notes and silver coinage.[194]

The depression actually began in 1893 with what historians now call the "Panic of 1893". It all started when European investors demanded payment only in gold, draining gold reserves in the U.S.

Again, America was being forced by the Europeans onto a gold-only money system. The results were as inevitable as before – a deep depression quickly set in as the major holders of gold in Europe choked the life out of the American economy.

---

[194] Lindbergh, Charles A, *Banking and Currency and The Money Trust* (Washington, D.C., National Capital Press, 1913), p. 106-7.

Chapter 18 – William Jennings Bryan

The presidential campaign of 1896 would see the explosive money issue dominant the election. The farmers of the west were sick and tired of the bankers not lending out their gold money. In fact, most of the money that was still in circulation was $346 million worth of Lincoln's old Greenbacks.

A virtually unknown former Congressman from Nebraska, William Jennings Bryan, ran for President as a Democrat and embraced the "Free Silver" issue that the Populist Party had unsuccessfully tried earlier.

The New York bankers were well aware of the anger and tried to control the 1896 Democratic convention.

McKinley vs. Bryan, the 1896 Presidential Campaign

Republican Governor of Ohio, William McKinley campaigned heavily in the 1896 presidential race on the tariff issue, positioning it as a positive solution to the 1893 depression – which was really only a subset of the entire post-Civil War depression of 1865-1896. McKinley promised protection and prosperity to every economic sector. How? By raising the tariff back up to 50% from the 42% of the second Grover Cleveland presidency.

Obviously this tariff issue was of minor import to the central question of the day; more money was needed in the system to break the depression – the issue that McKinley's opponent, William Jennings Bryan would champion in 1896.

Bryan's father had been an ardent Greenbacker, but Bryan also was politically practical. He knew that the Greenback Party had failed miserably in the past three presidential election cycles, so he chose the Free Silver issue as the way to increase the money supply in a way that would get more popular support due to the strong remaining anger over the "Crime of '73" when silver money was abandoned.

At the Democratic National Convention in Chicago in 1896, Bryan made an emotional speech entitled, "Crown of Thorns and Cross of Gold." Bryan's speech was so powerful that it propelled him from relative obscurity to the presidential nomination on the 5th ballot at the tender age of 36.

Amazingly we have Bryan's actual voice recreating portions of this famous speech, recorded years later with the advent of recording technology. Although the recording does not capture the power of the original moment, it does allow us to hear Bryan's voice:

URL: 7.tv/8acc

Here is the written text of Bryan's speech:

> I come to speak to you in defense of a cause as holy as the cause of liberty—the cause of humanity. Never before in the history of this country has there been witnessed such a contest as that through which we have passed.

Bryan's re-creation recording then skips significant portions of his original speech. According to the Official Proceedings of the Democratic National Convention, Bryan continued with these important references to America's monetary history:

> What we need is an Andrew Jackson to stand as Jackson stood, against the encroachments of aggregated wealth.
>
> We say in our platform that we believe that the right to coin money and issue money is a function of government. We believe it. We believe it is a part of sovereignty....
>
> Those who are opposed to this proposition tell us that the issue of paper money is a function of the bank and that the government ought to go out of the banking business. I stand with Jefferson rather than with them, and tell them, as he did, that the issue of money is a function of the government and that the banks should go out of the governing business.

Chapter 18: William Jennings Bryan 161

William Jennings Bryan with four Indian chiefs.

Bryan then explained why the money issue he would champion was more important than McKinley's tariff issue:

> They ask ... why it is we say more on the money question than we say upon the tariff question, I reply that if protection has slain its thousands, the gold standard has slain its tens of thousands....
>
> When we have restored the money of the Constitution, all other necessary reforms will be possible, and that until that is done there is no reform that can be accomplished.

However, the gold standard and it's 30-year-long restrictive impact on the money supply had become so unpopular that even most Republicans had come out against it. Now, Bryan's recording picks back up:

> They will search the pages of history in vain to find a single instance where the common people of any land have ever declared themselves in favor of

the gold standard. They can find where the holders of fixed investments have declared for a gold standard, but not for the masses have.

If they dare to come out in the open field and defend the gold standard as a good thing, we will fight them to the uttermost ... we will answer their demands for a gold standard by saying to them, you shall not press down upon the brow of labor this crown of thorns. You shall not crucify mankind upon a cross of gold.

The Tariff Issue

We see that in the "Cross of Gold" speech, Bryan mentions the tariff issue, harkening back to the days of Lincoln's chief economist, Henry C. Carey. Tariffs had always been a big deal in American politics. They were a major causative issue behind the Civil War. Tariffs can easily favor one industry over another, or one state over another.

So the electorate was easily divided on the tariff issue. Protective tariffs would be called "protectionism" today – as opposed to "free trading" -- and would be strongly opposed with those buying lots of goods from China where wages are a small fraction of what they are in the Western world.

Henry C. Carey believed that protective tariffs kept America's manufacturing might strong, and it also raised so much money for the government that without interest being paid on a national debt, the income from tariffs would replace most other forms of federal taxation. It would be difficult to argue with this economic system in today's world. If you are going to buy foreign goods produced at slave wages, you will have to pay a high import tariff to level the playing field to keep our own manufacturing base healthy, and eliminate income taxes. Sounds fair enough; but 150 years ago, the issue was more complex – and became a major political issue in many presidential campaigns.

Tariffs in the Constitution

The Tariff Act of 1789 provided the first national source of revenue for the newly formed United States. The new Constitution allowed only the federal government to levy tariffs, so the old system of state rates disappeared. The new law taxed all imports at rates from 5 to 15 percent. These rates were primarily designed to generate revenue to pay the expenses of the federal government.

Once industrialization started, the demand for higher and higher tariffs came from manufacturers and factory workers. Pro-tariff supporters believed that Americans should be protected from the low wages of Europe. Every Congressman was eager to apply for a higher rate to protect his local industry and so tariffs became a huge political issue with some tariffs tending to favor some states over others.

Eventually, tariffs got out of hand, peaking in 1828 at about 50%. From that point on, the pendulum of political justice began to swing the other way. Thirty years later, in 1857, tariffs had dropped to 18% as the "Free Traders" gained power.

Bryan's Campaign

In the wake of Bryan's whirlwind nomination, the bankers were scared. The average American farmer was mad about the lack of a plentiful money supply because farmers rely heavily on credit. Now it looked like they had finally gained sufficient political force to win the highest office in the land and disrupt all the banker's plans.

As a result, the 1896 campaign was among the most fiercely contested Presidential races in American history. Though Bryan was only 36 years old at the time, this speech is widely regarded as the most famous oration ever made before a political convention.

The McKinley campaign outspent Bryan by a 5-to1 margin. Bryan's strategy was to take his political campaign on the road. Bryan invented the national stumping tour. He made over 500 speeches in 27 states during the 4 month campaign – an average of 4 a day – many of them lasting over 2 hours. Across the nation, tens of thousands of Americans rallied around Bryan's appearances with torchlight parades.

The battle became so heated that thousands of miles away, in Alaska, the highest mountain in North America, Mount McKinley, was even named for Bryan's opponent, Republican William McKinley. It seems that the first gold miner on the mountain, a man named William Dickey, named the mountain in honor of the gold money candidate in retaliation because his many silver mining friends so zealously supported William Jennings Bryan.

McKinley got manufacturers and industrialists to inform their employees that if Bryan were elected, all factories and plants would close and there would be no work. The ruse succeeded. McKinley beat Bryan by a small margin.

Bryan ran for President again in 1900 and in 1908, falling short each time. But the threat his presence presented to the national bankers afforded the Republican alternatives. Roosevelt and Taft, a measure of independence from them. Roosevelt opposed their monopolies and Taft was unenthusiastic about their proposed central bank legislation that would finally be passed in 1913 as the Federal Reserve Act. The bankers therefore shifted their support to Democrat Woodrow Wilson in 1912.

Although William Jennings Bryan never gained the Presidency, his efforts delayed the moneychangers from attaining their next goal — a new, privately owned central bank for America — the Federal Reserve.

Chapter 19 – Silver Money

Many people today still point to the Bryan era, and say that it demonstrates the effectiveness of silver backing for money as the solution to today's problems. So let's take a quick look at that.

What if Bryan had won? How do you think the biggest bankers of them all, J.P. Morgan, the Rockefellers, etc., would have reacted as a silver bill marched its way through Congress? Without question, they – just like you or I -- would buy as much silver as they could afford. In today's marketplace, the silver futures market would explode. In Morgan's case, however, he wouldn't have entered the market simply to speculate, he would have attempted to corner the entire silver market.

Such would be the case if the national money were backed by anything of value – "value-backed" money, so to speak. Would a basket of commodities be an improvement, as some suggest? No, especially as it relates to any commodity currently traded electronically. Prices of every commodity in the so-called "basket" would spike due to speculation, long before the bill could even be voted on.

The Hunt Brothers Corner the Silver Market

The most illustrative example of this sort of "cornering of the market" is that of the Hunt Brothers in the 1970s. Nelson Bunker Hunt and his brother Herbert were the sons of Texas oil billionaire Haroldson Lafayette Hunt, Jr. The family fortune was sizeable, estimated at $5 billion. This, however, was far from being a dominant player in the world of New York finance. But the Hunts were determined to corner the market on silver.

The Hunts played the silver futures market perfectly at the dawn of electronic trading. They bought futures contracts, and then started taking physical delivery once the contract closed. Silver trader Larry LaBorde tells this hilarious story about how the Hunts started moving their physical silver hoard to Switzerland:

> In 1973 they started buying and by early 1974 they had accumulated silver contracts totaling 55 million oz. or about 8% of the world's silver supply at that time. The brothers then took delivery of all 55 million oz. of silver.

Chapter 19: Silver Money

Bunker was concerned about government confiscation of his silver. He could not bring it to Texas without paying a 5% franchise tax to the State [about $10 million]. The brothers decided to pick up the silver and drop it off in Switzerland for safekeeping.

Meanwhile, back at the ranch, (the Circle K Ranch in Texas) brother-in-law Randy Kreiling and his brother Tilmon held a shooting contest amongst the cowboys to find the best marksmen. The dozen best marksmen were hired for a special assignment to ride shotgun on one of the largest private silver transfers in history. The Circle K cowboys flew on 3 specially chartered 707 jets to Chicago and New York where they were met by a convoy of armored trucks during the middle of the night. Forty million oz. of silver was loaded onto the planes and they immediately flew to Zurich where they were met by another convoy of armored trucks. The cowboys loaded the trucks and silver was dispersed to six different storage locations in Switzerland. The transfer cost Bunker and Herbert $200,000. The storage costs for the 40 million oz. in Switzerland and the 15 million oz. still in the US amounted to $3 million/year.[195]

In 1979, the Hunts teamed up with two Saudi Arabian money men and formed a Bermuda corporation, International Metals Investment Company (IMIC), and IMIC then jumped into the silver market. In 1979, the price of silver skyrocketed from $6 per ounce up to an all-time high of $48.70 per ounce.

The brothers were estimated to hold one third of the entire world supply of silver (other than that held by governments). The situation for other prospective purchasers of silver was so dire that the jeweler Tiffanys took out a full page ad in the *New York Times*, condemning the Hunt Brothers and stating "We think it is unconscionable for anyone to hoard several billion, yes billions of dollars worth of silver and thus drive the price up so high that others must pay artificially high prices for articles made of silver".[196]

---

[195] http://www.321gold.com/editorials/laborde/laborde012904.html ; retrieved Jan. 10, 2011
[196] Wikipedia, *Silver Thursday*; quoting TIME Magazine. April 7, 1980, "He Has a Passion for Silver".

Chapter 19: Silver Money

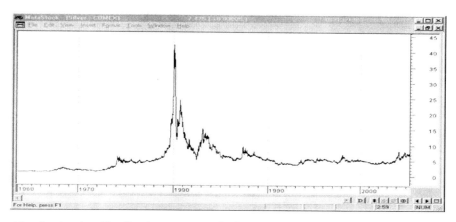

The Hunts had effectively cornered the silver market. On January 7, 1980, the COMEX (New York Mercantile Exchange and Commodity Exchange) had to change the rules to break the Hunts because they had nearly run out of physical silver to deliver.

> In response to the Hunt's accumulation, the exchange rules regarding leverage were changed, when COMEX adopted "Silver Rule 7" placing heavy restrictions on the purchase of commodities on margin. The Hunt brothers had borrowed heavily to finance their purchases, and as the price began to fall again, dropping over 50% in just four days, they were unable to meet their obligations, causing panic in the markets.[197]

As Jon Matonis recounted:

> They did nothing illegal, the Chicago Board of Trade (CBOT) and COMEX changed the rules in the middle of the game, the Commodity Futures Trading Commission (CFTC) implemented new regulations, and the Hunts were bankrupted, unjustly. All they really did was simply request the delivery of the physical metal for which they held valid, legal contracts.[198]

The Hunts may have been very well intentioned. Apparently they wanted to force a return to silver backed money to prevent inflation. They played

---

[197] http://en.wikipedia.org/wiki/Silver_Thursday
[198] *The Monetary Future*, Jan. 28, 2010, "Hunt Brothers Demanded Physical Delivery Too".
http://themonetaryfuture.blogspot.com/2009/01/hunt-brothers-demanded-physical.html

by the rules and won. Unfortunately, they didn't realize that the rules could be changed by those in control of the quantity of money.

Karl Denninger explains it best:

URL: 7.tv/8dda

> ...If you control the quantity of the money, nobody else cares about anything else. You can cause depressions, deflation, inflation, anytime you like for your own political and monetary benefit.
>
> If you can give people cheap credit that they cannot afford, human nature is that people will take whatever you give them for free, whether it ultimately destroys them or not, and so you can create these boom and bust cycles that ultimately asset strip the wealth of average people.[199]

Here is a HyperScan for a chart of one-year historical daily closing prices for silver:

URL: 7.tv/7cfa

---

[199] Karl Denninger, video interview from *The Secret of Oz* documentary (McLean, VA, Still Productions, 2010), at 37:00 min in the Jan. 08, 2011 revised version.

Chapter 20 - The Aldrich Bill

To understand the London connection to the U.S. Federal Reserve, we have to start with the American investment firm of J.P. Morgan and its link to the British Rothschilds.

Morgan started out when an American bond salesman by the name of George Peabody, traveled to London to sell bonds for the Chesapeake and Ohio Canal. There was no money in America thanks to the financial panic engineered in 1837 to punish America for President Jackson's veto of the Second Bank of the U.S. Peabody eventually sold his bonds and opened an import-export business in London specializing in transactions between Britain and the United States.

He befriended Nathan Rothschild, the dominant figure in the Bank of England. Peabody's business grew with the rapidly expanding trade between the two nations. By 1850, he needed an American partner. He selected a Boston merchant by the name of Junius Morgan and moved him to London to learn the business in 1854. Peabody, Morgan & Company not only sold bonds for American businesses and state governments, but during the American Civil War, they were the chief financial agent for the Union government.

After the War, in 1864, Peabody retired and completely turned the business over to Junius, who promptly changed the firm's name to J.S. Morgan and Company. Junius' son, John Pierpont Morgan was groomed for the business by taking his schooling in both Boston and Europe. In 1895, the firm's name changed to what it is today, J.P. Morgan & Company, by far the dominant American bank.

After his father's death, J.P. Morgan took on the longtime director of the Bank of England, Edward Grenfell, and changed the name of the London branch to Morgan, Grenfell & Company. In the post-Civil War period the connection between Morgan and the Rothschilds was certainly well known in financial circles. As one writer put it:

> Morgan's activities in 1895-1896 in selling U.S. gold bonds in Europe were based on his alliance with the House of Rothschild; these activities added to

Chapter 20: The Aldrich Bill

Morgan's reputation as a rescuer of governments. That reputation was often the key to his power....[200]

For more information on JP Morgan:

URL: 7.tv/4ab5

It is said that Morgan money dominated the election of McKinley over Bryan. As we've just seen, Bryan was opposed to the central banking system – at least early in his career -- and supported a silver-based money to keep monetary policy out of the hands of the moneychangers. Interestingly, before the 1896 Presidential campaign, McKinley, as a Congressman from Ohio, had favored limited coinage of silver. But during the campaign, he took the opposite position, advocating what Bryan repeatedly called "rule of the rich."

After McKinley's assassination by anarchist Leon F. Czolgosz, on September 6, 1901 — about six months into his second administration — Theodore Roosevelt ascended to the presidency. To appease Morgan interests, Roosevelt initially delayed an anti-trust prosecution that had been started by the Justice Department against Morgan and their affiliate, Kuhn-Loeb & Co. But on February 18, 1902, Roosevelt revived the Sherman Anti-Trust Act and went after another Morgan firm, Northern Securities Company, a giant combine of railroads owned by Morgan, John D. Rockefeller, Edward H. Harriman, and James Hill. During the following seven years, Roosevelt pursued his "trust-busting" policies by bringing suit against 43 other major corporations over the next seven years.

---

[200] Kolko, Gabriel. *The Triumph of Conservatism: A Reinterpretation of American History, 1900-1916.* (New York, The Free Press, 1963), p. 142

The Crash of 1907

After Roosevelt's election in 1904, he increased the pressure on the Money Trusts again. He asked Congress to pass the Hepburn Act of 1906, giving the Interstate Commerce Commission authority to set maximum rates for interstate railroad traffic. What is a "trust"? It is a term that was popular before World War I to indicate a monopoly held by a group of individuals. Today, we'd simply call it a "monopoly."

For more information on John D. Rockefeller:

URL: 7.tv/5a4d

By 1907, Morgan and the other moneychangers had had enough. First, they created a panic by attacking Morgan's primary Wall Street rival, the Heinze-Morse group, the holders of considerable banking, mining, steel and shipping interests. By cleverly manipulating the stock market, the Rockefellers drove down the stock of Heinze's Union Copper Company from as high as $60, down to $10 a share. In addition, Rockefeller spread the rumor that not only were Heinze copper interests were in trouble, but also Heinze banks as well. J.P. Morgan then jumped in, predicting that he thought the Knickerbocker Trust Company would be the first Heinze bank to go under. As historian Skousen explained:

> That was all it took to send depositors storming to the tellers' cages of the Knickerbocker Bank to get their money. Within a few days the bank was forced to close its doors. Similar fear spread to other Heinze banks and then to the whole banking world. The crash was on.[201]

Morgan interests called loans and refused to grant new ones. Before long, the panic had engulfed America. Thousands of banks were vastly

---

[201] W. Cleon Skousen, *Behind the Scenes* (Salt Lake City, UT: The Freemen Institute, 1980), p. 5.

overextended, some having maintained less than 1% reserves. The weaker banks went under first, closing their doors to their depositors. Compounding the effect was the fact that news spread more quickly than ever before, thanks to the new communications technologies. Telegraph communication now linked the nation and fledgling telephone service connected many major cities east of the Mississippi. Within days, every bank in the nation was trying to reassure its customers. Many closed their doors and never reopened. Skousen described the effect on the money supply:

> Circulating money was hoarded by any who happened to get some, so before long a viable medium of exchange became practically nonexistent. Many business concerns began printing IOU's on small pieces of paper and exchanging these for raw materials as well as giving them to their workers for wages. These 'tokens' passed around as a temporary medium of exchange.[202]

This can and will happen again. You may remember a similar recent situation which took place in the state of California in 1992, and again in 2009. Its state budget in shambles from illegal immigration, the State of California was forced to pay its workers for a time in IOUs.

J.P. Morgan to the Rescue

Now, the American people were really angry. Forty years on the financial roller coaster had worn thin. Americans desperately wanted safe banks that they could entrust with their money. They wanted a stable financial system and it seemed like Morgan was providing just the opposite.

At this critical moment, J.P. Morgan staged a brilliant public relations coup, with a very profitable solution. He offered to salvage the last Heinze bank, the Trust Company of America, if it would sell him their valuable Tennessee Coal and Iron Company for a small fraction of its real worth. Morgan wished to further reduce the competition to his vast U.S. Steel Corporation that he'd bought from Andrew Carnegie in 1902 for nearly half a billion dollars – the largest such industrial takeover in U.S. history at that point. Although the proposal violated U.S. anti-trust laws,

---

[202] Ibid.

Chapter 20: The Aldrich Bill

the country was so desperate that the deal was still approved by Washington.

Morgan then convinced Congress to allow him to circulate $200,000,000 of his own private money. Of course, this token money would be issued by Morgan banks. Morgan said this flow of new money might be just the thing to get the economy moving again. So, the plan was approved. Morgan printed $200,000,000 out of literally nothing! He bought things with the new funny money, paid for services with it, and sent it to his branch banks to lend out at interest.

It worked. Soon, the public had regained confidence in money in general, and quit hoarding their currency. By 1908, the panic was over and Morgan was seen as a hero for "saving" the nation from a crisis he had not only created, but also profited from. As incredible as it may seem, the president of Princeton University, Woodrow Wilson, actually applauded Morgan's efforts:

> All this trouble (the 1907 depression) could be averted if we appointed a committee of six or seven public-spirited men like J.P. Morgan to handle the affairs of our country.[203]

Keep in mind, the future President was referring to the man who owned (or owned for Rothschild interests) U.S. Steel (1902), AT&T (1875), General Electric (1892), and International Harvester (1902), as well as numerous banks and railroad interests — a man who would soon be his financial benefactor as well.

Just how powerful was J.P. Morgan? On November 1, 1913, Congressman Robert N. Page (D-NC), himself a small-town banker, entered this speech of Texas Representative, Robert Lee Henry, a direct descendent of Patrick Henry, into the Congressional Record concerning the vast wealth of what was then known as "The Money Trust":

> Monopoly first began to prey upon the people in the time of Queen Elizabeth. Privileges of monopoly were granted by her to courtiers and servants till they became intolerable and were terminated by the wrath of the people in the enactment of the "statute of monopolies" in 1624. Our antitrust act is but the

---

[203] Griffin, p. 448 quoting H.S. Kenan, *The Federal Reserve Bank* (Los Angeles: Noontide Press, 1966), p. 105

outgrowth of the spirit against monopolies which secured the passage of those ancient laws. Twenty-five years ago gigantic monopolies ... against trade in alarming proportions began to infest this country.... The people demanded their utter destruction.... In obedience to that demand, Congress passed what is known as the Sherman Antitrust Law, and on July 2, 1890, it was approved by Benjamin Harrison, the President....

This was the beginning of the struggle against monopoly in Federal legislation.... And patriots of whatever persuasion should preserve and perfect it to meet the emergencies of the hour....

J. Pierpont Morgan and his partner, George F. Baker, admitted before a committee in Washington that they dominated and controlled practically all of the great interstate railways and industrial corporations and trusts through interlocking directorates, voting trusts, and various financial conspiracies.... In aggregate they hold 385 directorates in 41 banks and trust companies, having total resources of $3,832,000,000 ... 50 directorships in 11 insurance companies, having total assets of $2,646,000,000; 155 directorships in 31 railroad systems, having a total capitalization of $12,193,000,000... 98 directorates in 28 producing and trading corporations, having a total capitalization of $3,583,000,000... and 48 directorships in 19 public utility corporations having a total capitalization of $2,826,000,000... in all, 746 directorships in 134 corporations, having total resources or capitalization of $25,325,000,000.

Henry then pointed out that the entire banking credit of the country was less, a mere $23,000,000,000.

The Boom/Bust Cycle

The real purposes for the repeated crashes since the Civil War had been threefold:

1. To concentrate more of America's rapidly developing wealth into the hands of a super-rich elite by the roller coaster effect, whereby booms and busts generate bankruptcies and foreclosures.
2. To make the independent, decentralized banking system look unstable.

Chapter 20: The Aldrich Bill

3. To make people so desperate for monetary security that they would be ready to accept practically any solution, namely the institution of a new central bank.

As mainline economics textbooks would later verify, the creation of the Federal Reserve System was a direct effect of the Panic of 1907:

> It sprang from the panic of 1907, with its alarming epidemic of bank failures: the country was fed up once and for all with the anarchy of unstable private banking.[204]

Minnesota Congressman Charles A. Lindbergh, Sr., the father of the famous aviator, "Lucky Lindy," later explained that the Panic of 1907 was the method by which:

> ...Those not favorable to the money trust could be squeezed out of business and the people frightened into demanding changes in the banking and currency laws which the Money Trust would frame.[205]

The stage was now set for the introduction of America's fourth attempt at central banking.

Roosevelt, duly chastened by the panic of 1907, signed into law the Aldrich-Vreeland Act, a bill creating the National Monetary Commission in 1908, which ordered Congress to study the problem of monetary instability. Roosevelt then retired from the political scene, declining to run for President again. He threw his political support to his Secretary of War, William Howard Taft. Later that year, Taft beat William Jennings Bryan (his third and final run) and Teddy Roosevelt strangely decided to withdraw from the rough and tumble of politics and with funding from the Carnegie Foundation (which had been newly chartered in 1906), took off on an African safari and other world globetrotting.

After Taft's election, the moneychangers opened the floodgates of money and the American economy boomed again. Taft was a popular President, just as most Presidents are when money is abundant. But as we will see,

---

[204] Paul A. Samuelson, *Economics*, 8th ed. (New York: McGraw-Hill, 1970), p. 272.
[205] Charles A. Lindbergh, Sr.; *Banking and Currency and The Money Trust* (Washington, D.C., National Capital Press, 1913), p. 94.

Taft ended up dealing the moneychangers another serious blow, and for that effrontery he would serve only one term.

Roosevelt to Africa

In March 1909, shortly after the end of his presidency, Roosevelt, ever the avid naturalist, decided to go on safari to Africa to collect specimens for the Smithsonian Institution and the American Museum of Natural History in New York.

> Roosevelt's party landed in Mombasa, British East Africa (now Kenya), traveled to the Belgian Congo (now Democratic Republic) before following the Nile up to Khartoum in modern Sudan. Financed by Andrew Carnegie and by his own proposed writings, Roosevelt's party ... included scientists from the Smithsonian and was led by the legendary hunter-tracker R. J. Cunninghame and was joined from time to time by Frederick Selous, the famous big game hunter and explorer. Among other items, Roosevelt brought with him four tons of salt for preserving animal hides, a lucky rabbit's foot given to him by boxer John L. Sullivan, an elephant-rifle donated by a group of 56 admiring Britons, and the famous Pigskin Library, a collection of classics bound in pig leather and transported in a single reinforced trunk.
>
> All told, Roosevelt and his companions killed or trapped more than 11,397 animals, from insects and moles to hippopotamuses and elephants. These included 512 big game animals, including six rare white rhinos. The expedition consumed 262 of the animals. Tons of salted animals and their skins were shipped to Washington; the quantity was so large that it took years to mount them all, and the Smithsonian was able to share many duplicate animals with other museums.[206]

President Taft

With Roosevelt out of the country, President Taft was happily making his mark on America. A large jovial man, Taft started the tradition of the President throwing out the "first ball" at the opening of the 1910 major league baseball season, in a game between the Washington Senators and the Philadelphia Athletics. More importantly, Taft pushed a bill

---

[206] Wikipedia: *Theodore Roosevelt,* retrieved Jan. 15, 2011.

Chapter 20: The Aldrich Bill

through Congress requiring that presidential campaign expenses be made public.

During his four years in office, President Taft's administration initiated 90 "trust-busting" prosecutions for violations of the Sherman Antitrust Act, including one against U.S. Steel (owned by Morgan) that his mentor, Theodore Roosevelt had personally approved.

Chapter 21 – The Jekyll Island Caper

On the evening of November 22, 1910 some of the wealthiest and most powerful men in America traveled in secrecy across the Hudson River to the Hoboken, New Jersey railroad station. There, they boarded the private railway car of Senator Nelson Aldrich (grandfather of Nelson Aldrich Rockefeller, Vice President of the U.S. under Gerald Ford), the Republican whip in the Senate, and chairman of the National Monetary Commission. Their destination would be a coastal resort off the Georgia coast. Their purpose was to plan America's new central bank. A friendly week of duck hunting was their cover.

The train traveled through the night and arrived at Jekyll Island, Georgia the next day. The group retreated to a private hideaway owned by J.P. Morgan. So secretive was the conclave, which actually lasted nine days, that the participants called themselves "The First Name Club," because during their stay, no one was to call any of the other participants by any other than their first name, lest the servants might spread the word.

Eventually, the story leaked out. The first inside look was published by *Leslie's Weekly*, in 1916, written by a financial reporter, B.C. Forbes (who later founded *Forbes* magazine).

> Picture a party of the nation's greatest bankers stealing out of New York on a private railroad car under cover of darkness, stealthily [traveling] hundreds of miles south, embarking on a mysterious launch, a full week under such rigid secrecy that the names of not one of them was once mentioned lest servants learn the identity and disclose to the world this strangest, most secret expedition in the history of American finance.

Chapter 21: The Jekyll Island Caper

> I am not romancing. I am giving the world, for the first time, the real story of how the famous Aldrich currency report, the foundation of our new currency system, was written. [207]

Senator Aldrich returned to Washington with the new central bank plan. The most difficult challenge was how to sell it to the American people. The name would be all-important. Certainly the word "bank" could not have any part of the name because the public was at this point well aware of what they called "the Money Trust."

> The law as enacted provided for twelve banks instead of one... but the intent of the law was to coordinate the twelve through the Federal Reserve Board in Washington, so that in effect they would operate as a central bank. [208]

URL: 7.tv/3bbb

Paul Warburg (photo triggered by HyperScan, above) wanted to entitle the legislation the "National Reserve Bill" or the "Federal Reserve Bill". Warburg was the personal representative of the Rothschild banking dynasty. The German-born Warburg was so well known wealth that he was the source of the famous fictional character "Daddy Warbucks" in the comic strip *Little Orphan Annie*.

Senator Aldrich, always the politician, wanted it named after himself, and so, the Aldrich Bill it eventually became. As Senator Aldrich would later admit in a magazine article:

> Before passage of this Act, the New York Bankers could only dominate the reserves of New York. Now, we are able to dominate the bank reserves of the entire country. [209]

---

[207] "Current Opinion" edited by Edward J. Wheeler, *How the Federal Reserve Bank was Evolved by Five Men on Jekyl Island*, (New York, The Current Literature Publishing Co., 1916), vol. 61, p. 382.

[208] "From Farm Boy to Financier," by Frank A. Vanderlip, *The Saturday Evening Post*, Feb. 9, 1933, pp. 25, 72.

This was a big deal for the big New York banks. Because of the rapid westward expansion, state banks were gaining an ever-increasing share of the new American financial pie.

The Name Game Deception

Now, the problem was how to convince Congress, the President and the American people to buy it. The name of this new central bank would be all-important. Aldrich felt that the word "bank" should not even be present in the name. Aldrich also felt that it would be most effective if it appeared that the power of the new bank was diffused — that not one central bank was created, but many The idea was to give the impression that power was dispersed along the same lines as the separation of powers concept that is inherent to our Constitution. The greatest fear was that the public would see the new bank as nothing but a creature of what had by then come to be known as The Money Trust. As Frank Vanderlip, one of the Jekyll Island participants, would admit over 20 years later:

> The law as enacted provided for twelve banks instead of one... but the intent of the law was to coordinate the twelve through the Federal Reserve Board in Washington, so that in effect they would operate as a central bank.[210]

For a photo of Frank Vanderlip:

URL: 7.tv/3d15

Warburg wanted to entitle the legislation the National Reserve Bill or the Federal Reserve Bill, but Aldrich, always the egotistical politician, wanted it named after him. And so, the Aldrich Bill it eventually became.

---

[209] Mullins, Eustace, *A Study of the Federal Reserve*, (New York, Kasper and Horton, 1952), p. 40.
[210] Vanderlip, pp. 25, 70.

Chapter 21: The Jekyll Island Caper

Selling It To Congress

After nine days at Jekyll Island, the group dispersed. Aldrich then undertook a tour of the central banks of Europe. To no one's surprise, Aldrich:

> ... Was impressed at how well ... the central banks in Britain and Germany handled the stabilization of the overall economy and the promotion of international trade.[211]

Upon his return from Europe, Aldrich presented the Aldrich Bill to Congress in 1912. The mechanism proposed was very similar to the old Bank of the United States. The bill gave the new bank the power to issue U.S. currency, lend the government money at interest, and then convert that federal debt into money to be loaned out by its member banks ten times over, or more, to their customers. What a deal! It would also control the affairs of other banks and be the depository of government funds.

But the differences between the new bank and the old BUS were important. Now, there was not even a sham of government ownership. The new bank would be owned privately by banks around the country, but dominated by the New York Federal Reserve Bank, which itself was dominated by a few powerful individuals — the Rockefellers, the Morgans, etc. The new bank would have total control over how much money was made available in the U.S. It could control lending policies of all its member banks in three ways:

1. By its "discount rate." This is the rate it could charge your local bank for loans.

2. By adjusting "reserve requirements" of your local bank. If the central bank set a 10% reserve requirement, that meant your local bank could loan out ten times as much money as it really had on deposit. In other words, the new central bank could control the "fraction" of fractional reserve banking.

---

[211] Wikipedia, *The History of Central Banking in the United States*, retrieved Jan. 15, 2011.

Chapter 21: The Jekyll Island Caper

3. By buying or selling government bonds (debt), the new central bank had another way to control how much money your local bank had to loan out. Under this system, your local bank could count federal government bonds as part of its reserves. If the new central bank wanted to contract the money supply of the nation, one way to do it would be to order local banks to sell some of their government bonds. This would reduce the local banks' available lending reserves. That way, even if the fraction of the "fractional reserve" remained the same, the base would have changed.

It was the most brazen proposal for a central bank the world had ever seen. Never before had a central bank sought such complete control over the banks of a nation and its supply of money. What was looming over the financial horizon was a debt monster, but few were sharp enough to see through the numerous deceptions the bankers would throw up.

According to Congressman Lindbergh, the initial proposal presented to Congress was to give the new central bank not a 20-year charter, as was granted to the old Bank of the United States, but a 50-year charter. He says that Aldrich's Monetary Commission:

> Spent over $300,000 in order to learn how to form a plan by which to create a greater money trust, and it afterwards recommended to Congress to give this proposed trust a fifty-year charter by means of which it could rob and plunder all humanity.[212]

Lindbergh's book has now been scanned by Google Books and can be read in its entirety at:

URL: 7.tv/3f70

---

[212] Lindbergh, Charles August, *Banking and Currency...*, p. 132.

Chapter 21: The Jekyll Island Caper

It's important to note here that when the Federal Reserve System was finally adopted, the 50-year charter provision was dropped entirely; it was given absolute control, permanently!

Selling It to the Public

Now, the public relations blitz began. The big New York banks (Morgans, Rockefellers, etc.) contributed to a $5 million "educational" fund to finance professors at respected universities to endorse the new concept. An organization called the National Citizens League was formed under the personal guidance of Paul Warburg. On April 8, 1912, *The New York Times* wrote a story passively justifying the enormous funding of the League to the National Banks:

> A million dollars doesn't go very far in a campaign of education such as is being carried on by the National Citizens League for the promotion of a sound banking system, yet the contribution of $1,000,000 for that purpose by individual Directors of the National banks of the country a short time ago provoked much comment and a suggestion that the electorate was to be corrupted by the use of these funds.[213]

The story goes on to include sample letters from banks to customers to enlist their aid in propagandizing for the League:

URL: 7.tv/2c12

But there were other initiatives as well. Funding was shuttled to the

---

[213] *The New York Times*, April 8, 1912, no date visible in a .pdf on the *NYT* site at: http://query.nytimes.com/mem/archive-free/pdf?res=F40A1FFA345517738DDDA10894DC405B828DF1D3

emerging schools of economics around the nation. As Galbraith explained it:

> Under Aldrich's direction a score or more of studies of monetary institutions in the United States and, more particularly, in other countries were commissioned from the emergent economics profession. It is at least possible that the reverence in which the Federal Reserve System has since been held by economists owes something to the circumstance that so many who pioneered in the profession participated also in its birth.[214]

Heading up the League's propaganda was J. Laurence Laughlin, a professor of economics at the University of Chicago. Congressman Lindbergh commented on the school's connection to the Money Trust:

> The University of Chicago is an institution endowed by John D. Rockefeller with nearly $50 million dollars. It may truly be said to be the Rockefeller University.[215]

Another academic called in to defend the central bank concept of the Aldrich Bill was the President of Princeton University, Woodrow Wilson, who was also a trustee of the Carnegie Foundation. Wilson had graduated from Princeton along with classmates Cleveland H. Dodge and Cyrus McCormick, now both directors of Rockefeller's National City Bank.

Wilson embraced John D. Rockefeller's maxim, "competition is sin," along with the idea of a central bank. He applauded the rise of vast corporations where competition was managed by the elite:

> The old time of individual competition is probably gone by. It may come back; I don't know; it will not come back within our time, I dare say.[216]

Truer words were never spoken! Wilson was the first prominent educator to speak in favor of the Aldrich Plan. Historian H.S. Kenan remarked that this gesture:

> ... Immediately brought him the Governorship of New Jersey and later the Presidency of the United States.[217]

---

[214] Galbraith, John Kenneth; *Money, Whence it Came....*, p. 123.
[215] Greider, p. 276
[216] Greider, p. 276.
[217] Kenan, H.S., *The Federal Reserve Bank* (Los Angeles: Noontide Press, 196), p. 1205.

Chapter 22 - The Election of 1912

When Roosevelt returned from his African hunting trip, he discovered that the right wing of the Republican Party had turned against Taft and urged him to run again. Roosevelt was a popular campaigner, and won most of the presidential primaries, but a majority of the convention delegates were already pledged to Taft who won on the first ballot. Enraged Roosevelt supporters bolted from the party and formed the Progressive Party that Roosevelt dubbed "The Bull Moose" party, and ran Roosevelt. This effectively split the Republican vote and therefore insured victory to a little-known Democrat governor from New Jersey, named Woodrow Wilson.

But was TR in the pocket of the Money Trust as some believe? Paul Warburg, the author of the Aldrich Plan at Jekyll Island, in his own book on the origins of the Federal Reserve System, says that in January 1912, ten months before the election, Roosevelt had been:

> ... Fairly won over to a favorable consideration of the Aldrich Plan.[218]

Of course, if you were politician Teddy Roosevelt, looking at an uphill fight as a third-party candidate, what would you tell the intellectual kingpin of the Money Trust? But was Roosevelt really a friend of the Money Trust – one of the bad guys? Some authors who support a gold money system seem to think so, but skepticism is necessary because these folks aren't always reliable when it comes to reporting quotes accurately. For example, the following TR quote was significantly altered:

> Roosevelt bellowed that "the issue of currency should be lodged with the government and be protected from domination and manipulation by Wall Street."[219]

The author's source, according to his footnotes, was Henry S. Commanger's *Documents of American History*, but the actual quote, both in Commanger's book and many older sources such as *The World Almanac and Book of Facts* from 1914, p. 781—as well as the oldest one cited in the footnote -- is far more detailed:

> The issue of currency is fundamentally a government function and the system should have as basic principles soundness and elasticity. The control should be lodged with the government and should be protected from domination and manipulation by Wall Street.[220]

Does Roosevelt sound like someone who is insincere? Hardly. It certainly seems that he was very knowledgeable on the money question. Another example: by shortening the following Roosevelt quote it removes a major theme of all monetary reformers: that the quantity of money <u>must</u> be under "effective control":

---

[218] Warburg, Paul. *The Federal Reserve System: Its Origins and Growth* (New York: Macmillan, 1930, Vol. I, p. 78

[219] Griffin, p. 456.

[220] Myers, L.T., *Great Leaders and National Issues of 1912* (no publisher mentioned, 1912), p. 291.

We are opposed to the so-called Aldrich Currency Bill because its provisions would place our currency and credit system in private hands.[221]

When, in fact, the quote continues thusly:

... Not subject to effective control. [222]

So Roosevelt here demonstrated that he knew the truth about money; the key factor being, *who controls the quantity*. Roosevelt knew it should be the government, and not the banks.

Theodore Roosevelt's Early Life

Teddy Roosevelt is a very interesting character placed right at the pivot point in American history when the great battle between the average American and financial capitalism or monopoly capitalism (not small-business capitalism) was being waged. Let's look at the roots of President Theodore Roosevelt to better understand the battle that was going on at this pivotal stage of American history.

Roosevelt was born in 1858 to a wealthy family in New York City. He was a sickly child, suffering from severe asthma back before there was any effective medical treatment for it. He was so sickly that he had to sleep propped up in bed or slouching in a chair. He could not attend school and so was home-schooled, and became a passionate student of nature.

> His lifelong interest in zoology was formed at age seven upon seeing a dead seal at a local market. After obtaining the seal's head, the young Roosevelt and two of his cousins formed what they called the "Roosevelt Museum of Natural History". Learning the rudiments of taxidermy, he filled his makeshift museum with many animals that he killed or caught, studied, and prepared for display. At age nine, he codified his observation of insects with a paper titled "The Natural History of Insects".[223]

From his grandparents' home, young Teddy witnessed the funeral procession of Abraham Lincoln when it came through New York. Teddy's

---

[221] Griffin, p. 456.
[222] *The New International Yearbook for the Year 1912*, editors Frank Moore Colby and Allen Leon Churchill, (New York, Dodd, Mead and Company, 1913), p. 585.
[223] http://en.wikipedia.org/wiki/*Theodore Roosevelt*

younger brother, Elliott, would become the father of First Lady Eleanor Roosevelt after marrying her 5th cousin, Franklin D. Roosevelt.

> As a young Sunday school teacher at Christ Church, Roosevelt was once reprimanded for rewarding a young man $1 who showed up to his class with a black eye for fighting a bully. The bully had supposedly pinched his sister and the young man was standing up for her. Roosevelt thought this to be honorable; however, the church deemed it too flagrant of support of fighting.[224]

Teddy gained admission to Harvard and took up boxing to combat his poor physical fitness. Always determined to give every endeavor his all, he was runner-up in the Harvard boxing championship. Only one year after graduation, the brilliant young Roosevelt was elected to the New York State Assembly, as a Republican, at age 25, as its youngest member. The next year, Teddy's first historical book, *The Naval War of 1812* (1882) established his professional reputation as a serious historian.

> He had a photographic memory and developed a life-long habit of devouring books, memorizing every detail. He was an eloquent conversationalist who, throughout his life, sought out the company of the smartest people. He could multitask in extraordinary fashion, dictating letters to one secretary and memoranda to another, while browsing through a new book.[225]

TR Enters Politics

Roosevelt attended the 1884 Republican National Convention and considered joining the "Mugwamp" reformers. The Mugwamps refused to support Republican candidate James G. Blaine because of his close ties to the Money Trust and general financial corruption. They supported Democratic candidate Grover Cleveland. It was the Mugwamps who supposedly swung New York State during the election, thereby electing Cleveland as president.

> Refusing to join other Mugwumps in supporting Democrat Grover Cleveland, the Democratic nominee, he debated with his friend Henry Cabot Lodge the pros and cons of staying loyal.

---

[224] Ibid
[225] Ibid

Chapter 22: The Election of 1912

> But, in probably the most crucial moment of his young political career, he resisted the very instinct to bolt from the Party....
>
> Leaving the convention, his idealism quite disillusioned by party politics, Roosevelt indicated that he had no further aspiration but to retire to his ranch in the wild Badlands of the Dakota Territory that he had purchased the previous year while on a buffalo hunting expedition.[226]

Roosevelt built a new ranch, which he named "Elk Horn", about 35 miles north of Medora, North Dakota.

> Roosevelt learned to ride western style, rope, and hunt. He rebuilt his life and began writing about frontier life for Eastern magazines. As a deputy sheriff, Roosevelt hunted down three outlaws who stole his riverboat and were escaping north with it up the Little Missouri. Capturing them, he decided against hanging them (apparently yielding to established law procedures in place of vigilante justice), and sending his foreman back by boat, he took the thieves back overland for trial in Dickinson, guarding them forty hours without sleep and reading Tolstoy to keep himself awake. When he ran out of his own books, he read a dime store western that one of the thieves was carrying.

In 1886, Roosevelt married his childhood sweetheart, Edith Kermit Carow. They honeymooned in Europe and TR led a party to the summit of Mont Blanc, a feat which resulted in his induction into the British Royal Society.

In 1888, Roosevelt campaigned for Benjamin Harrison. After the election, President Harrison appointed TR to the U.S. Civil Service Commission where he served for 7 years. Roosevelt jumped into his new task – attacking the spoils system in Washington. As TR biographer James Bucklin Bishop described the assault:

> The very citadel of spoils politics, the hitherto impregnable fortress that had existed unshaken since it was erected on the foundation laid by Andrew Jackson, was tottering to its fall under the assaults of this audacious and irrepressible young man.... Whatever may have been the feelings of the ... President (Harrison) — and there is little doubt that he had no idea when he appointed Roosevelt that he would prove to be so veritable a bull in a china

---

[226] Ibid

Chapter 22: The Election of 1912

shop—he refused to remove him and stood by him firmly till the end of his term.

During this time, the New York Sun described Roosevelt as "irrepressible, belligerent, and enthusiastic."

In spite of Roosevelt's support for Harrison's reelection bid in the presidential election of 1892, the eventual winner, Grover Cleveland (a Bourbon Democrat), reappointed him to the same post.[227]

Roosevelt only left this post when he was appointed New York City Police Commissioner in 1895. Again, TR dove in with unrelenting zeal tasked with the job of reforming the police force which was reputed as one of the most corrupt in the nation. The NYPD's division history records called Roosevelt:

... An iron-willed leader of unimpeachable honesty (who) brought a reforming zeal to the New York City Police Commission in 1895.

---

[227] Ibid

Chapter 22: The Election of 1912

TR as Badlands hunter in 1885

In 1894, Roosevelt met Jacob Riis, the muckraking Evening Sun newspaper journalist who opened the eyes of New York's rich to the terrible conditions of the city's millions of poor immigrants with such books as, *How the Other Half Lives*. In Riis' autobiography, he described his relationship with Roosevelt:

> When Roosevelt read [my] book ... he came to the Evening Sun office one day looking for me. I was out, and he left his card, merely writing on the back of it that he had read my book and had "come to help." That was all and it tells the whole story of the man. I loved him from the day I first saw him; nor ever in all the years that have passed has he failed of the promise made then. No one ever helped as he did.[228]

In 1897, the year after McKinley's victory over William Jennings Bryan, President McKinley appointed Roosevelt as Assistant Secretary of the

---

[228] Ibid

Navy. When the Spanish-American War broke out, a year later, Roosevelt resigned from the Navy Department and joined the Army where he organized the First U.S. Volunteer Cavalry Regiment which the newspapers called the "Rough Riders". Under his command, the Rough Riders made a famous charge up San Juan Hill on July 1, 1898. For his actions, Roosevelt was nominated for the Medal of Honor but it was later denied, probably because

Roosevelt angered Secretary of War, Russell Alger, by demanding that his troops be brought home after the war because malaria and other diseases were killing more of them than had died in battle.

Roosevelt was elected Governor of New York in 1898, and was elected as McKinley's Vice-President in 1900. When McKinley was assassinated in 1901, Roosevelt became president. In his first address to Congress, Roosevelt bashed the Money Trust and was from then on called a "trust-buster."

In May 1902, Roosevelt took on the unions as well. He put an end to a strike by the United Mine Workers but set up a fact-finding commission to study the situation that resulted in workers getting higher pay and working fewer hours.

The Democratic Ticket of 1912

The major money in the three-way presidential race between Roosevelt, Taft and Wilson, was definitely behind Wilson. Paul Warburg and Jacob Schiff, along with Morgan, the Rockefellers, and Bernard Baruch, backed Wilson. According to historian James Perloff:

> Baruch brought Wilson to the Democratic Party Headquarters in New York in 1912, 'leading him like one would a poodle on a string.' Wilson received an 'indoctrination course,' from the leaders convened there....[229]

Baruch and the Democrats extracted certain promises from Wilson. In exchange for their support, he pledged to:

---

[229] Perloff, James, *The Shadows of Power: The Council on Foreign Relations And The American Decline* (Appleton, Wisc: Western Islands, 1988), p. 27.

Chapter 22: The Election of 1912

- Support the soon-to-be-proposed Federal Reserve Act;
- Support income tax;
- Take their advice when war broke out in Europe;
- Allow them to suggest his cabinet appointments.

Despite these assurances, the Democratic platform stated that Wilson was dead set against a central bank. As Rep. Louis McFadden, himself a Democrat, explained 20 years later:

> The Aldrich bill was condemned in the platform upon which Theodore Roosevelt was nominated in the year 1912, and in that same year, when Woodrow Wilson was nominated, the Democratic platform as adopted at the Biltmore convention, expressly stated: 'We are opposed to the Aldrich plan or a central bank.' This was plain language. The men who ruled the Democratic Party then promised the people that if they were returned to power there would be no central bank established here while they held the reins of government. Thirteen months later that promise was broken, and the Wilson administration, under the tutelage of those sinister Wall Street figures who stood behind Colonel House, established here in our free country the worm-eaten monarchical institution of the 'king's bank' to control us from the top downward, and to shackle us from the cradle to the grave.[230]

Now all Baruch had to do was to get Wilson nominated. But the nomination was far from assured. At the Democratic convention of 1912, delegates gave the Speaker of the House of Representatives, Champ Clark, from Missouri, a majority on the 10th ballot. But it took 2/3rds of the convention to nominate. Wilson's big-money supporters stayed with him. On the 14th ballot, William Jennings Bryan swung his support to Wilson and the nomination was clinched.

> Wilson's nomination represented a personal triumph for Cleveland H. Dodge, director of National City Bank [owned by Rockefeller].... The nomination represented no less a triumph for ... J.P. Morgan and Company. Sitting with Dodge as co-directors of the National City Bank at the time were

---

[230] Speech made by McFadden on the floor of Congress, June 10, 1932, Collective Speeches p. 390.

the younger J.P. Morgan, now the head of the [Morgan] firm, Jacob Schiff, [and] William Rockefeller....[231]

Modern critics of Teddy Roosevelt brand him as a "progressive" and indeed in a March 30, 1912 speech, delivered at Carnegie Hall in New York City, entitled "The Right of the People to Rule" he said:

> Friends, our task as Americans is to strive for social and industrial justice, achieved through the genuine rule of the people.[232]

But if the essence of the American experiment is unprecedented freedom for the common man – of decentralization of power -- then how else is America supposed to escape the serfdom of old-world Europe – the ultimate centralization of power of that day -- other then by banding together in self-governance for the common good? How can this be seen as some sort of leftist radicalism, socialism or even communism? Those are the tools of power centralization, not de-centralization.

Roosevelt seemed to be an appropriately American mix, sometimes favoring labor, sometimes favoring big business, but always his focus seemed to be decentralization of power and self-governance. Also from his 1912 speech "The Right of the People to Rule" is this:

> The great fundamental issue now before our people can be stated briefly. It is: Are the American people fit to govern themselves, to rule themselves, to control themselves? I believe they are. My opponents do not. I believe in the right of the people to rule. I believe the majority of the plain people of the United States will, day in and day out, make fewer mistakes in governing themselves than any smaller class or body of men, no matter what their training, will make in trying to govern them. I believe, again, that the American people are, as a whole, capable of self—control and of learning by their mistakes. Our opponents pay lip—loyalty to this doctrine; but they show their real beliefs by the way in which they champion every device to make the nominal rule of the people a sham.[233]

---

[231] Lundberg, Ferdinand, *America's Sixty Families* (New York: Vanguard Press, 1937), pp. 109, 113.

[232] Roosevelt, Theodore. *The Right of the People to Rule*, made at Carnegie Hall, New York, NY 1912.

[233] http://en.wikisource.org/wiki/The_Right_of_the_People_to_Rule

Chapter 22: The Election of 1912

In this speech, Roosevelt touched on the selflessness of the ideal American leader. These might have just been words, but they were good words.

> The leader ... is but an instrument, to be used until broken and then to be cast aside; and if he is worth his salt he will care no more when he is broken than a soldier cares when he is sent where his life is forfeit in order that the victory may be won. In the long fight for righteousness the watchword for all of is spend and be spent.[234]

TR then explains the core of his populist message – the hope of all the world -- for the great American experiment:

> We, here in America, hold in our hands the hope of the world ... and shame and disgrace will be ours if ... we trail in the dust the golden hopes of men. If on this new continent we merely build another country of great ... material prosperity, we shall have done nothing; and we shall do as little if we merely set the greed of envy against the greed of arrogance, and thereby destroy the material well-being of all of us.
>
> To turn this Government either into government by a plutocracy or government by a mob would be to repeat on a larger scale the lamentable failures of the world that is dead.
>
> The worth of our great experiment depends upon its being in good faith an experiment – the first that has even been tried – in true democracy on the scale of a continent, on a scale as vast as that of the mightiest empires of the Old World. Surely this is a noble ideal ... for which ... it is worthwhile to sacrifice much....[235]

Interestingly, Thomas Edison was on the scene at that point, making the first audio recordings. Fortunately, this speech was one of his first attempts. You can hear an audio clip of TR's voice here:

---

[234] Hagedorn, Hermann, *Americanism of Theodore Roosevelt*, (Cambridge, Mass., Houghton Mifflin, 1923), p. 185.
[235] Hagedorn, Hermann, *Americanism of Theodore Roosevelt*, (Cambridge, Mass., Houghton Mifflin Company, 1923), p. 186.

URL: 7.tv/5bb5

TR's Assassination Attempt

On October 14, 1912, a saloonkeeper named John Schrank shot Teddy Roosevelt in the chest. Luckily the bullet had to penetrate his steel eyeglass case and a 50-page speech he was carrying in his jacket.

> Roosevelt, as an experienced hunter and anatomist, correctly concluded that since he wasn't coughing blood, the bullet had not completely penetrated the chest wall to his lung, and so declined suggestions he go to the hospital immediately. Instead, he delivered his scheduled speech with blood seeping into his shirt. He spoke for 90 minutes. His opening comments to the gathered crowd were, "Ladies and gentlemen, I don't know whether you fully understand that I have just been shot; but it takes more than that to kill a Bull Moose." Afterwards, probes and x-ray showed that the bullet had traversed three inches (76 mm) of tissue and lodged in Roosevelt's chest muscle but did not penetrate the pleura, and it would be more dangerous to attempt to remove the bullet than to leave it in place. Roosevelt carried it with him for the rest of his life.[236]

Within 5 minutes of being shot, Roosevelt approached the podium:

> Friends, I shall ask you to be as quiet as possible. I don't know whether you fully understand that I have just been shot; but it takes more than that to kill a Bull Moose. But fortunately I had my manuscript, so you see I was going to make a long speech, and there is a bullet - there is where the bullet went through - and it probably saved me from it going into my heart. The bullet is in me now, so that I cannot make a very long speech, but I will try my best.
>
> And now, friends, I want to take advantage of this incident to say a word of solemn warning to my fellow countrymen. First of all, I want to say this about myself: I have altogether too important things to think of to feel any concern over my own death; and now I cannot speak to you insincerely within five minutes of

---

[236] http://en.wikipedia.org/wiki/Theodore_Roosevelt

being shot. I am telling you the literal truth when I say that my concern is for many other things. It is not in the least for my own life. I want you to understand that I am ahead of the game, anyway. No man has had a happier life than I have led; a happier life in every way. I have been able to do certain things that I greatly wished to do, and I am interested in doing other things. I can tell you with absolute truthfulness that I am very much uninterested in whether I am shot or not. It was just as when I was colonel of my regiment. I always felt that a private was to be excused for feeling at times some pangs of anxiety about his personal safety, but I cannot understand a man fit to be a colonel who can pay any heed to his personal safety when he is occupied as he ought to be with the absorbing desire to do his duty.[237]

Then Roosevelt, bleeding profusely through his shirt, went after the Money Trust:

> Our opponents have said that we intend to legalize monopoly. Nonsense. They have legalized monopoly. At this moment the Standard Oil and Tobacco Trust monopolies are legalized; they are being carried on under the decree of the Supreme Court. Our proposal is really to break up monopoly. Our proposal is to lay down certain requirements, and then to require the commerce commission - the industrial commission - to see that the trusts live up to those requirements. Our opponents have spoken as if we were going to let the commission declare what those requirements should be. Not at all. We are going to put the requirements in the law and then see that the commission requires them to obey that law.
>
> And now, friends, as Mr. Wilson has invited the comparison, I only want to say this: Mr. Wilson has said that the States are the proper authorities to deal with the trusts. Well, about eighty percent of the trusts are organized in New Jersey. The Standard Oil, the Tobacco, the Sugar, the Beef, all those trusts are organized in the state of New Jersey and the laws of New Jersey say that their charters can at any time be amended or repealed if they misbehave themselves and give the government ample power to act about those laws, and Mr. Wilson has been governor a year and nine months and he has not opened his lips. The chapter describing what Mr. Wilson has done about trusts in New Jersey would read precisely like a chapter describing snakes in Ireland, which ran: "There are no snakes in Ireland." Mr. Wilson has done precisely and exactly nothing about the trusts.

---

[237] "I Have Just Been Shot" speech by Theodore Roosevelt delivered in Milwaukee, Wisconsin, October 14, 1912.
http://en.wikisource.org/wiki/I_have_just_been_shot, retrieved January 15, 2011.

The speech is available here:

URL: 7.tv/5b42

In the end, Roosevelt got 27.4% of the vote; Taft 23.2%, and Wilson won with only 41.8% of the vote, a situation that was not to be repeated until the presidential election of 1992, when William Jefferson Clinton — also in a three-way contest — won with only 43% of the popular vote. William McAdoo, Wilson's Secretary of the Treasury, viewed Wall Street's financing of his candidate with alarm:

> The fact is that there is a serious danger of this country becoming a pluto-democracy; that is, a sham republic with the real government in the hands of a small clique of enormously wealthy men, who speak through their money, and whose influence, even today, radiates to every corner of the United States.[238]

Political science now calls this a "plutocracy" – rule by the rich.

The Democrats Victory

Along with Wilson gaining the Presidency, Democrats won a majority in both houses of Congress. Democrats gained 7 seats in the Senate and 61 in the House to dominate that chamber with more than 2/3rds of the members. This meant that the Aldrich Plan was effectively dead.

Party	Total seats	(change)	Seat percentage
Democratic Party	291	+61	66.8%
Republican Party	134	-28	30.8%
Progressive Party	9	+9	2.0%
Independent	1	+0	0.2%
Totals	435	+41	100.0%

---

[238] McAdoo, William G., *Crowded Years* (New York: Weybright & Talley, 1971), p. 165.

Chapter 22: The Election of 1912

Morgan interests now began to advance the "Democratic" version of the legislation, which Warburg named the Federal Reserve System. Professor Laughlin of the University of Chicago and his Warburg-financed National Citizens' League weighed in. Excusing the failure of the Aldrich Plan as "progress" he said the League was now free to:

> Try to help in getting a proper bill adopted by the Democrats.[239]

---

[239] Kolko, p. 222.

Chapter 23 - Birth of the Federal Reserve

This time, the name of the new central bank had been more carefully considered. The word "bank" would not appear; it would be called a "System." The word system could not evoke thoughts of bank or corporations — it implied a remedy to problems — perhaps even a governmental remedy. This impression was aided, of course, by the use of the word "Federal." The federal government, however, would have virtually no control over this privately owned-and-run central bank. Finally, the word "Reserve" was added. Obviously, the one thing that had bothered the public more than anything else about banking was the threat of losing their savings if their local bank went under. Therefore the word "Reserve" was chosen to encourage the notion that all the banks were going to pool their resources to keep every bank solvent.

The Democrats appointed Congressman Carter Glass, the Democratic Chairman of the House Banking and Currency Committee, and one of the most outspoken critics of the Aldrich Plan, to develop the new bill which would eventually be called the Glass-Owen Bill.

America would certainly have never agreed to any bill containing the word "Bank" in it. Congressman Everis Hayes of California warned:

Chapter 23: Birth of the Federal Reserve System

> Our people have set their faces like steel against a central bank.[240]

By 1913, the new bill was ready for presentation to Congress. After reconciliation with a Senate version put forward by Senator Robert L. Owen, the bill emerged as the Glass-Owen Bill.

Glass was adamant that this bill was entirely different from the Aldrich Plan, though he had admitted that he had no technical expertise in the field of banking. The new bill was, in fact, virtually the same in every important detail, as the old. For public consumption, both Glass and Owen hailed the new bill as a substantial defeat for the Money Trust. So vehement was their verbiage that Paul Warburg admits he had to step in to reassure his friends in Congress that the two bills were virtually identical.

> Brushing aside the external differences affecting the 'shells,' we find the 'kernels' of the two systems very closely resembling and related to one another.[241]

Edward Mandell House

Woodrow Wilson's chief aid was Col. Edward Mandell House. House, though a native Texan, had a long family lineage in London. The elder House was one of the wealthiest men in Texas. His son, Edward, inherited his father's cotton plantations that paid him an income of $20,000 a year — a princely sum before World War I. He used his father's money to make himself the kingmaker of Texas politics of that era.

In 1911, Edward began supporting Woodrow Wilson. He threw the crucial Texas delegation to him, ensuring his nomination. House told his biographer that after the election, when he went to meet Wilson at the White House for the first time, he handed Wilson $35,000. This extravagant amount was exceeded only by a $50,000 contribution from Wall Street investor, Bernard Baruch — a man who would go on himself,

---

[240] Congressional Record, pt. 6, 1913, p. 6021
[241] Warburg, Paul Moritz; *The Federal Reserve System, Its Origins and Growth* (New York, Macmillan, 1930), p. 412.

to serve as an unpaid advisor to every President from Wilson to Eisenhower.

America's Future Revealed

Col. House had recently written a novel that had been published anonymously, entitled *Philip Dru, Administrator: A Story of Tomorrow*. The novel called for the enactment of the graduated income tax, excess profits tax, unemployment insurance, social security, and a flexible currency system — all of which would later be enacted by the Wilson and Franklin D. Roosevelt administrations.

> One of the institutions outlined in the book, though under another name, is the Federal Reserve System. The Schiffs, the Warburgs, the Kahns, the Rockefellers and Morgans put their faith in House.[242]

In Philip Dru, we get an interesting view of what House's plans for America were:

> America is the most undemocratic of democratic countries.... Our Constitution and our laws served us well for the first hundred years of our existence, but under the conditions of today they are not only obsolete, but even grotesque.[243]

> Nowhere in the world is wealth more defiant, and monopoly more insistent than in this mighty republic ... and it is here that the next great battle for human emancipation will be fought and won.[244]

House's solution for these vexing problems of capitalism was a revolution, which would install an omnipotent dictator after a bloody civil war. By these means alone, according to Colonel House's character, Philip Dru, could "Socialism as dreamed of by Karl Marx ...." be established in the United States?[245] House wished the same for Russia, which would see a communist revolution only five years after his book was published.

---

[242] Stang, Alan. *The Actor: The True Story of John Foster Dulles, Secretary of State, 1953-1959* (Western Islands, 1968), p. 17.

[243] House, Edward Mandell; *Philip Dru: Administrator: A Story of Tomorrow, 1920-1935* (New York, B.W. Huebsch, 1912), p. 222.

[244] Ibid.

[245] Ibid.

Chapter 23: Birth of the Federal Reserve System

Dru thought of Russia in its vastness, of the ignorance and hopeless outlook of the people, and wondered when her deliverance would come. There was, he knew, great work for someone to do in that despotic land.[246]

The Council on Foreign Relations

By 1921, Colonel House had written the charter for the American branch of the British Round Table group, which would be officially incorporated as "The Council on Foreign Relations," or CFR. The CFR has made no great attempt to hide its power consolidating intentions, either domestically or internationally. In the second edition of their prestigious quarterly journal *Foreign Affairs*, published in September 1922, they say:

> Obviously there is going to be no peace or prosperity for mankind as long as [America] remains divided into fifty or sixty independent states.... Equally obviously there is going to be no steady progress in civilization ... until some kind of international system is created which will put an end to the diplomatic struggles incident to the attempt of every nation to make itself secure.... The real problem today is that of world government.[247]

Lenin was an admirer of *Foreign Affairs*. The CFR is now in possession of Lenin's original copy containing underscored passages in which he was particularly interested.[248] It is clear that Col. House was the modern-day founder in the United States of the concept that would soon be known as the New World Order. But for now, his chief task was to bring about the Federal Reserve System.

Passage of the Glass-Owen Bill

Congressman Glass held public hearings on the Democrat's new central banking bill in the House Banking and Currency Committee, but vocal opponents of the measure, including Congressman Lindbergh, were not allowed to speak. As the Glass-Owen Bill moved closer to a vote in the

---

[246] Ibid.
[247] Armstrong, Hamilton Fish. *The Foreign Affairs Reader* (New York, Published for the Council on Foreign Affairs by Harper,1947), p. 75. Also, Perloff, James, *The Shadows of Power: The Council on Foreign Relations And The American Decline* (Appleton, Wisc: Western Islands, 1988), p. 11.
[248] Perloff, p. 13.

Chapter 23: Birth of the Federal Reserve System

fall of 1913, Senator Aldrich (recently retired from the Senate) and Frank A. Vanderlip, president of Rockefeller's National City Bank of New York, opposed it with great vigor. In an address to the American Academy of Political Science at Columbia University on October 15, 1913, Aldrich, in a breathtaking admission said this about the Federal Reserve Bill (the Glass-Owen Bill):

> I am aware that there seems to be a marked tendency in recent years, in some quarters, to abandon the doctrine that states have still any virile powers under our form of government, and to assent to the concentration of all powers and authority in the national government, to be exercised through Congress, or in later days, through agents of the executive. But this is, I think, the first attempt to give a government board the right to manage a great business, which is more important in its intimate relations to all the people than any other.[249]

Of course, as it would turn out, the Federal Reserve System was not really a part of the government, it would merely pretend to be managing the banking system so that the public would be deceived into believing that the government had taken charge over the Money Trust. Of course, such was not the case. This essential deception has been at the root of EVERY subsequent major financial disaster in American history. But then Aldrich goes on with this stunning assessment:

> If the attempt is successful it will be the first and most important step toward changing our form of government from a democracy to an autocracy. No imperial government in Europe would venture to suggest, much less enact, legislation of this kind.[250]

The entire text of his remarks is now available on Google Books at:

---

[249] *Proceedings of the Academy of Political Science in the City of New York*, edited by Mussey, Henry Raymond, (New York, The American Academy of Political Science, Columbia University, 1913), Vol. IV, No. 1 p. 85.
[250] Ibid.

Chapter 23: Birth of the Federal Reserve System

URL: 7.tv/5b08

Vanderlip later admitted in his 1935 *Saturday Evening Post* article that:

> Although the Aldrich Federal Reserve Plan was defeated when it bore the name Aldrich, nevertheless its essential points were all contained in the plan that finally was adopted.[251]

Wilson's Treasury Secretary, William McAdoo eventually saw through the deception:

> Bankers fought the Federal Reserve legislation — with the tireless energy of men fighting a forest fire. They said it was populistic, socialistic, half-baked, destructive, infantile, badly conceived, and unworkable....
>
> These interviews with bankers led me to an interesting conclusion. I perceived gradually, through all the haze and smoke of controversy that the banking world was not really as opposed to the bill as it pretended to be.[252]

The Remarkable Testimony of Alfred Crozier

As the Glass-Owen Bill neared a vote in Congress in the latter half of 1913, furor over its passage mounted rapidly. Congressional committees were forced to allow critics the opportunity to speak. An Ohio attorney, Alfred Crozier, was called before the Senate Banking and Currency Committee to answer questions about his book, *U.S. Money vs. Corporation Currency*, published the previous year.

Crozier attacked the Panic of 1907 as a deliberate attempt to stampede the American public and Congress into the Glass-Owen Bill.

> Within recent months, William McAdoo, Secretary of the Treasury of the United States, was reported in the open press as charging specifically that there was a conspiracy among certain of the large banking interests to put a contraction upon the currency and to raise interest rates for the sake of

---

[251] Vanderlip, Frank Arthur and Sparkes, Boyden, *From Farm Boy to Financier* (D. Appleton-Century Company, 1935), p. 218
[252] McAdoo, pp. 213, 225-6

forcing ... Congress into passing currency legislation desired by those institutions.[253]

Crozier noted the similarities between the Aldrich Bill and the Glass-Owen Bill.

> The ... bill grants just what Wall Street and the big banks for twenty-five years have been striving for, namely, private instead of public control of currency. It [the Glass-Owen bill] does this as completely as the Aldrich Bill. Both measures rob the Government and the people of all effective control over the public money supply and vest in the banks exclusively the dangerous power to make money among the people scarce or plenty.[254]

Crozier then pointed out one of the few modifications made in the Glass-Carter bill.

> The Aldrich Bill puts this power in one central bank. The Administration Bill puts it in twelve regional central banks, all owned exclusively by the identical private interests that would have owned and operated the Aldrich Bank. There is absolutely no difference between the two measures in legal effect as to the control of the volume of currency in circulation.
>
> If the Government is to retain absolute, instead of pretended, control, then one bank or public agency is all that is needed, and will be more simple and scientific than a dozen or any other number of scattered agencies exercising currency powers.[255]

The Congress-Is-Too-Corrupt-to-Have-the-Money-Power Argument

Alfred Crozier's remarkable 1913 testimony answers some objections you hear from metalists today.

> Now, if we are to assume, gentlemen, that in a republican form of government it is impossible for Congress to create a public body that it is safe to delegate these governmental powers to and that therefore we must

---

[253] Banking and Currency Hearings before the Committee on Banking and Currency, United States Senate (Washington, D.C., 1913), Vol. 3, p. 2893
[254] Ibid, p. 2897
[255] Ibid.

Chapter 23: Birth of the Federal Reserve System

> take these powers away from the Government and delegate them to some private corporation, run for profit, that is different: I do not agree with you.
>
> I believe in the republican form of government and in the ability of that form of government to construct a public agency, a department of government, that will be absolutely free from all political taint or partisan bias and free from control by the influence of Wall Street or anybody else—just the same as the Supreme Court is to-day. But it should be a separate department of the Government; it should not be intermixed or intermeddled with the Treasury Department work at all.[256]

Crozier then points out the results of the proposed system:

> By making money artificially scarce, interest rates throughout the country can be arbitrarily raised and the ... cost of living increased for the profit of the banks owning these regional central banks, and without the slightest benefit to the people. These 12 corporations together cover the whole country and monopolize and use for private gain every dollar of the public currency, and all public revenues of the United States. Not a dollar can be put into circulation among the people by their Government without the consent of and on terms fixed by these 12 private-money trusts.[257]

The Battle for Bryan's Support

For the most part, critics like Crozier were ignored. But there was one man of extreme influence who could not be ignored — William Jennings Bryan. Bryan had made it clear that he would not support any bill that resulted in a private monopoly issuing private money disguised as U.S. currency. Once Bryan actually read the bill, he demanded that the new Federal Reserve notes be Treasury currency – U.S. Notes -- issued and guaranteed by the U.S. government. He also demanded that the governing body of the new Federal Reserve System be appointed by the President and approved by the Senate, or he would speak out against the bill.

This was no small threat. Bryan still commanded the heart and soul of the Democratic Party. His sense of loyalty to the party had kept him from attacking the bill in the past, at least partially because he, like most

---

[256] Ibid.
[257] Ibid, p. 2898

everyone else, didn't fully understand it. But one thing was certain; the bill would never pass with his opposition.

Senator Glass was called to the White House to meet with President Wilson and Col. House. As Glass recounted years later in his book, *Adventures in Constructive Finance*, Wilson explained how they intended to deceive Bryan. They would tell him that the new Federal Reserve Notes would be made "obligations" of the government and thereby convince Bryan that this was actually a government issue, when, in fact, it would simply be money loaned into existence by private banks at interest. Glass was astonished at the proposal advanced by Wilson and House.

> It would be a pretense on its face. Was there ever a government note based primarily on the property of banking institutions? Was there ever a government issue not one dollar of which could be put out except by demand of a bank? The suggested government obligation is so remote it could never be discerned.[258]

President Wilson agreed that the logic was weak, but it was their only option:

> Exactly so, Glass. Every word you say is true; the government liability is a mere thought. And so, if we can hold the substance of the thing and give the other fellow [Bryan] the shadow, why not do it, if thereby we may save our bill?[259]

Many years later, Paul Warburg, in his book, *The Federal Reserve System: Its Origins and Growth*, explained the only way the tenuous logic was actually true:

> While technically and legally the Federal Reserve Note is an obligation of the United States Government, in reality it is an obligation ... [of] the reserve banks.... The government could only be called upon to [bail them out] after the reserve banks had failed.[260]

Perhaps Wilson, Morgan and Warburg never imagined that their system of debt would ever get out of control, but it has. Failed banks now feel they can march into Congress seeking handouts to cover their losses, so

---

[258] Smith, Rixey, and Beasley, Norman. *Carter Glass: A Biography* (Ayer Company Publishers, 1939), p. 117.
[259] Ibid
[260] Warburg, p. 409.

Chapter 23: Birth of the Federal Reserve System

they can continue to pursue the highest profit margins from the most risky investments, at the expense of the American taxpayer.

In any case, what is amazing is that Bryan actually bought all this. Wilson promised to make the Federal Reserve Board of Governors subject to Presidential appointment and consent by the Senate, but the terms were so lengthy — 14 years — that no President would be able to appoint a majority. Wilson boldly proclaimed that through these new modifications:

> ...The banks may be instruments, not the masters, of business and of individual enterprise and initiative.[261]

To further grease the deal, in March 1913, Bryan was rescued from an obscure retirement when Wilson appointed him to be his new Secretary of State. Predictably, Bryan decided in favor of the bill, saying:

> The right of the government to issue money is not surrendered to the banks; the control over the money so issued is not relinquished by the government.... I am glad to endorse earnestly and unreservedly the currency bill....[262]

The Final Vote

On September 18, 1913, the House of Representatives passed its version of the bill by an overwhelming 287-to-5 vote. Now the measure, known as the Federal Reserve Act, went to the Senate for consideration. As the bill neared passage in mid-December, Senator Stone attacked the methods the proponents had used to secure support for the legislation over the previous two years:

> I myself have known more than one occasion when bankers refused credit to men who opposed their political views and purposes. When Senator Aldrich and others were going around the country exploiting this scheme, the big banks of New York and Chicago were engaged in raising a munificent fund to bolster up the Aldrich propaganda. I have been told by bankers of my own state that contributions to this exploitation fund had been demanded of them and that they had contributed because they were afraid of being blacklisted or boycotted. There are bankers in this country who are enemies of the public welfare. In the

---

[261] Greider, p. 277.
[262] Glass, Carter; *As Adventure in Constructive Finance*. (New York, Doubleday, 1927), p. 142.

past, a few great banks have followed policies and projects that have paralyzed the industrial energies of the country to perpetuate their tremendous power over the financial and business industries of America.[263]

Seven days after these comments were made, on December 19, 1913, the Senate passed their version of the Federal Reserve Act by a vote of 54-34. But this was not the final vote. There were forty important differences between the House version and the one adopted by the Senate. Some opponents believed that it would be many weeks after the Christmas recess before the differences could be ironed out and a conference bill would be ready for consideration. As foolish Congressmen rushed home for the Christmas recess, they were assured by the proponents of the measure that nothing would happen on the bill until January.

The moneychangers waited silently until Sunday, December 21. Then, in a single day, those remaining in Congress miraculously ironed out all forty disputed points and quickly brought the new bill to a vote. On Monday, December 22, 1913, the bill passed the House by a vote of 282-60 and the next day, December 23, passed Senate by a margin of 43-25 with 27 members not voting. These had probably headed home for the Christmas break.

Here is the Congressional Record from that day:

URL: 7.tv/5bb7

---

[263] Mullins, Eustace; *The Federal Reserve Conspiracy* (Palmdale, CA, Omni Publications, 1954), p. 35.

Chapter 23: Birth of the Federal Reserve System

The Christmas Surprise

Miraculously, the Sunday, December 21, 1913 edition of the New York Times commented editorially that, as a result of the soon forthcoming passage of the Act:

> New York will be on a firmer basis of financial growth, and we shall soon see her the money centre of the world.[264]

The next morning — hours before the Federal Reserve Act was even passed — *The New York Times*' headline read:

> Money Bill May Be Law Today — Conferees Had Adjusted Nearly All Differences At 1:30 This Morning — No Deposit Guarantees — Senate Yields On This Point But Puts Through Many Other Changes.
>
> With almost unprecedented speed, the conference to adjust the House and Senate differences on the Currency Bill practically completed its labours early this morning. On Saturday the Conferees did little more than dispose of the preliminaries, leaving forty essential differences to be thrashed out Sunday.... No other legislation of importance will be taken up in either House of Congress this week.[265]

The *Times* buried a brief quote from Congressman Lindbergh that:

> The bill would establish the most gigantic trust on earth.

The speed of the bill's passage caught even President Wilson off guard. He objected to some rather obscure provisions concerning the selection of some of the regional banks' Directors. Both Paul Warburg and Bernard Baruch had camped in Washington to assist in overseeing the bill's passage. Upon hearing the news of Wilson's foot dragging, Baruch rushed to the White House. After hearing the President's complaints he assured him that the difficulty could be resolved through "administrative processes," and Wilson caved in.

Interestingly, none of the original seven participants at the Jekyll Island meeting were present at the signing. They had prudently decided not to be present. But their motivations were clear. As Bernard Baruch would

---

[264] *The New York Times*, Dec. 22, 1913, front page.
[265] Ibid.

write in the *Knickerbocker Press* of Albany, New York nearly five years later — in the August 8, 1918 edition:

> We are living in a highly organized state of socialism.[266]

Let's compare Wilson's actions as President to his idealism just two years earlier. In 1911, while still Governor of New Jersey and yet to burst upon the national scene, Wilson wrote:

> The great monopoly in this country is the money monopoly. Our system of credit is concentrated. The growth of the Nation, therefore, and all our activities are in the hands of a few men, who, even if their action be honest and intended for the public interest, are necessarily concentrated upon the great undertaking in which their money is involved, and who necessarily, by very reason of their limitations, chill and check and destroy genuine economic freedom. This is the greatest question of all, and to this statesmen must adjust themselves with an earnest determination to serve the long future and the true liberties of men.[267]

As late as November 1, Democratic Congressmen were lionizing Wilson:

> By a strange coincidence of history there have come out of the bosom of New Jersey the great trusts ... and the gigantic monopolies. From this proud Commonwealth have come the dragon's teeth, and now it seems as if the very providence and wisdom of God there has come from her borders the giant this year sent forth to exterminate the dragons infesting the land. When history is finally recorded, [President Andrew] Jackson and New Jersey's governor will stand forth as the two great figures triumphing in memorable struggles as the champions of popular rights.[268]

Early in his presidency, Wilson was also deeply troubled by the Money Trust. In 1913 – just a few months before J.P. Morgan came to Washington to help usher the Federal Reserve Act through Congress -- Wilson in his book, *The New Freedom*, wrote:

> Since I entered politics, I have chiefly had men's views confided to me privately. Some of the biggest men in the United States, in the field of commerce and manufacture, are afraid of somebody, are afraid of something. They know that there is a power somewhere so organized, so

---

[266] *Congressional Serial Set* (Washington, D.C., Government Printing Office, 1919), p. 12
[267] *Bills and Debates in Congress Relating to Trusts*. Committee on the Judiciary, United States House of Representatives, Sixty-Third Congress, November 1, 1913, p. 3406.
[268] Ibid, p. 3408.

Chapter 23: Birth of the Federal Reserve System

subtle, so watchful, so interlocked, so complete, so pervasive, that they had better not speak above their breath when they speak in condemnation of it.

They know that America is not a place of which it can be said, as it used to be, that a man may choose his own calling and pursue it just as far as his abilities enable him to pursue it; because to-day, if he enters certain fields, there are organizations which will use means against him that will prevent his building up a business which they do not want to have built up; organizations that will see to it that the ground is cut from under him and the markets shut against him. For if he begins to sell to certain retail dealers, to any retail dealers, the monopoly will refuse to sell to those dealers, and those dealers, afraid, will not buy the new man's wares.

And this is the country which has lifted to the admiration of the world its ideals of absolutely free opportunity, where no man is supposed to be under any limitation except the limitations of his character and of his mind; where there is supposed to be no distinction of class, no distinction of blood, no distinction of social status, but where men win or lose on their merits.

I lay it very close to my own conscience as a public man whether we can any longer stand at our doors and welcome all newcomers upon those terms. American industry is not free, as once it was free; American enterprise is not free; the man with only a little capital is finding it harder to get into the field, more and more impossible to compete with the big fellow. Why? Because the laws of this country do not prevent the strong from crushing the weak. That is the reason, and because the strong have crushed the weak the strong dominate the industry and the economic life of this country.[269]

Wilson's book can be found in its entirety at:

URL: 7.tv/5bcd

---

[269] Wilson, Woodrow, *The New Freedom* (New York: Doubleday,1913), p. 13-14.

The Communist Manifesto

It is interesting to note that the Communist Manifesto, written in 1848, halfway between President Jackson's and Abraham Lincoln's administrations, laid out a ten-plank plan for establishing a Communist state. Plank 5 called for; "Centralization of credit in the hands of the State, by means of a national bank with state capital and an exclusive monopoly." Plank 2 called for; "A heavy progressive or graduated income tax." Here's the list of all ten:

1. Abolition of property in land and application of all rents of land to public purposes.
2. A heavy progressive or graduated income tax.
3. Abolition of all right of inheritance.
4. Confiscation of the property of all emigrants and rebels.
5. Centralisation of credit in the hands of the State, by means of a national bank with State capital and an exclusive monopoly.
6. Centralisation of the means of communication and transport in the hands of the State.
7. Extension of factories and instruments of production owned by the State; the bringing into cultivation of waste-lands, and the improvement of the soil generally in accordance with a common plan.
8. Equal liability of all to labour. Establishment of industrial armies, especially for agriculture.
9. Combination of agriculture with manufacturing industries; gradual abolition of the distinction between town and country, by a more equitable distribution of the population over the country.
10. Free education for all children in public schools. Abolition of children's factory labour in its present form. Combination of education with industrial production.[270]

Today, 2011, the careful reader will be appalled by the similarities of the above list to what passes for sovereign national governments today.

---

[270] http://www.gutenberg.org/etext/61

What's the Monetary Reform Difference?

How does monetary reform differ from Plank #5? Monetary reform is all about de-centralizing power to the greatest extent practical. For example once upon a time a beloved monetary reformer proposed just such a system as Plank #5, where a single central bank would issue all the credit. I said, "Suppose I go to this national bank seeking a mortgage loan but I am rejected as an enemy of money monopoly state; what would be my remedy? There would be no competition at all, much less a vibrant competitive market for borrowing and lending."

My friend thought about it for a while, and then finally responded, "Well, you could sue them!"

Obviously, that wouldn't work to foster freedom. In a rightly constructed system, the issuers of credit would be many and varied. There would be a bank which favored Democrats; a bank which favored Republicans; even a bank which favored enemies of the Money Trust. There would be a state-chartered banking system in every state, further de-centralizing the money power.

The Graduated Income Tax

Key to the plan of the debt-based money system in America was the graduated income tax. If the government was to start running up bigger debts, it had to propose some way of paying them off. Federal debt had risen slowly since President Jackson paid it off entirely in 1836. At the start of the Civil war, federal debt was a mere $90,582,000. At the end of the war, debt had risen to $2,755,764,000. Over the following 25 years, federal debt had slowly been paid down to just over one billion dollars by 1913. Only six years after the passage of the Federal Reserve Act, federal debt would swell to over $25 billion! As James Perloff put it:

> The solution was income tax. Prior to 1913, there was no income tax in America (except during the War Between the States and early Reconstruction period). The U.S. government survived on other revenue sources, such as tariffs and excise taxes. As a result, it could neither spend nor borrow heavily.

Chapter 23: Birth of the Federal Reserve System

Because income tax had been declared unconstitutional by the Supreme Court in 1895, it had to be instituted by constitutional amendment. The man who brought forward the amendment in Congress was the same senator who proposed the plan for the Federal Reserve — Nelson Aldrich.[271]

The same Nelson Aldrich who participated at the Jekyll Island meeting was obviously doing their bidding once again in proposing the very income tax that is killing the American wage earner. President Taft had pushed the 16th Amendment through Congress in July of that year. It states:

> The Congress shall have power to lay and collect taxes on incomes....

Debate was heated throughout the land. Speaker of the Virginia House of Delegates, Richard E. Byrd, feared the 16th Amendment with prophetic clarity:

> A hand from Washington will be stretched out and placed upon every man's business; the eye of the inspector will be in every man's counting house ... the law will of necessity have inquisitorial features, it will provide penalties, it will create complicated machinery. Under it men will be hauled into court distant from their homes. Heavy fines imposed by distant and unfamiliar tribunals will constantly menace the taxpayer.[272]

The 16th Amendment was declared ratified on February 25, 1913, just a week before President Wilson's inauguration. However critics claim that ratification was actually never achieved; that ratification fell several states short and so officials in Wilson's administration simply declared it ratified. Whether Wilson was aware of this is not known at this hour of historical reconstruction of the period, but during Wilson's inauguration speech on March 4, the crowd was told:

> No one can mistake the purpose for which the nation now seeks to use the Democratic Party.[273]

---

[271] Perloff, p. 25
[272] Ekrich, Arthur A., "The Sixteenth Amendment: The Historical Background," *Cato Journal, I* (Spring, 1982), p. 170; as quoted by Dr. Murray Sabrin, *Tax-Free 2000* (Lafayette, LA: Prescott Press, 1994), p. 79.
[273] *World Book Encyclopedia*; (1980), s.v. "Wilson, Woodrow;" v. 21, p. 270b.

Chapter 23: Birth of the Federal Reserve System

Truer words were never spoken. Within a year, Wilson would shove through Congress two of the most economically repressive measures in America's history, the income tax bill and the Federal Reserve Act. If it weren't so pathetic, the story of President Wilson's first cabinet meeting would be comical. The cabinet, as agreed, was suggested by Morgan, Schiff, Baruch, Warburg and company. During that first meeting, some of the new cabinet members weren't even sure which post they were there to fill. Franklin K. Lane introduced himself at the meeting, saying:

> My name is Lane, Mr. President. I believe I am the Secretary of the Interior.[274]

In April, Wilson called the Congress into special session (in 1913, Congress had not yet implemented year-round sessions). Enabling legislation was needed to make the graduated income tax a fact. To make it more palatable at first, the rates were very low — one-percent on incomes up to $20,000, with a maximum rate of seven percent. The bill was finally passed on October 3, 1913, just in time for Congress to begin debate on the Federal Reserve Bill before Christmas.

Why the big push for the income tax? The central bankers knew war was brewing, and they knew someone had to pay for it. World War I broke out less than a year later.

The income tax bill was actually called the Underwood Tariff Bill because it lowered tariffs on imports and exports as well. This was key to those who were about to profit mightily from the upcoming war because J.P. Morgan, Bernard Baruch and many others were about to reap huge profits arming the combatants in Europe.

As James Perloff put it:

> Income tax didn't soak the rich, it soaked the middle class. Because it was a graduated tax, it tended to prevent anyone from rising into affluence. Thus it acted to consolidate the wealth of the entrenched interests, and protect them from new competition.[275]

---

[274] Perloff, p. 28.
[275] Perloff, p. 26.

"Business Cycle" A Sham

A year after the passage of the Federal Reserve Act, on January 20, 1915, Congressman Lindbergh gave his assessment of the results of the Act. First, he pointed out a secretive way Fed insiders make huge profits:

> Congress, by the passage of the Federal Reserve Act, put into the control of the big banks ... the means by which they may obtain information in regard to the financial standing of every subsidiary bank, railway and industrial corporation, and use such information for purposes of speculation to their enormous advantage over others not having access to the same means of information. It has placed it in the power of the Money Trust to make and determine prices of speculative and other commodities at its will.[276]

Then, he went on to explain how the Fed members utilize the so-called "business cycle" to their advantage:

> To cause high prices, all the Federal Reserve Board will do will be to lower the rediscount rate [what the Fed charges local banks when they borrow money] so that the associated banks will more generally apply for and receive the Federal Reserve notes, producing an expansion of credit and a rising stock market; then when ... business men are adjusted to these conditions, it can check ... prosperity in mid-career by arbitrarily raising the rate of interest. It can cause the pendulum of a rising and falling market to swing gently back and forth by slight changes in the discount rate, or cause violent fluctuations by a greater rate variation, and in either case it will possess inside information as to financial conditions and advance knowledge of the coming change, either up or down. This is the strangest, most dangerous advantage ever placed in the hands of a special privilege class by any Government that ever existed. This act makes it ... easy for the Money Trust to control banks....
>
> The President, in creating the Federal Reserve Board, appointed men who had been educated by the Money Trust system, believed in it and knew no other.[277]

Congressman Lindbergh also mentions the vital fact that the Fed had cornered the market in gold:

---

[276] Lindbergh, p. 87.
[277] Ibid, p. 88.

Chapter 23: Birth of the Federal Reserve System

> Already the Federal Reserve banks have cornered the gold and gold certificates....[278]

Other People's Money

Despite the fact that his colleagues in the House must have thought him at least ill advised to point it out, Lindbergh explained another secret of the Fed — the use of O.P.M. (Other People's Money) to get rich:

> The system is private, conducted for the sole purpose of obtaining the greatest possible profits from the use of other people's money, and in the interest of the stockholders and those allied with them. It is inconsistent with free government to subject every industry and enterprise in the country to the domination of the big banks that have been granted the exclusive privilege to control our finances.[279]

Without going into a detailed explanation of the mechanism of the Federal Reserve System, in light of the preceding comments on the use of O.P.M., it is interesting to note another similarity between the Fed structure and that of the old Bank of the United States (BUS).

According to the Federal Reserve Act, Section 2.3, whenever a bank wished to join the Federal Reserve, it was required to put up 6% of its "paid-up capital stock" in cash as a reserve in order to join. But guess what? The joining bank was authorized to make time payments. One percent whenever the Board of Governors asked for it, then an additional one-percent three months later, than an additional one-percent six months after that. The balance would be paid whenever the Board of Governors chose to make them pay up ... or not![280]

If you were a sharp operator, you might get away with putting up only a percent or two before you were using government money to make money

---

[278] Ibid, p. 88.
[279] Lindbergh, Charles August; *The Economic Pinch* (Palmdale, CA; Omni Publications, 1968), p. 89.
[280] *Federal Reserve Act And Other Statutory Provisions Affecting the Federal Reserve System* (Washington, D.C.: Board of Governors of the Federal Reserve System, as amended through August 1990), p. 4

— probably enough money to more than cover the remaining payments. In short, O.P.M.

There was one very important difference from the old BUS system, and that is, federal government ownership of stock. Recall that with the BUS, the government bought 20% of the initial stock and put up cash. Once funded, the insiders could leverage that cash through fractional reserve banking, creating "new" money, sufficient in quantity to fund loans to the insiders, with which to fund the balance of cash needed to purchase the remaining 80% of the stock at little or no risk or cost to themselves.

As noted earlier, in the Fed system, the government owns no stock. But the organizing committee did put in a trap door provision in the 1913 bill providing for the government to temporarily put up taxpayer funds to help the system get going if initial stock subscriptions were slow coming in. Section 2.10 states:

> Stock Allotted to United States
>
> Should the total subscriptions by banks and the public to the stock of said Federal reserve banks ... be, in the judgment of the organizing committee, insufficient to provide the amount of capital required therefore, then and in that event the said organization committee shall allot to the United States such an amount of said stock as said committee shall determine. Said United States stock shall be paid for at par out of any money in the Treasury not otherwise appropriated, and shall be held by the Secretary of the Treasury and disposed of for the benefit of the United States in such manner, at such times, and at such price, not less than par, as the Secretary of the Treasury shall determine.[281]

In other words, after enough cash was sucked out of the Treasury to give the bankers a good fractional reserve base from which to loan money to each other, providing seed capital or reserves for one of the 12 Federal Reserve Regional Banks, than the government was to sell the stock back to them, with no profit or interest. Nice work if you can get it! How would you like unlimited access to the U.S. Treasury to get your business up and running?

---

[281] Ibid.

Chapter 23: Birth of the Federal Reserve System 221

In any case, Lindbergh went on to explain that panics could now be scientifically created, moderated, or stopped — all to the advantage of Fed insiders:

> They know in advance when to create panics to their advantage. They also know when to stop panic. Inflation and deflation work equally well for them when they control finance.... They quickly turned the War [World War I] into the most profitable thing for them that had ever at any time taken place.[282]

In 1971, *The New York Times Magazine* reported that Congressman Louis McFadden chairman of the House Committee on Banking and Currency from 1920 to 1931 remarked that the passage of the Federal Reserve Act brought about:

> ...A super-state controlled by international bankers and international industrialists acting together to enslave the world for their own pleasure.[283]

In the 1960s, Congressman Wright Patman, former chairman of the House Banking Committee, and a powerful critic of the central banking system agreed that:

> In the United States today we have in effect two governments .... We have the duly constituted Government .... Then we have an independent, uncontrolled and uncoordinated government in the Federal Reserve System, operating the money powers which are reserved to Congress by the Constitution.[284]

Even Thomas A. Edison, the inventor of the electric light joined the fray in criticizing the system of the Federal Reserve:

> If our nation can issue a dollar bond, it can issue a dollar bill. The element that makes the bond good, makes the bill good, also. The difference between the bond and the bill is the bond lets money brokers collect twice the amount of the bond and an additional 20%, whereas the currency pays nobody but those who contribute directly in some useful way. It is absurd to say that our country can issue $30 million in bonds and not $30 million in

---

[282] Lindbergh, p. 90
[283] Perloff, p. 23.
[284] *Grassroot Hearings on the Economy:* Part 2, United States Congress. House. Committee on Banking, Finance, and Urban Affairs, (Washington, D.C., Government Printing Office, 1981), p. 126.

currency. Both are promises to pay, but one promise fattens the usurers and the other helps the people.[285]

In 1922, the Mayor of New York, John F. Hylan, made a speech in Chicago that slammed the Money Trust, calling it an "octopus":

> Some years ago, a sterling American – Theodore Roosevelt – condemned the "invisible government." That warning has much timeliness today, for the real menace of our republic is this invisible government which, like a giant octopus, sprawls its slimy length over city, state and nation.
>
> To depart from mere generalizations, let me say that at the head of this octopus are the Rockefeller Standard Oil interests and a small group of powerful banking houses generally referred to as the international bankers.

---

[285] *The New York Times*, Dec. 6, 1921, p. 6.

Chapter 23: Birth of the Federal Reserve System

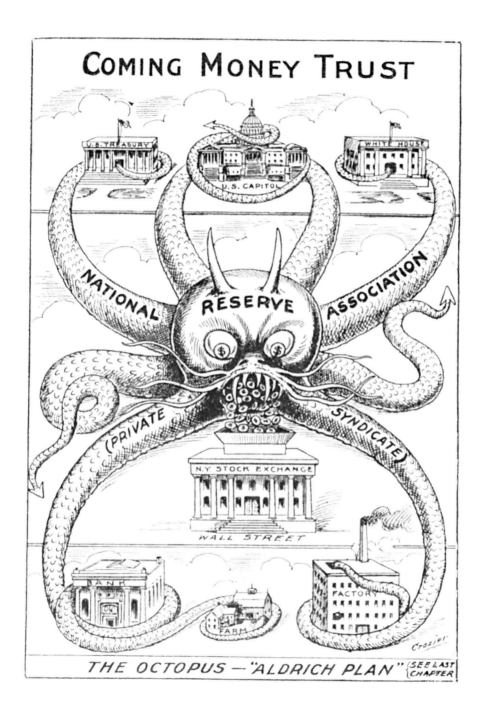

> The little coterie of powerful international bankers virtually run the United States government for their own selfish purposes. They practically control both parties, write political platforms, use leading men of private organizations and resort to every device to place in nomination for high public office only such candidates as will be amenable to the dictates of corrupt big business.
>
> They connive at centralization of government on the theory that a small group of hand-picked, privately controlled individuals in power can be more easily handled than a larger group among whom there will most likely be men sincerely interested in public welfare.[286]

By 1922, farmers and at least one labor union were already seeing through the Federal Reserve's money monopoly:

> To end the monopoly of credit under our present banking, money and credit system, which compels farmers and legitimate business enterprises to pay as high is 12 per cent interest, while speculative business interests can get their credit at 6 per cent or 5 per cent, or less, through the Federal Reserve System. Farmers have to put up adequate security and borrow real money, while the interests which exploit farmers ... and financial interests which control our entire transportation system get their credit through the Federal Reserve System, which can manufacture and pyramid fiat money and credit.[287]

---

[286] *Amalgamated Sheet Metal Workers' Journal*, (New York, The Sheet Metal Publication Co., Jan. 1922), Vol. 27-28, p. 33.
[287] *Amalgamated Sheet Metal Workers' Journal*, (New York, The Sheet Metal Publication Co., Jan. 1922), Vol. 27-28, p. 33.

Chapter 24 – The Crash of 1929

League of Nations

As soon as World War I was concluded, influential groups in the United States and Britain began a push for the world's first international government, the League of Nations. As Perloff explained:

> In 1917, [Col.] House had assembled a group in New York called 'the Inquiry,' consisting of about one hundred men ... they developed plans for the peace settlement. Some twenty members of the Inquiry went with Wilson to Paris in 1919, as did House and bankers Paul Warburg and Bernard Baruch.[288]

Agreement on the new world government proposal, the League of Nations, was given top priority at the post-World-War-I Paris Peace conference, which opened on January 18, 1919. Although the League was adopted at the Paris conference, the world was not yet ready for the notion of world government. Lord Curzon, the British foreign secretary, called the League of Nations "a good joke," even though it was the stated policy of Great Britain to support the League. The French Secretary to the Ministry of Foreign Affairs, M. Philippe Berthelot, said it would never be anything but "a grotesque hoax."[289]

To the humiliation of President Wilson and Colonel House, the U.S. Congress wouldn't ratify U.S. membership in the League. From that point on, the League became virtually powerless and gradually atrophied until it was replaced by the United Nations in 1946.

John Maynard Keynes

Having been successful at consolidating financial power within the United States with the implementation of the Federal Reserve System, the central bankers now began to search for a way to erect a totally

---

[288] Perloff, p. 32.
[289] Fuller, John Frederick Charles, *Decisive Battles: Their Influence Upon History and Civilisation*: Vol. 1 (New York, C. Scribner's Sons,1949), p. 1004

centralized international structure. But after the rejection of the League of Nations by the U.S. Senate in 1920, the central bankers knew they had to move very carefully.

Their leading theoretician was British economist, John Maynard Keynes. Keynes was a Fabian socialist — a statist — who would later be appointed as a director of the Bank of England. He popularized the notion that governments could spend their way out of depressions, but what is never mentioned in the discussion of Keynesian economics is that all the money he advocated spending would actually be borrowed — by the sale of bonds — primarily to banks.

Keynes tried to develop a way to get the nations of the world to accept a global currency, backed by gold, called the Bancor, which he introduced after World War II. Fortunately, to date, the Bancor has not gained acceptance. It seems that most nations are attached to their sovereign currencies and distrusting of handing over national sovereignty to anyone in any form.

And then in 1929, less than 16 years after the passage of the Federal Reserve Act, and only nine months after the inauguration of Herbert Hoover, the third consecutive Republican President, and the American economy was deliberately taken down.

The Fed Begins to Squeeze

On August 9, the Fed began to tighten money. It raised the discount rate — the interest rate the Fed charges your local bank to borrow money — sharply. A few days later, the Bank of England followed suit. At the same time, the Fed began to sell government securities, another money contracting move. This was the final signal to the insiders to get out of the stock market and put all their assets in cash or gold bullion. It is said that the biographies of all the Wall Street giants — John D. Rockefeller, J.P. Morgan, Joseph P. Kennedy, Bernard Baruch, Henry Morganthau, and Douglas Dillon — remarked on the wisdom of these men in getting out of the market just before the crash.

It is far more likely that they were given a secret advisory similar to the one sent out in March of 1929 by the father of the Federal Reserve System, Paul Warburg, which read:

> If the orgies of unrestrained speculation are permitted to spread, the ultimate collapse is certain not only to affect the speculators themselves, but to bring a general depression involving the entire country.[290]

After the Fed began the double-barreled approach to tighten the American money supply, in August 1929, the market didn't crash immediately. The effects of moves by the Fed can take up to a year to be felt. But with Wall Street strung out to the maximum extent on easy money and a form of credit known as "24-hour broker call loans," the system began to sink about six weeks later.

24-Hour Broker Call Loans

With a 24-hour broker call loan, one could buy $1,000 worth of stock on a 10% margin — that is, one would only have to put down $100 in cash. If the stock went up, the borrower could sell and make a quick leveraged profit on a risk of only $100. The problem is, when these 24-hour loans were called, the investor had to come up with the full amount within 24 hours. For most investors, that meant they had to liquidate their stock, no matter what the price.

The Crash

The stock market peaked on September 19, 1929. Then it began to slide. Few investors were worried. There had been ups and downs before. They continued to buy for five more weeks as the market slid down still further. Then on "Black Thursday," October 24, the stock market crashed. As one writer explained events:

> When everything was ready, the New York financiers started calling 24-hour broker call loans. This meant that the stockbrokers and the customers had to dump their stock on the market in order to pay the loans. This naturally

---

[290] *The Bankers Magazine*, (New York, 1929), vol. 118, p. 569. Also quoted by Smith, Rixy; and Beasley, Norman; *Carter Glass: A Biography* (Ayer Publishing,1939), p. 476. Also quoted by Watkins, T.H., *The Hungry Years* (New York, Henry Holt, 1999), p. 29.

collapsed the stock market and brought a banking collapse all over the country because the banks not owned by the oligarchy were heavily involved in broker call claims at this time, and bank runs soon exhausted their coin and currency and they had to close. The Federal Reserve System would not come to their aid, although they were instructed under the law to maintain an elastic currency.[291]

On Friday and Saturday, stock prices leveled out and held firm. But the next Monday, prices began to fall again, and on Tuesday, the bottom totally dropped out of the market. Thousands of investors, large and small, were wiped out and America was hurled into "The Great Depression." According to John Kenneth Galbraith, writing in *The Great Crash, 1929*, at the height of the selling frenzy, Bernard Baruch brought Winston Churchill into the visitor's gallery to witness the panic and perhaps impress him with his power.[292]

Congressman Louis McFadden, chairman of the House Committee on Banking and Currency from 1920 to 1931 knew whom to blame. He accused the Fed and the international bankers of orchestrating the Crash:

> It was not accidental. It was a carefully contrived occurrence.... The international bankers sought to bring about a condition of despair here so that they might emerge as rulers of us all.[293]

But McFadden went even farther. He openly accused them of causing the Crash in order to steal America's gold. In, February of 1931, in the midst of the Depression, he put it this way:

> I think it can hardly be disputed that the statesmen and financiers of Europe are ready to take almost any means to reacquire rapidly the gold stock which Europe lost to America as a result of the War [WWI].[294]

Curtis Dall, a broker for Lehman Brothers, was on the floor of the New York Stock Exchange the day of the Crash. In his 1970 book, FDR: *My*

---

[291] Galbraith, *The Great Crash, 1929*, (New York, Houghton Mifflin Harcourt Publishing, 1954) p. 105.
[292] Ibid.
[293] Perloff, p. 56.
[294] Speech made by Rep. Louis T. McFadden on the floor of Congress, February 14, 1931, *Collective Speeches of Congressman Louis T. McFadden* (Palmdale, CA, Omni Publications, 1970) p. 144.

Exploited Father-In-Law, Dall explained that the Crash was triggered by the planned sudden shortage of call money in the New York money market. Actually, it was the calculated 'shearing' of the public by the World-Money powers triggered by the planned sudden shortage of call money in the New York Money Market.[295]

Hoover Struggles

President Hoover complained to the Secretary of Treasury. Andrew Mellon that nothing was being done by either Treasury or the Fed to improve the economic situation:

> Mr. Mellon ... insisted that when the people get an inflation brainstorm, the only way to get it out of their blood is to let it collapse. He held that even a panic was not altogether a bad thing. He said: 'It will purge the rottenness out of the system. High costs of living and high living will come down. People will work harder, live a normal life. Values will be adjusted, and enterprising people will pick up the wrecks from less competent people.[296]

Within a few weeks, billions of dollars of wealth was destroyed. But did it really disappear? Or was it simply consolidated in fewer hands? By way of example, insiders like Joseph P. Kennedy saw his net worth grow from $4 million in 1929 to $100 million by 1935.[297]

At first, the Crash didn't affect the average American. Its effect was more immediately felt on the speculators in New York, and unemployment didn't become widespread until later. Of course, the newspapers blamed President Hoover for the Crash. Over the remaining three years of his term, Hoover tried to repair the economic damage. He launched government programs to beef up wages, prop up businesses, encourage construction, subsidize farmers and rescue banks, but to no avail. Instead of moving to help the economy out by quickly lowering interest rates to stimulate the economy, the Fed continued to brutally contract the money supply further, deepening the depression. Between 1929 and 1933, the

---

[295] Dall, Curtis B.; *FDR: My Exploited Father-In-Law*, (Washington, D.C., Action Associates, 1970), p. 49.
[296] Hersh, Burton; *The Mellon Family: A Fortune in History* (New York: William Morrow and Co., 1978), p. 290.
[297] Griffin, p. 499.

Chapter 24: The Crash of 1929

Fed reduced the money supply by an additional 33%. If money was scarce, jobs were even harder to come by.

But the money didn't just vanish. It was somewhere. In fact, it seems that some money that was being taken out of the starving American economy was being shuttled into the rebuilding of Germany. In 1931, eight years before Hitler would invade Poland, Rep. Louis McFadden, Chairman of the House Banking and Currency Committee, warned Congress about the German buildup and complained that Americans had to pay for it:

> After WWI, Germany fell into the hands of the German international bankers. Those bankers bought her and they now own her, lock, stock, and barrel. They have purchased her industries, they have mortgages on her soil, they control her production, and they control all her public utilities. There is no country in the world today of which the inhabitants are so enslaved as are the Germans.
>
> The international German bankers have subsidized the present Government of Germany and they have also supplied every dollar of the money Adolph Hitler has used in his lavish campaign to build up a threat to the government of Bruening. When Bruening fails to obey the orders of the German International Bankers, Hitler is brought forth to scare the Germans into submission.... Through the Federal Reserve Board... over $30 billions of American money over and above the German bonds that have been sold here has been pumped into Germany.... You have all heard of the spending that has taken place in Germany.... modernistic dwellings, her great planetariums, her gymnasiums, her swimming pools, her fine public highways, her perfect factories. All this was done on our money. All this was given to Germany through the Federal Reserve Board ... and what is worse, Federal Reserve notes were issued for it....
>
> Here you have a banking system which has financed Germany from start to finish with the Federal Reserve notes and has unlawfully taken from the Government and the people of the United States. The Federal Reserve

Chapter 24: The Crash of 1929

Board ... has pumped so many billions of dollars into Germany that they dare not name the total.[298]

In his last year in office, Hoover put forward a plan to bail out the failing banks, but he needed support from the Democratic Congress and that was not to be had. Franklin Roosevelt (FDR) was swept into office in the 1932 presidential election.

> Roosevelt's first act as President was to declare a national bank holiday for the period March 4-9, 1933. In his inaugural address, Roosevelt, referring to the financial collapse, stated that: "The money changers have fled from their high seats in the temple of our civilization."
>
> Despite the eloquent rhetoric against bankers ... Roosevelt never definitively set forth his own views on banking.
>
> Roosevelt was against federal deposit insurance, at least when he took office. During his first press conference he was asked to comment on federal deposit insurance and he did so, but asked that his remarks be kept off the record. Roosevelt said:
>
> "The general underlying thought behind the use of the word 'guarantee' with respect to bank deposits is that you guarantee bad banks as well as good banks. The minute the Government starts to do that the Government runs into a probable loss.... We do not wish to make the United States Government liable for the mistakes and errors of individual banks, and put a premium on unsound banking in the future."[299]

This sounds good in today's context, but keep in mind, the real moneychangers had just deliberately crashed the American economy and the biggest banks would no doubt once again to feed on the smaller banking fish. As the year wore on and there was no improvement, FDR became frustrated as well. He wrote to Secretary of the Treasury William Woodin, blasting the bankers and economists for their neglect of the problem:

> I wish our banking and economists friends would realize the seriousness of the situation from the point of view of the debtor class, -- i.e., 90% of the

---

[298] Speech made by Rep. Louis T. McFadden on the floor of Congress, February 14, 1931, *Collective Speeches of Congressman Louis T. McFadden* (Palmdale, CA, Omni Publications, 1970) p. 236.
[299] Phillips, Ronnie J., *The 'Chicago Plan' and New Deal Banking Reform* The Jerome Levy Economics Institute of Bard College, Working Paper No. 76, June 1992, p. 4-5.

human beings in this country – and think less from the point of view of the 10 per cent who constitute the creditor classes.[300]

The Secretive Chicago Plan

With the situation desperate, eight economists from the University of Chicago proposed a secret plan to pull America out of its tailspin. Only 40 copies of the confidential plan were distributed on March 16, 1933. The plan would essentially gut the 20-year-old Federal Reserve Act and take America off the gold standard. Here are some of the points:

The government would take back ownership of all the Federal Reserve Banks, liquidate their assets, and create (or encourage) new banks to be created which from then on would not practice fractional reserve lending – in other words, a 100% reserve system!

> "The Federal Reserve Banks should liquidate the assets of all member banks, pay off liabilities, and dissolve all existing banks and new institutions should be created which accepted only demand deposits subject to a 100% reserve requirement in lawful money and/or deposits with the Reserve Banks. Savings would be handled through the incorporation of investment trusts. Present banking institutions would continue deposit and lending functions under Federal Reserve supervision until the new institutions can be put into place."[301]

Federal Reserve Notes would be made "legal tender". Previously, Federal Reserve Notes were "demand notes" that is, the notes stated on their face "The United States of America will pay to the bearer on demand" the face value in gold or silver coin. For an image of a $1 demand note:

URL: 7.tv/5c6a

---

[300] Ibid, p. 5.
[301] Ibid, p. 7-8.

In other words, the Chicago Plan would cut the gold and silver backing to the Federal Reserve Notes.

There would be a Federal guarantee of deposits. Once gold and silver backing was removed, then the government could print up sufficient Federal Reserve Notes to make good all the depositors, or as the paper puts it: "...in any amounts which may be necessary to meet demands for payment by depositors...." This was exactly the opposite of what FDR had wanted.[302]

Frederick Soddy

The ideas presented in the Chicago Plan were radical, but nothing new. They were actually conceived by an "amateur" economist, Oxford University professor of Chemistry, Frederick Soddy, who won the Nobel prize in chemistry in 1921. Soddy won the prize for his theory of radioactive decay and was first to use the term "isotope." His essays popularizing the understanding of radioactivity was the main inspiration for H.G. Wells' *The World Set Free* (1914), which features atomic bombs dropped from biplanes in a war set many years in the future.

From 1921 to 1934, Soddy wrote four books on monetary reform offering a perspective on economics rooted in "the laws of thermodynamics." Although at the time, Soddy was dismissed as a crank, most of his ideas have come to fruition such as:

- The abandonment of the gold standard
- Letting international exchange rates float
- Using the quantity of money to counter cyclical trends
- Establishing a consumer price index to monitor the quantity of money

But Soddy's last suggestion has not yet come to fruition: banning fractional reserve banking. At the height of the depression, American economist started to pay attention to Soddy. Professor Frank Knight of the University of Chicago, the lead author of the Chicago Plan, wrote regarding one of Soddy's books:

---

[302] Ibid, p. 8.

> The practical thesis of the book is distinctly unorthodox, but is in our opinion both highly significant and theoretically correct. In the abstract, it is absurd and monstrous for society to pay the commercial banking system "interest" for multiplying several fold the quantity of medium of exchange when ... a public agency could do it at negligible cost....[303]

In 1933, Soddy published his theories in the *Economic Forum*. According to Prof. Ronnie Phillips:

> His basic argument was that technology had created an age of plenty, and that only the structure of the banking system prevented the full realization of this abundance and the elimination of poverty.[304]

Soddy argued that all economic problems stemmed from fluctuations in the quantity of the money supply – the vast majority of which was created by banks and:

> ... That these fluctuations could be minimized if the government alone had the power to create money and created it in order to maintain a stable price level. In order to achieve a government monopoly on the creation of money, it would be necessary to eliminate the money created by banks in the process of making loans.... The growing bank failures of the early thirties ... provided Knight and others at Chicago with the opportunity to restate and refine the Soddy proposal.[305]

Soddy urged his fellow scientists to take up the monetary issue and even dared to use the word "plutocracy":

> The monetary system is actually based the very error [that strikes at the heart of that to which] Western civilization owes its greatness. It serves only the convenience of a parasitic and upstart plutocracy practising a worldly wisdom the exact opposite of that which is the foundation of our age. It prefers dark in times when all men seek the light, and is sowing the seeds of hatred and war in a world weary to death of strife. It is poisoning the wells of Western civilization, and science must turn from the conquest of Nature to deal with a more sinister antagonist, or lose all it has won.[306]

---

[303] Ibid, p. 46.
[304] Ibid.
[305] Ibid.
[306] Soddy, p. 220.

Chapter 24: The Crash of 1929

Henry Wallace, the Secretary of Agriculture, gave the Chicago Plan to FDR less than a week after it was distributed with a note for the President:

> The memorandum from the Chicago economists which I gave you at [the] Cabinet meeting Tuesday, is really awfully good and I hope that you or Secretary Woodin will have the time and energy to study it. Of course the plan outlined is quite a complete break with our present banking history. It would be an even more decisive break than the founding of the Federal Reserve System.[307]

The Chicago Plan was the first prototype response to the debt monster the bankers had erected to suck the life out of the United States. These were leading academics in this new field of economics who were genuinely interested in trying to bring immediate relief to the economic suffering they saw all around them. These brave economists knew the Fed system wasn't working and so they embarked on a rescue mission: create the best monetary system possible for the United States. It was not as robust, and not nearly as well thought out as the 1939 plan, "A Program for Monetary Reform," that would be issued 6 years later by the same core economists, but it was a good first start created under difficult times. Unfortunately, President Roosevelt ignored the Chicago Plan.

1933 Gold Seizure

On April 5, 1933, FDR ordered all gold in the possession of the American public to be sold to the Treasury at the going rate of $20.67 per ounce, payable in Federal Reserve Notes, but the other major recommendations were not implemented. Violations were punishable by a fine of up to $10,000 or up to ten years in prison, or both, but the belief was widespread that most citizens who owned large amounts of gold had it transferred to countries such as Switzerland.

For an image of Executive Order 6102:

---

[307] Phillips, p. 8.

Chapter 24: The Crash of 1929

URL: 7.tv/5c11

There were some exceptions for coin collectors. Anyone could keep up to $100 in gold coins and "gold coins having recognized special value to collectors of rare and unusual coins," were exempted from the seizure. Rumors persist that all safe deposit boxes were seized and searched for gold by the IRS. These rumors proved to be false. [308]

Approximately 500 tons of gold were voluntarily turned into the Treasury voluntarily at the exchange rate of $20.67. On January 30, 1934, the official price of gold was raised to $35 per ounce, a 75% increase.

The Glass-Steagall Act of 1933

On June 16, 1933, Congress passed the Glass-Steagall Act. Before that, the banks were allowed to own investment houses. As the Congressional Research Service of the Library of Congress puts it:

> In the nineteenth and early twentieth centuries, bankers and brokers were sometimes indistinguishable. Then, in the Great Depression after 1929, Congress examined the mixing of the "commercial" and "investment" banking industries that occurred in the 1920s. Hearings revealed conflicts of interest and fraud in some banking institutions' securities activities. A formidable barrier to the mixing of these activities was then set up by the Glass Steagall Act. [309]

The result was that at many banks, you could actually buy stocks and banks were using their huge resources to speculate as well. Throughout much of the 1990s an ongoing debate raged to try to get the Glass-Steagall Act of 1933 repealed.

In 1995, I wrote the following in my first attempt on the topic:

---

[308] http://en.wikipedia.org/wiki/Executive_Order_6102
[309] http://en.wikipedia.org/wiki/Glass–Steagall_Act, retrieved Jan. 16, 2011.

Chapter 24: The Crash of 1929

But today, President Clinton has endorsed new legislation that would repeal the Glass-Steagall Act and allows banks to function as stockbrokers once again.

Informed sources call this the most dangerous banking legislation proposed in a generation. Why? Because ... once reinstituted, another wave of wild speculation will occur. This will inevitably make the U.S. economy even more vulnerable to a manipulated stock market crash than before which this time will drag the entire world down with it.[310]

The repeal bill met stiff resistance in Congress, but was finally passed in 1999 and signed into law by President Clinton.

---

[310] Still, Bill. *On the Horns of the Beast* (Winchester, VA, Reinhart & Still Publishers, 1995), p. 95.

Chapter 25 – Program for Monetary Reform

In July of 1939, a group of the leading professors of economics of the day wrote a consensus paper in an attempt to once again push through monetary reform once again. Called "A Program for Monetary Reform," or "PMR," its lead author was Paul H. Douglas, an esteemed professor of economics at the University of Chicago who later in his career became a U.S. Senator. Douglas was described by Dr. Martin Luther King, Jr. as "the greatest of all the Senators."

Douglas was truly a remarkable American. Despite being a Quaker, and a professor of economics at the University of Chicago, in 1942, Douglas, at age 50, joined the Marine Corps and received a Bronze Star, two Purple Hearts, and a permanently disabled left arm.[311]

Other professors of economics who were authors of the paper were:

- Irving Fisher – Yale University
- Frank D. Graham – Princeton University
- Earl J. Hamilton – Duke University
- Willford I. King – New York University
- Charles R. Whittlesey – Princeton University

The document states that 235 economists from 157 universities and colleges had approved it, without reservations. Additionally, 40 more economists had approved it with some reservations and 43 had expressed disapproval. I'm not sure how many professors of economics there were in the United States in 1939, but I'm willing to bet this was most of them.

It opens with a foreboding warning to the world, painting a picture of a way of life toward which we are rapidly heading towards today.

> The great task confronting us today is that of making our American system, which we call "democracy," work. No one can doubt that it is threatened. However, the danger lies less in the propaganda of autocratic Governments

---

[311] Sledge, Eugene B. (1990). *With the Old Breed: At Peleliu and Okinawa*. Oxford University Press. ISBN 0-19506-714-2.

Chapter 25: Program for Monetary Reform 239

> from abroad than in the existence, here in America, of ten millions of unemployed workers, sharecroppers living barely at subsistence level, and hundreds of thousands of idle machines. On such a soul fascist and communist propaganda can thrive. With full employment such propaganda would be futile.[312]

The document then lays out the basic problem with the current system – as it was in 1939, and still remains today.

> If the purpose of money and credit were to discourage the exchange of goods and services, to destroy periodically the wealth produced, to frustrate and trip those who work and save, our present monetary system would seem a most effective instrument to that end.
>
> Practically every period of economic hope and promise has been a mere inflationary boom, characterized by an expansion of the means of payment, and has been followed by a depression, characterized by a detrimental contraction of the means of payment *[the money supply]*. In boom times, the expansion of [money] accelerates the pace by raising prices, and rising prices conjuring up new money, the inflation proceeds in an upward spiral till a collapse occurs, after which the contraction of our supply of money and credit, with falling prices and losses in place of profits, produces a downward spiral generating bankruptcy, unemployment, and all of the other evils of depression.
>
> The monetary reforms here proposed are intended primarily to prevent these ups and downs in the volume of our means of payment with their harmful influences on business.[313]

The professors then review the problems with the "gold standard".

> During the last ten years the world has largely given up the gold standard....
>
> In September 1931 England found it impossible to maintain her gold reserves and was forced off the gold standard. Since then, every other gold-standard nation has either been forced off gold or has abandoned it voluntarily. Those countries which bowed first to this pressure were also the

---

[312] *A Program for Monetary Reform* by Paul H. Douglas of the University of Chicago, et al, July 1939, p. 2.
[313] Ibid, p. 4.

first to recover from the depression. France was among the last to abandon gold; and she is still suffering from her mistake in waiting so long.

The depression experience of all countries under the gold standard has shown that it is scarcely worthy of being called a "standard" at all. It has shown that the so-called "stability" of gold and of foreign exchange destroyed the stability of the buying power of money and thereby the stability of economic conditions generally. In fact, the effort to retain gold as a "standard" has had such disastrous results all over the world that, for the time being, international trade has been deprived of some of the useful services which gold might still render it....

After the experience of the past decade, it is improbable that many countries will want to give their currencies arbitrary gold values at the cost of domestic deflation and depression....[314]

Some countries, especially the Scandinavian and others included in the so-called "Sterling Bloc", have gone further than the United States in formulating and in carrying out these new monetary policies.

On abandoning the gold standard in 1931, the Scandinavian countries took steps to maintain for the consumer a constant buying power for their respective currencies. Finland's central bank made a declaration to this effect. The Riksbank of Sweden has done the same.... As a result, since then, people of those fortunate lands have never lost confidence in their money. The buying power of their monetary units have been maintained constant within a few percent since 1931. At the same time, these countries have made conscious use of monetary policy as an essential part of their efforts to promote domestic prosperity. They have been so successful as to have practically eliminated unemployment; to have raised their production figures to new peaks; and to have improved steadily the scale of living of their people.[315]

The document then lays out what a correct monetary system should do, namely create and maintain stability in the quantity of money.

---

[314] Ibid, p. 5-7.
[315] Ibid, p. 8.

Chapter 25: Program for Monetary Reform

> Our own monetary policy should... be directed toward avoiding inflation as well as deflation, and in attaining and maintaining as nearly as possible full production and employment.[316]

The PMR document then proposes the establishment of a Monetary Authority to control the quantity of money, and to keep it at arms length from the political tides of direct Congressional manipulation. As a counter-balance, the Monetary Authority would be subject to strict guidelines established by law by Congress to manage the quantity of the American money supply, in order to achieve the above objectives.

> The criteria for monetary management adopted should be so clearly defined and safeguarded by law as to eliminate the need of permitting any wide discretion to our Monetary Authority.[317]

Constant-per-Capita Standard

They then propose two ways of keeping the money supply stable. The first is called the "Constant-per-Capita Standard".

> Establish a constant-average-per-capita supply or volume of the circulating medium, including both "pocket-book money" and "check-book money".... One great advantage of this "constant-per-capita-money" standard is that it would require a minimum of discretion on the part of the Monetary Authority....
>
> Under [this system] all the Monetary Authority would have to do would be to ascertain the amount of circulating medium in active circulation, and whatever amount of circulating medium seemed necessary to keep unchanged the amount of money per head of population. For this purpose, the statistical information regarding the volume of [the money supply] should be improved.[318]

Of course, this is exactly the opposite of our current situation where, since 2006, the Federal Reserve has hidden the broadest measure of the money supply (M3) from public view.

---

[316] Ibid.
[317] Ibid, p. 12.
[318] Ibid, p. 13.

Constant-Cost-of-Living Standard

The second proposed method of keeping the money supply stable is called the "constant-cost-of-living standard". By this method, the cost of a number of commodities would be regularly sampled and then the volume of money would be adjusted to keep the average cost of this basket of commodities constant.

Unfortunately, we see today that this method is employed by the Federal Reserve to try to gauge inflation, and the weakness in this system is that when a certain commodity fluctuates in price in a way that does not suit the political need of those in power, it is removed from this market basket of commodities. So, this method has been proven to be ineffective.

Fractional Reserve Lending

In order for the Monetary Authority to be able to keep the volume of money constant, the ability of the commercial banks to create their own fractional reserve money must be eliminated.

The astounding truth of our money system is that banks get to loan out many times the amount of money they actually have. Back in late 1930s when the *Program for Monetary Reform (PMR)* was written, the reserve requirement was 20%. In other words, banks could loan $100 for every $20 they actually had in the bank.

This was gradually lowered over the years from a 20% reserve requirement to a 10% reserve requirement. After the economic collapse in 2008, we discovered that banks had been totally ignoring the reserve requirement. Some of the biggest banks had loaned out 50 times the amount of their reserves (in other words, a 2% reserve). Mortgage giants Freddie Mac and Fannie Mae had loaned out over 70 times their reserves.

In other words, it is impossible to control the amount of money in circulation when the commercial banks are creating money out of thin air, and loaning it out, with the government (and therefore, we, the people) having no idea how much money they are creating. Included, too, in this money creation is credit card "money," which creates additional money in the money supply chain whenever you make a purchase with your credit

Chapter 25: Program for Monetary Reform

card, it spends just as well as a $100 bill. And let's not overlook that when banks have complete discretion over how much they will loan out and to whom, it becomes fairly easy for them to buy influence with the various nodes of power in any nation, such as its politicians and its media. This is the very definition of the word "plutocracy."

As the 1921 Nobel laureate in Chemistry, Frederick Soddy put in 1934, money must be created in the public interest and serve merely as the distributive mechanism of society:

> To allow it to become a source of revenue to private issuers is to create, first, a secret and illicit arm of the government and last, a rival power strong enough ultimately to overthrow all other forms of government.[319]

As the *PMR* put it:

> A chief loose screw in our present American money and banking system is the requirement of only fractional reserves behind demand deposits. Fractional reserves give our thousands of commercial banks power to increase or decrease the volume of [money] by increasing or decreasing bank loans and investments. The banks thus exercise what has always, and justly, been considered a prerogative of sovereign power. As each bank exercises this power independently without any centralized control, the resulting changes in the volume of the circulating medium are largely haphazard. This situation is a most important factor in booms and depressions....[320]
>
> It is a system which permits, and practically compels, the banks to lend and owe five times as much money as they must have on hand if they are to survive in the competitive struggle, which causes much of the trouble.

Flash forward to today's world — or the world of 2007, that is. During an interview with the *Financial Times*, on July 9, 2007, Citigroup CEO Charles Prince tried to excuse his bank's excessive money creation through the issuance of risky sub-prime loans.

> When the music stops, in terms of liquidity, things will get complicated. But as long as the music is playing, you've got to get up and dance."

---

[319] Soddy, p. x.
[320] *A Program for Monetary Reform* ...., p. 19.

In other words, under the fractional reserve system, banks are driven to ever-greater distortions of the reserve requirements by the competitive demands for profits.

As the *PMR* put it:

> Despite these inherent flaws in the fractional reserve system, a Monetary Authority could unquestionably, by wise management, give us a far more beneficial monetary policy than the Federal Reserve Board has done in the past. But the task would be much simplified if we did away altogether with the fractional reserve system; for it is this system which makes the banking system so vulnerable....
>
> The 100% reserve system was the original system of deposit banking, but the fractional reserve system was introduced by private Venetian bankers not later than the middle of the Fourteenth century.... bankers began to lend some of this [money], though it belonged not to them but to the depositors. The same thing happened in the public banks of deposit at Venice, Amsterdam, and other cities, and the London goldsmiths of the Seventeenth century found that handsome profits would accrue from lending out other people's money... a practice which, when first discovered by the public, was considered to be a breach of trust. <u>But what thus began as a breach of trust has now become the accepted and lawful practice.</u> Nevertheless, the practice is incomparably more harmful today than it was centuries ago, because, with increased banking, and the increasing pyramiding now practiced by banks, it results in violent fluctuations in the volume of the circulating medium and in economic activity in general.[321]

How To Establish the 100% Reserve System

According to the *PMR*:

> The simplest method of making the transition from fractional to 100% reserves would be to authorize the Monetary Authority to lend, without interest, to every bank or other agency carrying demand deposits, sufficient cash ... to make the reserve of each bank equal to its demand deposits.
>
> The present situation would be made the starting point of the 100%

---

[321] Ibid, p. 21-22.

Chapter 25: Program for Monetary Reform

reserve system by simply lending to the banks whatever money they might need to bring the reserves behind their demand deposits up to 100%. While this money might largely be newly issued for the occasion ... it would not inflate the volume of anything that can circulate. It would merely change the nature of the reserves behind the money that circulates.... The bank would simply serve as a big pocket book to hold its depositors' money in storage.[322]

One objection to the 100% reserve solution is that banks might still try to cause depressions by coordinated action to get their way politically, as they have done time and time again in American history. The *PMR* addressed this directly:

> In such a case, it would, of course, be imperative for the Monetary Authority to increase the volume of circulating medium still further.

This would be literally free money the Government could spend into the economy without debt or increasing taxes. In fact, the Government could even reduce taxes while increasing spending levels.

> The profit to the Government from the creation of new circulating medium would be a fitting reward for supplying us with such increased means of payment as might become necessary to care for an increased volume of business....
>
> In early times, the creation of money was the sole privilege of the kings or other sovereigns — namely the sovereign people, acting through their Government. This principle is firmly anchored in our Constitution and it is a perversion to transfer the privilege to private parties to use in their own real, or presumed, interest.
>
> The founders of the Republic did not expect the banks to create the money they lend. John Adams, when President, looked with horror upon the exercise of control over our money by the banks.

The *PMR* then rightly reassures us that banks would not disappear under the 100% reserve system.

> Lest anyone think that the 100% reserve system would be injurious to the banks, it should be emphasized that the banks would gain, quite as truly as

---

[322] Ibid, p. 22-23.

the Government and the people in general. Government control of the money supply would save the banks from themselves – from the uncoordinated action of some 15,000 independent banks, manufacturing and destroying our check-book money in a haphazard way.

With the new steadiness in supplying the nation's increasing monetary needs, and with the consequent alleviation of severe depressions, the people's savings would, in all probability, accumulate more rapidly and with less interruption than at present. Loans and investments would become larger and safer, thus swelling the total business of banks....

Incidentally, there would no longer be any need of deposit insurance on demand deposits. [323]

No More National Debt

The *PMR* then tackles the thorny problem of what to do about the existing National Debt.

A by-product of the 100% reserve system would be that it would enable the Government gradually to reduce its debt, through purchases of *[existing outstanding]* Government bonds by the Monetary Authority as new money was needed to take care of expanding business. Under the fractional reserve system, any attempt to pay off the Government debt, whether by decreasing Government expenditures or by increasing taxation, threatens to bring about deflation and depression.[324]

In other words, since all our money is created out of debt under the existing system, paying down the debt during a deflationary period is an impossibility since it would further reduce the money supply.

Whatever increase in the circulating medium is necessary to accommodate national growth could be accomplished without compelling more and more people to go into debt to the banks, and without increasing the Federal interest-bearing debt.[325]

The *PMR* concludes with a solemn warning that is just as applicable to today's situation as it was in 1939.

---

[323] Ibid, p. 36.
[324] Ibid, p. 41.
[325] Ibid.

Chapter 25: Program for Monetary Reform

If we do not adopt the 100% reserve system, and if the present movement for balancing the budget succeeds without providing for an adequate money supply, the resulting reduction in the volume of our circulating medium may throw us into another terrible deflation and depression, at least as severe as that through which we have just been passing.

When violent booms and depressions, in which fluctuations in the supply of money play so vital a part, rob millions of their savings and prevent millions from working, Constitutions are likely to become scraps of paper.[326]

The entire paper, in PDF form, can be found at:

URL: 7.tv/5abd

(Note: PDF's are not optimized for mobile phone displays; you may elect to forward the resulting link to your desktop email address for subsequent viewing).

---

[326] Ibid, p. 42.

Chapter 26 - State Level Solutions

The Bank of North Dakota Model

Solutions at the state level will probably be easier to achieve initially then a federal-level solution. An interesting fact is that you don't have to have a federal charter to create a bank. States can charter banks as well; all it takes is a bill passed by the state legislature. Many states already allow state chartered banks.

The state then deposits all their funds into their new bank and can then utilize the fractional reserve principle to their advantage by making loans to themselves for roads, bridges, etc., at low or no interest. Just like you and I, we can loan money to each other with or without interest. What's different with a bank – under current laws – is that they can loan out more money than they actually have in deposits and capital. Until we can change this system at the national level, at least states can utilize it to their financial advantage to get back on a more solid financial footing.

The Bank of North Dakota is the only state owned bank in America. It was created in 1919, as a populist movement swept thru the debt ridden farmers of the Northern Plains. Even in these worst of times, the Bank of North Dakota is earning record profits and helping fund their state. It's been doing this for the last 90 years, hardly a radical startup idea. According to the Bank's President, Eric Hardmeyer:

> Our funding model, our deposit model is really what is unique as the engine that drives the bank. And that is we are the depository for all state tax collections and fees and so we have a captive deposit base, we pay a competitive rate to the state treasurer…. We take those funds and then … we plow those deposits back into the state … in the form of [low-interest] loans.
>
> Over the last 10-12 years, we've turned back a third of a billion dollars just to the general fund to offset taxes or to aid in funding public sector needs. Not bad for a state with a population of 600,000.
>
> [In 2009] the State of North Dakota does not have any funding issues at all. We, in fact, are dealing with the largest surplus we've ever had.

Chapter 26: State Level Solutions

There are four benefits to a State Bank:

1. States can use their great financial clout to benefit their state and keep taxes low. Now, we are <u>not</u> talking about mortgaging the State Capitol building. North Dakota does <u>not</u> include these assets as backing for the Bank of North Dakota. States, however, can conservatively double or triple what's called their "Tier 1 capital" and still be more fiscally sound than any other commercial bank on the planet.
2. No interest payments. States never have to float bonds for projects at the New York money center banks. They can simply borrow at zero interest from their own bank. Remember, it is a bank just like any other and it is allowed to lend out many times more money than it actually has – like 10 to 12 times as much. Again, to be extra-conservative, a state should limit this credit expansion to 2 to 3 times. States have a guaranteed income stream from taxation. All this goes into satisfying the capital requirements of the state bank just like any other bank.

Most people don't realize how expensive it is for a state to borrow by issuing long-term bonds. Just like your long-term mortgage on your house, it ends up at least doubling the cost. In the spring of 2010, I was walked onto the floor of the Missouri House of Representatives while it was in session discussing hotly contested cuts in the state budget. The House Budget Chairman, Allen Icet, stopped the proceedings of the entire House and introduced me from the podium and suggested to all members that my film, *The Secret of Oz*, was playing in the Rotunda of the State Capitol and I would be available to answer questions.

Icet later told me that he believed creating a State Bank of Missouri would cut their budget deficit in half, as a byproduct of no longer having to pay the interest on the state's bonded indebtedness. Ask your state legislator, "Would you like something completely safe that would cut the deficit in half this year?"

3. The State Bank should NOT compete with local banking. In fact, it should support local banks by providing them with various types of short-term loans at low interest rates. This does produce a profit that the State Bank turns back to the State government. Typically,

Chapter 26: State Level Solutions

local banks are not big enough to compete for a state's requirements for floating bond issues, so they lose no business there. Legislators must work with local bankers to be sure that they understand that a State Bank can help their business models, not hurt them. The Bank of North Dakota is a good cooperative model.

4. State sovereignty. All State legislators are anxious to regain some semblance of state sovereignty, which has been effectively decreased in recent years to the ever-increasing power of the federal government. The State Bank satisfies to a great degree the longing of state legislators to take back some power from the federal government.

URL: 7.tv/4b15

Ellen Brown, author of *Web of Debt*, recently wrote an excellent article on the State Bank issue. It can be found at the above HyperScan (4b15.) She has also given me permission to link to her latest at: http://publicbanking,wordpress.com/.

The Virginia Study Plan

At last count, 13 states are currently considering some sort of variation on the State Bank concept. Here is a plan simply calling for a one-year study put forward in Virginia in January 2010:

HOUSE JOINT RESOLUTION NO. 62

    Offered January 13, 2010

    Prefiled January 11, 2010

Chapter 26: State Level Solutions

Establishing a joint subcommittee to study whether to establish a bank operated by the Commonwealth. Report.

Patron-- Marshall, R.G.

WHEREAS, the Commonwealth does not currently engage in the business of banking or own, control, or operate a bank; and

WHEREAS, the state of North Dakota currently engages in the business of banking, owns, controls, and operates a bank known as the Bank of North Dakota; and

WHEREAS, the Bank of North Dakota was established pursuant to North Dakota Century Code 6-09-01 for the purpose of encouraging and promoting agriculture, commerce, and industry; and

WHEREAS, the Bank of North Dakota is not a member of the Federal Deposit Insurance Corporation but pursuant to North Dakota Century Code 6-09-10, all deposits in the Bank of North Dakota are guaranteed by the state; and

WHEREAS, the deposit base of the Bank of North Dakota is unique in that its primary deposit base is the State of North Dakota and all state funds and funds of state institutions are deposited with the Bank of North Dakota, as required by law; and....

WHEREAS, the Commonwealth is expected to have a budget shortfall of between $ 1.8 billion and $ 3.6 billion in 2010 and North Dakota is expected to have an $ 800 million budget surplus by the end of 2010; and

WHEREAS, the Commonwealth would benefit from loaning funds to develop agriculture, commerce and industry in lieu of granting tax revenues to newly established businesses; and

WHEREAS, by opening accounts in a bank owned, controlled, and operated by the Commonwealth, Virginians would be able to invest in the growth of agriculture, commerce and industry in the Commonwealth; and....

WHEREAS, a need exists to determine if the Commonwealth would benefit from the creation and operation of a similar financial institution; now, therefore, be it

RESOLVED by the House of Delegates, the Senate concurring, That a joint subcommittee be established to study whether to establish a bank operated by the Commonwealth. In conducting its study, the joint subcommittee shall consider recommendations for legislation to establish a state owned, controlled, and operated bank....

As of the spring of 2010, North Dakota was also the only state sporting a major budget surplus; it had the lowest unemployment and default rates in the country; and it had the most community banks per capita, suggesting that the presence of a state-owned bank has not only not hurt, but has helped the local banks.

The Bank of North Dakota makes low interest loans to students, existing small businesses and start-ups. It partners with private banks to provide a secondary market for mortgages, and supports local governments by buying their municipal bonds. This exact model will not work in all states because of a variety of different local statutes, so the BND model must be adjusted to fix existing state law, or state law can be changed to accommodate it.

The strongest argument for debt-free State-chartered, State-owned banks is the very existence of BND. This is not some crackpot economics theory. It's not an experiment. It's been working for 90+ years, serving its citizens to keep their standard of living high, and their taxes low.

Here is the HyperScan link to BND. Click on "About BND" to see a page about their deposit base, which is "all state funds and funds of state institutions":

URL: 7.tv/8c36

The State Bank of Washington

In Washington State, legislation was proposed in the 2010 legislative session by six legislators, Hasegawa, Hudgins, Chase, Simpson, Dickerson and Goodman, to authorize the creation of a state bank.

Chapter 26: State Level Solutions

The legislature finds that access to capital is vitally important for the health, security, and well-being of all individuals and businesses in our state. They are the economic drivers that help Washington's commerce run smoothly. The lack of accessible capital, as currently experienced due to the economic downturn, is exacerbating the economic hardships being faced by working families and businesses.

The legislature further finds that it can best direct economic development policy initiatives in a responsive and efficient manner with a state bank at its disposal.

The mission of the state bank of Washington is to promote agriculture, education, community development, economic development, commerce, and industry in Washington state. In this role, the bank acts as a funding resource in partnership with other financial institutions, economic development groups, and guaranty agencies.

Accuracy of financial reporting and compliance with all applicable laws and regulations is an integral part of the state bank of Washington's overall risk management strategy.

It is the intent of the legislature that all state funds and funds of state institutions are deposited at the state bank of Washington and are guaranteed by the state. Other deposits may be accepted from any private or public source.

Unfortunately, this legislation requires two amendments to its Constitution to become effective.

This act takes effect if the proposed amendments to Article VIII and Article XII of the Constitution, allowing the state legislature to create a state bank that may make decisions to lend, borrow, and invest state moneys (H-4717/10), is validly submitted to and is approved and ratified by the voters at the next general election. If the proposed amendment is not approved and ratified, this act is void in its entirety.

There is the link to a PDF version of the legislation:

Chapter 26: State Level Solutions

URL: 7.tv/7b23

More on this legislation in a few pages.

Start a Movement in Your State

Want to get involved in your state? A good place to start is a new website dedicated to this purpose, the Public Banking Institute:

URL: 7.tv/6eb0

The Commonwealth Group

This topic of public banking is so dynamic – that is, fast moving – that it is hard to keep up. Another relatively new group has appeared, called the Commonwealth Group, which offers some very interesting alternatives for states and is designed as a resource for state legislators.

For information on the Commonwealth Group:

URL: 7.tv/8fdc

Chapter 26: State Level Solutions

Michael Sauvante is the Executive Director of The Commonwealth Group. He can be reached at 650-641-1246 or via email at:

sauvante@commonwealthgroup.net

They prefer the alternative of a state bank owned by a holding company. Most of the following can be found on their website:

Bank Charters and Regulatory Oversight

Banks are established in the United States through one of two means – they receive a charter (legal permission to be a bank and perform banking functions) from a state regulatory banking agency, or from a federal agency. The banks so chartered are called state chartered banks or federally chartered banks. With rare exceptions, the entity granted such a charter is a corporation.

As attractive as public banking might be to a state, county or city, some might not want or be able to establish a bank on their own. For example, a clause in Michigan's constitution states:

No state money shall be deposited in any bank, savings and loan association, or credit union, in excess of 50 percent of the net worth of the bank, savings and loan association, or credit union.[327]

This clause makes it difficult for Michigan to form a wholly owned bank through which it processes all its revenues. Other entities may have concerns about risking their assets, or face high legislative hurdles.

Bank ownership falls into two generic categories:

1. Stand-alone banks, i.e. banks owned directly by one or more individual stockholders. This is the way that most states and other government entities would probably prefer to own their own banks, provided they have the ability to create one without complication and delays. For example, the Bank of North Dakota is a DBA of the state and would most closely fit under this category.

---

[327] Article IX, section 20

2. Banks owned by a bank holding company, which in turn is owned by one or more stockholders (stockholders can be individuals, partnerships, corporations, LLCs, or even government entities, etc.). Holding companies are companies that own all or portions of other things, which could be real estate, airplanes or other companies. In this case the companies would be one or more banks. Thus a bank holding company owns an interest in one or more banks and the holding company is owned by shareholders.

A bank holding company (commonly known as a BHC) would allow multiple government entities to join forces so that they can collectively own an interest in one or more banks for their mutual benefit and the benefit of society. Such a BHC could be jointly owned by a state, one or more of its counties or cities, bodies like utility districts, school districts and agencies that manage government pension funds, etc., and even non-profit organizations, which collectively represent the public as the ultimate owners.

That jointly owned bank holding company would in turn own one or more banks in whole or in part. If the former, then the bank holding company would need to establish a bank from scratch or take over one or more as described below. Alternatively, the BHC can acquire a minority interest by investing in an existing bank. There are benefits to both approaches, and the BHC could do one or both.

Either model would work well for Native American Indian tribes looking to invest their new-found wealth in a sustainable model. More on the Native American Bank later.

A State Sovereignty Issue

Buying a bank is probably the fastest path to ownership for a state legislature. There are plenty of small banks in every state that are in trouble. A state can also start from scratch and set up an entirely new bank completely outside the Federal Reserve System. A state need not even apply for Federal Deposit Insurance; it can self-insure all its needs. It would only be seeking a charter from the state legislature – itself. This is a long-recognized tradition in American banking that far preceded the notion of "National Banks" which didn't even exist until the Civil War. This method is probably the best way for a state to claw back a huge chunk of state sovereignty from the Federal Reserve System and the federal government in general.

Public Banking Around the Nation

> "Hundreds of job-creating projects are still on hold because Michigan businesses and entrepreneurs cannot get bank financing. We can break the credit crunch and beat Wall Street at their own game by keeping our money right here in Michigan and investing it to retool our economy and create jobs."

So says Virg Bernero, mayor of Michigan's capitol city of Lansing and a leading Democratic candidate for governor. Bernero proposes that Michigan open a state-owned bank, which could protect consumers by making low-interest loans to those most in need, including students and small businesses. It could also help community banks, by buying mortgages off their books and working with them to fund development projects. Bernero's campaign spokesman Jamaine Dickens says the Bank is not a partisan issue but is a "common-sense approach to a financial crisis that Michigan is facing."

Bernero joins a growing list of candidates proposing this sensible solution to the states' fiscal ills. Local economies have collapsed because of the Wall Street credit freeze. To reinvigorate local business, Main Street needs a heavy infusion of credit; and publicly owned banks could fill that need.

Candidates in seven states are running on a state-bank platform, in Florida, Oregon, Illinois, California, Washington State, Vermont and Idaho, including three Democrats, two Greens, one Republican and one Independent.

Vermont's Gaelan Brown, says, "Washington, DC has lost all moral authority over Vermont." Among other proposals, he maintains that "Vermont should explore creating a State-owned bank that would work with private VT-based banks, to insulate VT from Wall Street corruption, and to increase investment capital for VT businesses, modeled after the very successful State-owned Bank of North Dakota..."

The Community Bank of Illinois

A third bill is on its way through the legislative process in Illinois. Introduced by Representative Mary Flowers, the Community Bank of Illinois would establish a state bank with the express purpose of boosting agriculture, commerce and industry. State funds and money held by penal, educational, and industrial institutions owned by the state would be deposited in the bank and would serve as reserves for loans. The bank could also serve as a clearinghouse for other banks, including handling domestic and foreign exchange; and it could buy property under Eminent Domain. All deposits would be guaranteed with the assets of the state. The Bank would be managed and controlled by the Department of Financial and Professional Regulation, with input from an advisory board representing private banking and public interests.

An amendment to the initial bill would enable the Community Bank of Illinois to make loans directly to the state's General Revenue Fund, helping the state to cope with its current budget challenges.

A Massachusetts-Owned Bank

The Associated Press reported on March 12, 2010, that a jobs bill sponsored by Massachusetts Senate President Therese Murray includes a call to study a Massachusetts-owned bank. Murray is floating the idea of a state-owned bank to spur job creation and free up lending to Massachusetts businesses. She told a business group that a state-owned bank has worked in North Dakota, helping to insulate that state from the worst of the recession while also keeping its foreclosure rate down.

The Michigan Development Bank

The Michigan bill has gotten the most press. Introduced into the legislature in January 2011, it mirrors Bernero's state bank idea. The bill's stated aim is to "keep Michigan's money in Michigan" by putting tax dollars into a proposed "Michigan Development Bank". Michigan has been hit hard by the nation's economic downturn, with an official unemployment rate of 14%. The Michigan Development Bank would function like a traditional bank but would focus on economic development rather than profit.

"Investing in the state's economy is the greatest way to create jobs, and this proposal will provide small businesses and entrepreneurs the funding they need to invest and grow," said Senator Gretchen Whitmer (D-East Lansing). "Our economy has stagnated due in part to stale thinking in Lansing, and this is just the type of innovative idea we need to create real economic change, using our own money to rebuild the state."

In a press release issued on March 9, Senate Democrats suggested that Michigan sell voter-approved bonds to jump-start the Development Bank. With an initial capitalization of $150 million, they estimate the bank could lend up to $1 billion to small businesses, students and farmers, and offer low-interest credit cards to consumers.

"Michigan's economy has been suffering, and working families in the state have had difficulty keeping up with credit card bills, college tuition prices and mortgage payments," said Senate Democratic Leader Mike Prusi (D-Ishpeming). "Establishing the Michigan Development Bank will keep our hard-earned dollars right here in the state to invest in small business, create good-paying jobs to get people back to work, and help protect the middle class."

Senator Hansen Clarke (D-Detroit) added, "With the current state of our economy, every dollar counts, yet we're depositing our money in other people's pockets by investing in big corporate banks without seeing much lending in return. It's time for the Mitten State to lend itself a helping hand and establish a bank that is willing to invest in our small businesses and offer the financial support necessary to see job growth."

Gene Taliercio, one of six Republicans and two Democrats seeking the 12th District state Senate seat in upcoming elections, has also put his weight behind the Michigan Development Bank.

The State Bank of Washington

A similar bill was introduced to the Washington State legislature on February 1, 2010. The bill, HB 3162, has generated so much interest that

Steve Kirby, chair of the Financial Institutions and Insurance Committee, has scheduled a special work session on it.

According to John Nichols in *The Nation*, the State Bank of Washington was formally proposed by House finance committee vice chair Bob Hasegawa, a Seattle Democrat. "Imagine financing student aid, infrastructure, industry and community development," said Hasegawa. "Imagine providing access to capital for small businesses, or otherwise leveraging our resources instead of having to do it with tax incentives. Imagine keeping our resources local instead of exporting them as profits, never to be seen again—that's what this bank could do."

A nonpartisan analysis of the bill prepared for the state legislature said that the bank would be the depository for all state funds and the funds of state institutions, and that these deposits would be guaranteed by the state. The bank would be run by a board of 11 members, would be chaired by the State Treasurer, and would have the same rules and privileges as a private bank chartered in the state. To get the bank off the ground, voters would have to approve amendments to the state Constitution, since current law prohibits the state from lending credit and investing in private firms.

Anyone who wants this book to be updated with their state's or their nation's efforts to promote public banking can send their information to:

billstill3@gmail.com

Chapter 26: State Level Solutions

HyperScan UPDATES: Please check back often for any updates regarding State Banking initiatives, by scanning:

URL: 7.tv/6f54

Chapter 27 – Sound Money Initiatives

The 2011 legislative session throughout the various state legislatures of America saw a new phenomenon, an explosion of no confidence in the Federal Reserve System and their money. A website called "Citizens for Sound Money" accumulates the various initiatives:

URL: 7.tv/7f08

Virginia

During the 2010 legislative session, Delegate Bob Marshall of the Commonwealth of Virginia, proposed a bill to fund a study of the Bank of North Dakota idea, HR62:

URL: 7.tv/8fb8

Unfortunately HJ62 was tabled and during 2011, no other legislator picked it up.

Utah

Another more robust initiative has been proposed in Utah. The bill, drawn by attorney Larry Hilton, fills a void in Article 1, Section 10 of the United States Constitution:

> No State shall ... coin Money; emit Bills of Credit; make any Thing but gold and silver Coin a Tender in Payment of Debts....

I support the Utah Sound Money Act and sent its author a note of endorsement, as per his request in January 2011:

> "I fully support the Utah Sound Money Act. I have always supported complimentary currencies, especially those based on gold and silver coin. I think this a good backstop to runaway inflation. This Act is carefully thought out and will send a message to other states that it's time to claw back state sovereignty from not only the federal government, but the Federal Reserve System.
>
> "But an important caveat to my support is that at the federal level, it is essential to reinstitute a debt-free money system, i.e. the re-issuance of U.S. Notes with gold and silver coin as a complimentary currency at a floating rate. In other words, coins would not be denominated in dollars, but by weight. The main regulator for controlling the QUANTITY of U.S. Notes issued, would be a National Monetary Authority (NMA) made up of one elected representative from each of the several States, serving a 2-year term only, limited to two terms. That way, Congress would set a target inflation rate, and the NMA would be responsible for hitting that target by using appropriate tools to control the QUANTITY of U.S. Notes issued. Of course, a mandatory feature of this system would be an end of fractional reserve lending by commercial banks, i.e. a full-reserve banking system.
>
> "Utah should also consider founding a state-chartered, state-owned bank to operate strictly in the public interest, such as that of the Bank of North Dakota, which has been in successful operation for over 90 years. This would completely break the State of Utah free of the Federal Reserve System for all the State's financial affairs. These state-chartered banks have never been disallowed. They are an American tradition and a vital -- and nearly forgotten -- remnant of state sovereignty They were the first banking institutions in the nation, and outside of

the first three failed central banks, the only banking institutions in the nation until the passage of the National Banking Act of 1863."[328]

---

[328] Bill Still's email to Larry Hilton, author of the *Utah Sound Money Act*, January 13, 2011.

Chapter 28 – U.S. National Solutions

The solution to the economic problems of every nation is to eliminate national debt, either by banning it entirely, or by retiring it with debt-free money issuance, and a tight control over the future quantity.

Governments don't need to borrow. In fact, the most important power of a sovereign nation is the creation of its national money – without debt. Then the main challenge to producing a good, stable economy is preventing government from creating too much, or too little, money. As the U.S. Constitution puts it: in Article 1, Section 8:

> The Congress shall have Power … To coin Money, regulate the Value thereof….

There is no way to regulate the value of money other than to control its quantity. In fact, tying money to a gold standard effectively puts Congress in the business of regulating the price and value of a commodity, gold – something it is not technically authorized to do.

Until sufficient political will can be generated at the national level, however, Probably the most effective way to move forward is to start creating State-owned, State-chartered banks, but recently an interesting national solution was proposed by Ohio Congressman Dennis Kucinich that is worth reviewing.

The Kucinich Bill

This bill, introduced in December 2010 is oddly titled the "National Emergency Employment Defense Act of 2010."

It starts out really making a case for monetary reform in superb fashion:

> (17) The authority to create money is a sovereign power vested in the Congress under Article I, Section 8 of the Constitution.
>
> (18) The enactment of the Federal Reserve Act in 1913 by Congress effectively delegated the sovereign power to create money, to the Federal Reserve System and private financial industry.
>
> (19) This ceding of Constitutional power has contributed materially to a multitude of monetary and financial afflictions, including--

(A) Growing and unreasonable concentration of wealth;

(B) Unbridled expansion of national debt, both public and private;

(C) Excessive reliance on taxation of citizens for raising public revenues;

(D) Inflation of the currency;

(E) Drastic increases in the cost of public infrastructure investments;

(F) Record levels of unemployment and underemployment; and

(G) Persistent erosion of the ability of Congress to exercise its Constitutional responsibilities to provide resources for the general welfare of all the American people.

(20) A debt-based monetary system, where money comes into existence primarily through private bank lending, can neither create, nor sustain, a stable economic environment, but has proven to be a source of chronic financial instability and frequent crisis, as evidenced by the near collapse of the financial system in 2008.

(21) Banks pyramided their value by spending money into existence, greatly inflating the value of bank holdings, inflating the value of their asset bases, enticing unknowing investors to participate in financing schemes like the bundling of subprime mortgages, and ultimately bringing undercapitalized banks and the entire financial system to the edge of ruin, creating circumstances where the taxpayers of the United States were called upon to save the banks from their own imprudent money-issuing practices, misspending and mis-investments. The banks' ability to create money out of nothing ultimately became the taxpayers' liability, and raises a fundamental question about a practice of money creation which threatens the wealth of the American people.

(22) Abolishing private money creation can be achieved with minimal disruption to current banking operations, regulation, and supervision.

(23) The creation of money by private financial institutions as interest-bearing debts should cease once and for all.

(24) Reclaiming the power of the Federal Government to create money, and to spend or lend money into circulation as needed, eliminates the need to treat money as a Federal liability or to pay interest charges on the Nation's money supply to financial institutions; it also renders unnecessary the undue influence of private financial institutions over public policy.

(25) Under the current Federal Reserve System, the persons responsible for the conduct of United States monetary policy have been unaccountable to the

Chapter 28: U.S. National Solutions 267

Congress and the Nation, have resisted auditing by the General Accounting Office, and have claimed exemptions from some Federal statutes, including the Civil Rights Act of 1964, that apply to all agencies of the Federal Government.

(26) The conduct of United States monetary policy by the Board of Governors of the Federal Reserve System, and specifically the failure of Board members to safeguard the financial system against wholesale fraud and abuse of citizens, demonstrates the risks of maintaining a system wherein the power to create and regulate money has been delegated to private individuals who are unaccountable to the People of the United States in any way, even through their representatives in Congress.

(27) The Board of Governors of the Federal Reserve System has acted unilaterally to create and spend $1.25 trillion for the purpose of acquiring mortgage-backed securities, in disregard for the Constitutional requirement that all Federal Government spending originate in the House of Representatives.

(28) An examination of the historical record demonstrates that the exercise of control by the United States Government over the money system has provided greater moderation in the supply of money and promoting the general welfare, and has been indispensable in times of national emergency for generating resources required to support public investment, provide for national defense, and promote the general welfare, and is therefore superior to private control over the money system.

(29) As our money system is a key pillar in maintaining general economic welfare and as the Federal Reserve System and its private banking partners has consistently failed to promote or preserve the general welfare, it is essential that Congress, in the name of protecting the economic lives of the American people and the long-term security of our Nation, reassume the powers and responsibilities granted to it by the Constitution.

Then, when it goes into the Purposes of the Act, which also look good:

(1) To create a full employment economy as a matter of national economic defense; to provide for public investment in capital infrastructure; to provide for reducing the cost of public investment; to retire public debt; to stabilize the Social Security retirement system; to restore the authority of Congress to create and regulate money, to modernize and provide stability for the monetary system of the United States, and for other public purposes.

(2) To abolish the creation of money, or purchasing power, by private persons through lending against deposits, by means of fractional reserve banking, or by any other means.

(3) To enable the Federal Government to invest or lend new money into circulation as authorized by Congress and to provide means for public investment in capital infrastructure.

Some have criticized it for retaining the Federal Reserve System.

(4) To incorporate the Federal Reserve System into the Executive Branch under the United States Treasury, and to make other provisions for reorganization of the Federal Reserve System.

However, I think this is entirely reasonable. Abolishing the Fed sounds more radical than it needs to sound. Abolishing its key functions onerous is more politically acceptable. Thereby, the Fed can be relegated in the future to clearing check to the end of time.

Now, let's look at the rest. My comments will be in ***bold italics***:

TITLE I--ORIGINATION OF UNITED STATES MONEY

SEC. 101. EXERCISE OF CONSTITUTIONAL AUTHORITY TO CREATE MONEY.

(a) In General- Pursuant to the exercise by the Congress of the authority contained in the 5th clause of section 8 of Article I of the Constitution of the United States of America--

(1) The authority to create money within the United States shall hereafter reside exclusively with the Federal Government; and

(2) The money so created shall be known as United States Money and denominated and expressed as provided in section 5101 of title 31, United States Code.

(b) Exercise of Sovereign Power- The creation of United States Money under this Act is the legal expression of the sovereign power of the Nation and confers upon its bearer an unconditional means of payment.

I couldn't agree more.

SEC. 102. UNLAWFUL FOR PERSONS TO CREATE MONEY.

Any person who creates or originates United States money by lending against deposits, through so-called fractional reserve banking, or by any other means, after the effective date shall be fined under title 18, United States Code, imprisoned for not more than 5 years, or both.

Again, this is great stuff.

Chapter 28: U.S. National Solutions

SEC. 103. PRODUCTION OF UNITED STATES MONEY.

(a) Commencing Full Production of United States Currency- Section 5115 of title 31, United States Code, is amended by striking subsections (a) and (b) and inserting the following new subsections:

> '(a) In General- In order to furnish suitable notes for circulation as United States money, the Secretary of the Treasury shall cause plates and dies to be engraved in the best manner to guard against counterfeits and fraudulent alterations, and shall have printed therefrom and numbered such quantities of such notes of the denominations of $1, $2, $5, $10, $20, $50, $100, $500, $1,000, $5,000, $10,000 as may be required.

Hmmmm, I wonder why the big notes. I don't have anything against it, just wondering.

> '(b) Form and Tenor- United States currency notes for circulation as United States money shall be in form and tenor as directed by the Secretary of the Treasury.'.

(b) Ceasing Production of Federal Reserve Notes- The Secretary of the Treasury shall wind-down and cease production of Federal reserve notes under the 8th undesignated paragraph of section 16 of the Federal Reserve Act (12 U.S.C. 418) as quickly as practicable after the date of the enactment of this Act, but no later than the effective date, in coordination with the start-up and maintenance of production of United States currency under section 5115 of title 31, United States Code. The Secretary shall ensure that at all times the amount of Federal Reserve notes in circulation is sufficient to meet demand until the production of United States currency is sufficient to meet such demand.

(c) Continuing Circulation Until Retirement- Any Federal Reserve notes in circulation shall continue to be legal tender until retired in accordance with applicable provisions of law.

SEC. 104. LEGAL TENDER.

(a) In General- United States Money shall enter into general domestic circulation as full legal tender in payment of all debts public and private.

SEC. 106. ORIGINATION IN LIEU OF BORROWING.

(a) In General- After the effective date, and subject to limitations established by the United States Monetary Authority under provisions of section 302, the Secretary shall originate United States Money to address any negative fund balances resulting from a shortfall in available Government receipts to fund Government appropriations authorized by Congress under law.

In other words, Kucinich, a Democrat, is insisting that the new money completely fund the existing budget deficit, including President Obama's controversial health care law passed in 2009. This, of course will be a non-starter with Republicans, and I have to agree. Although budgetary "austerity" measures will NOT fix our current economic problems, spending reductions at the federal level are absolutely necessary – if for no other reason than to reduce the burgeoning power of the federal government.

> (b) Prohibition on Government Borrowing - After the effective date, unless otherwise provided by an Act of the Congress enacted after such date--
>
> (1) No amount may be borrowed by the Secretary from any source; and
>
> (2) No amount may be borrowed by any Federal agency or department, any independent establishment of the executive branch, or any other instrumentality of the United States (other than a national bank, Federal savings association, or Federal credit union) from any source other than the Secretary.

So what Kucinich is attempting to do is to fund all current spending programs, before "slamming the door" shut:

> (c) Rule of Construction - No provision of this Act shall be construed as preventing the Congress from exercising its constitutional authority to borrow money on the full faith and credit of the United States.

You might ask, "Why this is in there?" I suspect this is to avoid having to go to a Constitutional amendment to implement this law, because the Congress is given the express right "To borrow Money on the credit of the United States...." in Article 1, Section 8. I think this is a very artful dodge around this provision. The point being, if you can create money, why would you even need to borrow again? However, in the long run, this provision of the U.S. Constitution needs to be removed by amendment, and new wording inserted, forbidding government borrowing. That can be accomplished in due time.

> SEC. 107. RETIREMENT OF INSTRUMENTS OF INDEBTEDNESS.
>
> Before the effective date, the Secretary shall commence to retire all outstanding instruments of indebtedness of the United States by payment in full of the amount legally due the bearer in United States Money, as such amounts become due.

Chapter 28: U.S. National Solutions

I agree with this with some hesitation, however. Yes, it's true that the biggest banks own a huge percentage of these debt instruments, and it's true that it may not be fair to give them all that money, but also you, the citizenry, own a huge percentage of these debt instruments in your 401K and other pension plans. It may be impractical to renounce that debt. I think society can afford to right itself in this manner, though further analysis would be in order.

TITLE II--ENTRY OF U.S. MONEY INTO CIRCULATION

SEC. 201. ENTRY OF U.S. MONEY INTO CIRCULATION.

The Secretary shall cause United States Money to enter into circulation by and through any of the following means:

(1) Any origination or disbursement of funds to accomplish Federal expenditures authorized and appropriated by an Act of the Congress.

(2) Any disbursement to retire outstanding instruments of indebtedness of the Federal Government or the Secretary of the Treasury as such instruments become due.

(3) Any contribution authorized by an Act of the Congress subject to any limitation established by the Monetary Authority to the Revolving Fund established in section 302 of this Act.

(4) Any action provided for in the transitional arrangements specified in title IV of this Act, including the conversion of all deposits in transaction accounts into United States Money.

(5) Any exercise of 'lender of last resort' emergency authorities under the emergency procedures specified in section 305.

(6) Any purchase of stock in a Federal reserve bank from a member bank and of any other assets as prescribed under the Federal Reserve Act as required accomplishing the purposes of section 301.

(7) Any other means, and for any other purpose explicitly authorized by an Act of the Congress that becomes law after the effective date of this Act.

Now we start getting into some very troubling language deep inside this bill:

SEC. 302. ESTABLISHMENT OF THE UNITED STATES MONETARY AUTHORITY.

(a) Monetary Authority-

    (1) ESTABLISHMENT-

        (A) IN GENERAL- There is hereby established the Monetary Authority as an authority within the Department of the Treasury under the general oversight of the Secretary of the Treasury.

I don't like this. It should have COMPLETE independence from any other arm of government.

        (B) AUTONOMY OF MONETARY AUTHORITY- The Secretary of the Treasury may not intervene in any matter or proceeding before the Monetary Authority, unless otherwise specifically provided by law.

I still don't like it. The Monetary Authority should be independent.

        (C) INDEPENDENCE OF MONETARY AUTHORITY- The Secretary of the Treasury may not delay, prevent, or intervene in the issuance of any regulation or other determination of the Monetary Authority, including the determination of the amounts of money to be originated and most efficient method of disbursement consistent with the appropriations of Congress and the statutory objectives of monetary policy as specified in this Act.

    (2) MEMBERSHIP-

        (A) IN GENERAL- The Monetary Authority shall consist of 9 public members appointed by the president, by and with the advice and consent of the Senate.

This is a huge problem. In other words, the "new" Monetary Authority would be constituted similarly to the current Federal Reserve Board of Governors.

        (B) TERMS-

            (i) IN GENERAL- Except as provided in subparagraph (E), each member of the Monetary Authority shall be appointed to a term of 6 years.

            (ii) CONTINUATION OF SERVICE- Each member of the Monetary Authority may continue to serve after the expiration of the term of office to which such member was appointed until a successor has been appointed and qualified.

Chapter 28: U.S. National Solutions   273

(C) POLITICAL AFFILIATION- Not more than 4 of the members of the Monetary Authority may be members of the same political party.

(D) VACANCY-

(i) IN GENERAL- Any vacancy on the Monetary Authority shall be filled in the manner in which the original appointment was made.

(ii) INTERIM APPOINTMENTS- Any member appointed to fill a vacancy occurring before the expiration of the term for which such member's predecessor was appointed shall be appointed only for the remainder of such term.

(E) STAGGERED TERMS- Of the members first appointed to the Monetary Authority after the enactment of this Act--

(i) 1 shall be appointed for a term of 2 years;

(ii) 2 shall be appointed for a term of 3 years;

(iii) 2 shall be appointed for a term of 4 years;

(iv) 2 shall be appointed for a term of 5 years; and

(v) 2 shall be appointed for the full term of 6 years.

(3) CHAIRPERSON- One of the members of the Monetary Authority shall be designated by the President as the Chairperson of the Monetary Authority.

Unbelievable! You mean this august group of 9 sages cannot even have the power to elect their own leader? I smell a rat.

(4) DUTIES- The Monetary Authority shall--

(A) establish monetary supply policy and monitor the Nation's monetary status; and

(B) carry out such other responsibilities as the President may delegate to the Monetary Authority or that may be provided by an Act of Congress.

(5) GOVERNING PRINCIPLE OF MONETARY POLICY- The Monetary Authority shall pursue a monetary policy based on the governing principle that the supply of money in circulation should not become inflationary nor deflationary in and of itself, but will be sufficient to allow goods and services to move freely in trade in a balanced manner. The Monetary Authority shall maintain long run growth of the monetary and credit aggregates commensurate with the economy's long run potential to increase production,

so as to promote effectively the goals of maximum employment, stable prices, and moderate long-term interest rates.

(6) MEETINGS- The Monetary Authority shall meet on a regular basis subject to the call of the Chairperson, the Secretary, or a majority of the members.

(7) PAY- The members of the Monetary Authority shall receive a salary at annual rates equal to the annual rate determined under section 5 of title 28, United States Code, for an associate justice.

(8) STAFF - The Monetary Authority may appoint and establish the pay of such employees as the Monetary Authority determines is appropriate to assist the Monetary Authority to carry out the duties imposed under this section.

(b) Responsibility of Secretary- The Secretary shall regulate the monetary supply in reasonable accordance with targets established by the Monetary Authority.

(c) Reports on Discrepancies- The Secretary shall report to the Congress any discrepancy between any monetary target and the monetary supply in excess of 0.5 percent at the end of each quarter.

So, this all-powerful Secretary – accountable to the President and to the President alone – is singularly charged with making this report, and thereby controlling the important decision-making function of this body. This is not de-consolidation of power in my book.

The full text of the NEED bill can be found at:

URL: 7.tv/8b20

The MoneyMasters Solution

Attorney Patrick Carmack wrote a national solution, The Monetary Reform Act, for my 1996 film, "The MoneyMasters". However, I no longer support this film because it contains many quotes that are either dubious or outright forgeries. Although I still support the basic thrust of the film, since the edit is out of my hands, I cannot correct it and therefore no longer support it. I fell victim to these quotes, repeated over and over in books down through the years, and I hope to correct the record here in the last chapter in this book where I list all the quotes known to be fakes.

That said, the Monetary Reform Act does provide some simple solutions worth sharing:

The Monetary Reform Act

Step 1: Directs the Treasury to issue U.S. Notes (Lincoln's old Greenbacks) or their electronic equivalents to pay off the National Debt.

Step 2: Proportionally increases the reserve ratio of private banks to 100% reserves, thereby terminating their ability to create money, while simultaneously absorbing the funds created to retire the national debt.

> These two relatively simple steps, which Congress has the power to enact, would extinguish the national debt, without inflation or deflation, and end the unjust practice of private banks creating money as loans (i.e., fractional reserve banking). Paying off the national debt would wipe out the $400+ billion annual interest payments and thereby balance the budget. This Act would stabilize the economy and end the boom-bust economic cycles caused by fractional reserve banking.[329]

Pat Carmack's "Monetary Reform Bill" can be found here:

URL: 7.tv/8fb0

---

[329] http://www.themoneymasters.com/monetary-reform-act/

Chapter 28: U.S. National Solutions

Check back often for updates to U.S. National Solutions:

URL: 7.tv/1b00

Chapter 29 – Competing Currencies

My take on competing currencies is going to be very short and perhaps anger some in the huge, international competing currency crowd.

I don't mind competing currency existing in a system where debt-free money is issued in the public interest; however, in that environment, I think competing currencies would be little more than an ineffective novelty.

If it makes people feel more secure to have competition in the marketplace of money in the wake of this last century of national debt and the resulting permanent interest payments – mostly to bankers -- created by the British-American debt-money system, then by all means, people should employ it. It is completely understandable. So let's examine some of the major themes in the competing currency world.

Gold Money

If you want to use your gold coins – commodity money – fine with me, use them. Engrave "One Ounce .995 Gold" on them and then try going to the grocery store to spend it. The problem is, that gold is likely to be valued at $2,000 per ounce or more, so you might need something smaller. A $1/10^{th}$ ounce gold coin – worth $200 -- is smaller than a U.S. dime, at 16.5 mm in diameter. The Dime ($1/10^{th}$ of a Dollar) is a whopping 17.91 mm in diameter and if made of gold would be worth about $320. A $10 gold coin would be about 32 times smaller than a U.S. dime, about the size of a BB. Good luck writing anything on that "coin".

But, no problem, perhaps we could design little coin dispensers, sort of like the old PEZ candy dispensers so we would not lose our $10 coins amidst pocked fluff.

Counterfeit Gold

But that is not the only problem; it is very <u>unlikely</u> that you could take any gold coin down to the grocery store and spend it. Why? Because who knows what's inside that gold coin? It could just be gold-plated tungsten.

Chapter 29: Competing Currencies

Recently, the world has been flooded with gold coins and gold bars – even those held in central banks – counterfeited with tungsten cores. Tungsten has the same density as gold, so it is very difficult to recognize by weight, and tungsten is a fraction of the price of gold.

Gold expert Ron Kirby, writing in Goldseek.com on 12 November 2009, put it this way:

> When the news of tungsten "salted" gold bars in Hong Kong first surfaced, many people who I am acquainted with automatically assumed that these bars were manufactured in China – because China is generally viewed as "the knock-off capital of the world".
>
> Here's what I now understand really happened:
>
> The amount of "salted tungsten" gold bars in question was allegedly between 5,600 and 5,700 – 400 oz. – good delivery bars [roughly 60 metric tonnes].
>
> This was apparently all highly orchestrated by an extremely well financed criminal operation.
>
> Within mere hours of this scam being identified – Chinese officials had many of the perpetrators in custody.
>
> And here's what the Chinese allegedly uncovered:
>
> Roughly 15 years ago – during the Clinton Administration [think Robert Rubin, Sir Alan Greenspan and Lawrence Summers] – between 1.3 and 1.5 million 400 oz. tungsten blanks were allegedly manufactured by a very high-end, sophisticated refiner in the USA [more than 16 Thousand metric tonnes]. Subsequently, 640,000 of these tungsten blanks received their gold plating and WERE shipped to Ft. Knox and remain there to this day. I know folks who have copies of the original shipping docs with dates and exact weights of "tungsten" bars shipped to Ft. Knox.
>
> The balance of this 1.3 million – 1.5 million 400 oz. tungsten cache was also plated and then allegedly "sold" into the international market.
>
> Apparently, the global market is literally "stuffed full of 400 oz. salted bars".
>
> http://news.goldseek.com/GoldSeek/1258049769.php

Gold coins with cheap tungsten cores would be much easier to counterfeit than currently issued paper money. Therefore, you would have to have gold coins assayed every time you try to use them. Granted, tungsten can be identified by sophisticated scanning technology. But even if this became so inexpensive that it became as ubiquitous as cheap credit card scanners, counterfeiters would simply change direction and begin watering down the percentage of gold from 99.5% to, let's say, 95% gold, then 85%, etc. So a full assay of gold coins would be necessary to trade with a knowledgeable merchant. Here is what one person did to determine that a gold coin was only 90% pure gold:

URL: 7.tv/08fb

In other words, your money would not be fully liquid, certainly not as liquid as paper money issued by the government and backed by national counterfeiting laws, which, in the case of the United States, are enforced by the U.S. Secret Service. Gold coins would never become as easy to use as reliable paper money, and in this convenience-driven world, that would pose a serious disadvantage.

And then there is the reality that there is no gold left in Fort Knox. This makes moving to a gold standard a further impossibility in the United States as discussed elsewhere in this book.

Gold Paper Money

Just remember, as soon as you start printing paper money backed by gold -- beautiful, official-looking receipts for your gold or silver bullion -- watch out. Greed will naturally get to the issuers of the beautiful, official-looking receipts and they will start printing more of them then they actually have gold in reserve.

The Implementation Problem

History has shown that gold money and other commodities are highly manipulate-able by those who favor plutocracy as the preferred system of national and world governance instead of the Founders dream of decentralization of power at every level of government. Gold money advocates are long on rhetoric and short on an effective implementation plan. Of course, the reason is that there can't be a plan that doesn't further favor the current holders of gold.

Even one of the most intellectual of the goldbugs, Gary North, admits this implementation dilemma:

> There is no conceivable way to establish a full gold coin standard that doesn't involve either massive deflation or else a huge hike in the price of gold …. A rise in the price of gold … would validate the central banks' ownership of most of the world's gold, which is the opposite of the traditional free market economist's case for gold: individual consumer sovereignty.[330]

Other Competing Currencies

Other experiments with competing currency have been based on monetizing labor -- hours of work. These beautiful, official-looking receipts representing work output, are all wonderful experiments in the tradition of America's ingrained need to experiment with public interest money systems. However, they suffer from the same challenges, plus, they are not useful outside a small geographic range, where the public understands (and accepts) their worth.

Bottom Line

Debt-free legal tender, issued in proper quantity will be least costly and maximally effective as a money system. No privately issued competing currency can possibly be issued at less cost or more convenience for the user.

---

[330] "Gold Isn't Money, Yet", Gary North, December 30, 2002, www.lewrockwell.com

Legal Tender Laws

American Congressman Ron Paul argues that Federal legal tender laws are a significant problem:

> One of the main stumbling blocks is **Federal legal tender law**, which state that government-controlled fiat currency MUST be accepted for many kinds of monetary transactions.
>
> In light of this, **Gresham's Law** takes effect. Gresham's Law states that bad money drives out good money. Meaning, if someone is forced to accept your bad money, it is to your advantage to pass it off, like a hot potato, in exchange for something of value. Any good money you have, you will hoard. Eventually, real money is driven out of circulation and under people's mattresses, so to speak. In the absence of legal tender laws, people are free to accept the medium of exchange of their choice, and are likely to insist on payment in something of real value.
>
> Ron Paul, RonPaul.com, September 28, 2008

On the surface, this argument makes sense to the metalist crowd, but it may be in direct violation of the U.S. Constitution. In Article 1, Section 8, the Constitution commands Congress to "regulate the Value...." of US money. How are you going to regulate the value of money if you don't regulate one form that everyone must accept? The Constitution does not prohibit in any way people trading in gold. In fact, to prevent States from manufacturing their own money, Article 1, Section 10 states:

> No State shall ... shall coin Money; emit Bills of Credit; make any Thing but gold and silver Coin a Tender in Payment of Debts...."

Why? Because the Founders recognized that regulating the money was one of the most important functions of a sovereign nation. It is THE most important concept to cement national cohesion. Remember, in the post-revolutionary war period, the American States were all printing and coining their own money. It was a chaotic situation. No one in South Carolina knew the value of Massachusetts's paper money – or even coins. One uniform, national money had to be created to make commerce more efficient.

Legal tender laws are an absolute necessity to make some kind of money – any kind of money -- ubiquitous and useable by anyone and everyone, any time and any place within the United States.

This is only common sense. Without legal tender laws, no grocery store would allow you to exchange gold coins for groceries due to the aforementioned counterfeiting problems. Without legal tender laws, customers might sue a grocery store if it did not allow payment in Icelandic Króna – perhaps ever on the basis of perceived discrimination against Vikings.

Dr. Paul acknowledges this argument 3 paragraphs later:

> Congress has the Constitutional duty to protect the integrity of our money. However, since it has passed this duty off, and the Federal Reserve has only debased our currency, Congress should no longer force Americans to do business in dollars if they would prefer to transact in gold, or silver, or cigarettes or seashells, for that matter.
>
> Ron Paul, RonPaul.com, September 28, 2008

So Dr. Paul's answer to the unconstitutional activities of the Federal Reserve Act is to allow the nation to further stray from the original intent of the Constitution, instead of having Congress merely fix the problem by repealing the Federal Reserve Act.

Don't Fear Competing Currencies

Dr. Bob Welham, a retired a retired academic mathematician and industrial researcher, provides the most succinct explanation of why competing currencies are not to be feared by monetary reformers:

> Let's assume that a national, publicly issued, debt-free, non-commodity fiat currency is well established, ... that it is good for the payment of taxes. Then we have a universal means of exchange ... issued by, used by, and received back (for tax payments) by the maximally inclusive collective of people, which is usually the nation state. This utility is provided at negligible ... cost by that nation to itself for its people to conduct their business.
>
> Can any alternative currency compete successfully against this? The national currency is ubiquitous and hence maximally convenient and liquid. Backed by

Chapter 29: Competing Currencies

legal tender law (everyone is obliged to accept it as payment) it is maximally robust and risk-free. Every taxpayer needs it so it is always in demand.

Any competing debt-based commercially issued currency would necessarily impose upon its user base the cost of its own existence, specifically the quantity of it in issue multiplied by the average interest rate spread between its borrowers and its depositors. This is the system that we have now, and by its nature any debt-based currency entails continuous transfer of wealth from its user base to its issuer-lenders. This inherent cost ensures that any such debt-based currency cannot compete in general against the proposed debt-free, persistently circulating national currency. What user base would willingly pay extra for an inferior, riskier, less than universal currency? Why participate in a costly commercial rent-a-currency scheme when you don't have to?

So how about a debt-free, non-commodity competing currency? Since there is no built-in profit for the commercial issuers of a debt-free currency, this too would tend to be economically uncompetitive. Its issuers' overheads would have to be passed on to its users who, through their taxes, would be paying already their share of the cost of the national currency. Why pay again for something which, even at best, can be no better than what you've already paid for?

Presumably also tax laws would ensure that any taxable transaction conducted in an alternative currency would be taxed just as if it were conducted in the national currency at the prevailing exchange rate. Moreover any tax due would be payable in the national currency. This imposes upon the users of any alternative currency the further cost of the exchange rate spread between that currency and the national currency, plus the volatility risk of that exchange rate.

Lastly, any competing commodity-backed currency would effectively be a proxy for that commodity and would float against the national currency accordingly.

Again, administration and exchange rate volatility and costs, in addition to the lack of universal convenience, would make it uncompetitive as a general currency.

So, in view of the cost and convenience advantages that the proposed national currency would enjoy, there is no pressing need to suppress competition. If the debt-free national currency is ubiquitous, issued in appropriate quantity, and well understood and trusted by the nation's citizens, then it need not fear competition. The free market would ensure that the debt-free national currency prevailed as the currency of choice in almost all circumstances.[331]

---

[331] Personal email from Dr. Robert Welham, December, 2011

Chapter 30 - Karl Denninger on MERS

MERS is a privately held company that operates an electronic registry designed to keep track of the title of properties that were sliced into securities which were then sold off and traded in markets in the U.S. and abroad.

Unfortunately for the banks originating these mortgages, things were moving so fast that proper recording was not done to insure a legal chain of title. The result is the largest possible impending disaster for the nation's banks.

This example from the New York Times:

> On Feb. 11, a circuit court judge in Miami-Dade County in Florida set aside a judgment against Ana L. Fernandez, a borrower whose home had been foreclosed and repurchased on Jan. 21 by Chevy Chase Bank, the institution claiming to hold the note. But the bank had been unable to produce evidence that the original lender had assigned the note, which was in the amount of $225,000, to Chevy Chase.
>
> With the sale set aside, Ms. Fernandez remains in the home. "We believe this loan was never assigned," said Ray Garcia, the lawyer in Miami who represented the borrower. Now, he said, it is up to whoever can produce the underlying note to litigate the case. The statute of limitations on such a matter runs for five years, he said....
>
> Mr. Garcia has another case in which a borrower tried to sell his home but could not because the note underlying a $60,000 second mortgage cannot be found. The statute of limitations on the matter will expire in October, he said, and if the note holder has not come forward by then, the borrower will be free of his obligation on the second mortgage.[332]

No one knows how many mortgages are at risk at this point, but it is potentially in the millions with potential losses in the trillions of dollars – a devastating hammer blow for the already shaky banking system at this point.

---

[332] *The New York Times*, "Guess What Got Lost in the Loan Pool?", Feb. 28, 2009. http://www.nytimes.com/2009/03/01/business/01gret.html?_r=2&em

Chapter 30: Denninger on MERS

Karl Denninger, author of "Market Ticker" has been following the MERS problem for many years:

URL: 7.tv/9cb5

For more information, contact Legal Aid in your state. *The New York Times* has mentioned attorney April Charney, a foreclosure lawyer at Jacksonville Legal Aid of Florida, who has been training consumer lawyers nationwide on how to litigate these cases.

HyperScan UPDATES:

Check back often for updates to MERS developments:

URL: 7.tv/1d13

Chapter 31 –Kennedy Assassination Myth

The red-sealed U.S. notes – Lincoln's old Greenbacks – were last issued in 1971, were also reissued in 1963, but that had nothing to do with the assassination of President John F. Kennedy. They were merely Lincoln's old Greenbacks issued 11 different times since the 1860s. They now trade among collectors at 5-to-10 times face value, less than a generation after being demonetized.

U.S. Notes became redeemable in gold or silver in 1879. After private ownership of gold was banned in 1933, they were only redeemable for silver. However, by 1960, a silver dollar contained $1.29 of silver, so in March 1964 redemption of U.S. Notes and Silver Certificates for silver dollars stopped and the U.S. government sold off its supply of silver dollars to collectors.

Executive Order 11110

Over the years I have been frequently asked if the Kennedy assassination had anything to do with the money question. The theory goes that the issuance of Executive Order 11110 by President Kennedy in 1963 concerning Silver Certificates may have led to his assassination. Supposedly Kennedy was going to issue massive amounts of silver certificates to undercut Federal Reserve notes and thereby diminish the power of the Fed and return America to "honest" money – the Austrian economic mantra.

This is completely false. Executive Order 11110 was signed by President Kennedy on June 4, 1963. It merely transferred the power to issue Silver Certificates from the President to the Secretary of the Treasury. It did not authorize an increase in Silver Certificates. Remember, in the face of the rising price of silver, these Silver Certificates were being rapidly phased out and replaced by lower denomination Federal Reserve Notes; not the other way around. For a scholarly explanation of this matter please see:

Chapter 31: Kennedy Assassination Myth

URL: 7.tv/9dce

Chapter 32: Fake Quotes

This topic of monetary reform has been liberally salted down through the years with a substantial number of fake quotes from famous personalities. The problem is these errors are repeated time and time again throughout the years as one author quotes another. I have fallen victim to this, as have hundreds of other authors. In the past, this sort of research has been very time consuming and expensive. Now, with the advent of the Internet, things are easier, but still it is no small task.

Since I've been writing in this field for a number of years, I have been the recipient of many dissertations pointing to the use of fake quotes in my work. Unfortunately, these errors offer an easy target to critics who want to attack and discredit the entire monetary reform thesis.

I have gone to great time and expense editing up revisions to "The Secret of Oz" in an attempt to weed out these fake quotes. Hopefully this web location will serve as a clearinghouse for authors into the future. If you would like to add to the "Fake Quotes" debate, make your submissions here:

URL: 7.tv/19bd

What follows are just a few examples of fake quotes.

Thomas Jefferson

I have used all three of these so-called Jefferson quotes in the past:

> If the American people ever allow private banks to control the issue of their currency, first by inflation, then by deflation, the banks and corporations that will grow up around them will deprive the people of all property until their children wake up homeless on the continent their Fathers conquered...

Chapter 32: Fake Quotes

I believe that banking institutions are more dangerous to our liberties than standing armies...

The issuing power should be taken from the banks and restored to the people, to whom it properly belongs.

According to Monticello, Jefferson's home:

http://www.monticello.org/site/jefferson/private-banks-quotation

Earliest known appearance in print: 1937[1][2]

Other attributions: None known.

Status: This quotation is at least partly spurious; see comments below.

Comments: This quotation is often cited as being in an 1802 letter to Secretary of the Treasury Albert Gallatin, and/or "later published in *The Debate Over the Recharter of the Bank Bill* (1809)."

The first part of the quotation ("If the American people ever allow private banks to control the issue of their currency, first by inflation, then by deflation, the banks and corporations that will grow up around them will deprive the people of all property until their children wake up homeless on the continent their Fathers conquered") has not been found anywhere in Thomas Jefferson's writings, to Albert Gallatin or otherwise. It is identified in *Respectfully Quoted* as spurious, and the editor further points out that the words "inflation" and "deflation" are not documented until after Jefferson's lifetime. [3]

The second part of the quotation ("I believe that banking institutions are more dangerous to our liberties than standing armies...") may well be a paraphrase of a statement Jefferson made in a letter to John Taylor in 1816. He wrote, "And I sincerely believe, with you, that banking establishments are more dangerous than standing armies; and that the principle of spending money to be paid by posterity, under the name of funding, is but swindling futurity on a large scale."[4]

The third part of this quotation ("The issuing power should be taken from the banks and restored to the people, to whom it properly belongs") may be a misquotation of Jefferson's comment to John Wayles Eppes, "Bank-paper must be suppressed, and the circulating medium must be restored to the nation to whom it belongs." [5]

Lastly, we have not found a record of any publication called *The Debate Over the Recharter of the Bank Bill*. There was certainly debate over the recharter of the National Bank leading up to its expiration in 1811, but a search of Congressional documents of that period yields none of the verbiage discussed above.

See this article's Discussion page for further insight into the formation and use of the latter portion of this quotation.

Footnotes

1. United States Congress. Senate. Committee on Agriculture and Forestry, Committee on Agriculture and Forestry, General Farm Legislation: Hearings Before a Subcommittee of the Committee on Agriculture and Forestry, United States Senate, Seventy-fifth Congress, Second Session, Pursuant to S. Res. 158, a Resolution to Provide for an Investigation of Agricultural Commodity Prices, of an Ever-normal Granary... (Washington, D.C.: GPO, 1937), 3607.

2. To establish the earliest appearance of this phrase in print, the following sources were searched for the phrase, "If the American people ever allow private banks to control the issue of their currency": Google Books, Google Scholar, Amazon.com, Internet Archive, America's Historical Newspapers, American Broadsides and Ephemera Series I, Early American Imprints Series I and II, Early English Books Online, Eighteenth Century Collections Online, 19th Century U.S. Newspapers, American Periodicals Series Online, JSTOR.

3. Suzy Platt, ed., *Respectfully Quoted: A Dictionary of Quotations Requested from the Congressional Research Service* (Washington D.C.: Library of Congress, 1989; Bartleby.com, 2003), http://www.bartleby.com/73/1204.html.

4. Thomas Jefferson to John Taylor, Monticello, 28 May 1816. Ford 11:533.

5. Thomas Jefferson to John Wayles Eppes, Monticello, 24 June 1813. Ford 11:303.

Here's what Jefferson DID say: in a letter to John Taylor in 1816. He wrote:

And I sincerely believe, with you, that banking establishments are more dangerous than standing armies; and that the principle of spending money to be paid by posterity, under the name of funding, is but swindling futurity on a large scale.

And Jefferson's comment to John Wayles Eppes,

Bank-paper must be suppressed, and the circulating medium must be restored to the nation to whom it belongs.

Notice how Jefferson understood that it was money issued by private banks that was the problem.

Ben Franklin

In the Colonies, we issue our own paper money. It is called Colonial Scrip. We issue it to pay the government's approved expenses and charities. We make sure it is issued in proper proportions to make the goods pass easily from the producers to the consumers. . . . In this manner, creating ourselves our own paper money, we control its purchasing power and we have no interest to pay to no one.

I have previously attributed this quote to *The Autobiography of Benjamin Franklin*. These words do not appear in Franklin's Autobiography or any other work of his.[333]

Abraham Lincoln

The government should create, issue and circulate all the currency and credit needed to satisfy the spending power of the government and the buying power of consumers..... The privilege of creating and issuing money is not only the supreme prerogative of Government, but it is the Government's greatest creative opportunity. By the adoption of these principles, the long-felt want for a uniform medium will be satisfied. The taxpayers will be saved immense sums of interest, discounts and exchanges. The financing of all public enterprises, the maintenance of stable government and ordered progress, and the conduct of the Treasury will become matters of practical administration. The people can and will be furnished with a currency as safe as their own government. Money will

---

[333] http://en.wikiquote.org/wiki/Money

cease to be the master and become the servant of humanity. Democracy will rise superior to the money power.

These are not Lincoln's own words, but just Gerry McGeer's interpretation of Lincoln's policy.[334]

The Times of London

Oh how I hated to give this quote up:

> If this mischievous financial policy, which has its origin in North America, shall become indurated down to a fixture, then that Government will furnish its own money without cost. It will pay off debts and be without debt. It will have all the money necessary to carry on its commerce. It will become prosperous without precedent in the history of the world. The brains, and wealth of all countries will go to North America. That country must be destroyed or it will destroy every monarchy on the globe.

Attributed to an editorial in *The Times* of *London* in 1865. No such editorial ever appeared. The earliest known appearance is in *The Flaming Sword*, Vol. XII, No. 42 (2 September 1898), p. 7

Andrew Jackson

> I killed the bank.

Reputedly from Jackson's tombstone at the Hermitage in Nashville, TN. On my first visit I didn't find it, and just assumed that it was my mistake, but on my second visit in 2010, I discovered that this quote is entirely fake.

Rothschild Related Quotes

> Permit me to issue and control the money of a nation, and I care not who makes its laws!

---

[334] McGeer, Gerald Grattan (1935). "5 - Lincoln, Practical Economist". *The Conquest of Poverty*. Gardenvale, Quebec: Garden City Press. pp. pp. 186ff.

Chapter 32: Fake Quotes

Attributed to Mayer Amschel Rothschild (1744 - 1812). No primary source for this is known and the earliest attribution to him known is 1935 (*Money Creators*, Gertrude M. Coogan). Before that, "Let us control the money of a nation, and we care not who makes its laws" was said to be a "maxim" of the House of Rothschilds, or, even more vaguely, of the "money lenders of the Old World".[335]

And then there is this one:

> The few who understand the system, will either be so interested in its profits, or so dependent on its favors that there will be no opposition from that class, while on the other hand, the great body of people, mentally incapable of comprehending the tremendous advantages...will bear its burden without complaint, and perhaps without suspecting that the system is inimical to their best interests.

Attributed to Senator John Sherman in a letter supposedly sent from the Rothschild Brothers of London to New York bankers Ikleheimer, Morton, and Vandergould, June 25, 1863. The letters are forgeries that could not have been written before 1876. Further, no evidence of a firm with the name "Ikleheimer, Morton, and Vandergould" has been found.[336]

Bismarck

> The division of the United States into federations of equal force was decided long before the Civil War by the high financial powers of Europe. These bankers were afraid that the US, if they remained as one block, and as one nation, would attain economic and financial independence, which would upset their financial domination over the world.

This quote is listed as "unsourced" by Wikiquote. And then the other quote I have used from Bismarck is much more difficult to research, but I have cut it anyway because of its dubious and anti-Semitic source:

> The death of Lincoln was a disaster for Christendom. There was no man in the United States great enough to wear his boots. And Israel went anew to garner the riches of the world. I fear that Jewish banks with their craftiness

---

[335] http://en.wikiquote.org/wiki/Money
[336] http://en.wikiquote.org/wiki/Money

and tortuous tricks will entirely control the exuberant riches of America and will use it to systematically corrupt modern civilization.

The source of this quote only goes back to 1826, *The Secret World Government Or "The Hidden Hand"*. This was written by the anti-Semitic author Count Cherep-Spirdovich. He got it from someone named Conrad Siem. G. Edward Griffin also uses this quote. According to both Gary North and Griffin, Siem was a German native who became an American citizen and wrote about the life and views of Bismarck. North even claims that Siem's source was a personal letter from Bismarck to Siem, who North says was only 15 at the time. North bases this claim on a 1930 census record saying that a "Conrad Siem" was living in Washington, D.C. at that time who was born about 1861. North, however does not divulge how he determined that this was the Conrad Siem in question.

As you can see, this all gets very murky very quickly. Unless further documentation is offered, I will not use this quote again.

The Earnest Seyd Controversy

For over a century, a story has circulated that a London based banker named Ernest Seyd bribed key members of Congress in 1873 to get them to vote for a gold-only money system, known as "The Crime of '73":

> In 1872, a British banker named Ernest Seyd was given £100,000 (about $5,000,000 in today's money) by the Bank of England and sent to America to bribe the necessary Congressmen to get silver demonetized to further reduce the money supply.

The above quote was included in original cut of my award winning 2010 documentary, "The Secret of Oz" and it is also part of my 1995 documentary "The MoneyMasters". However, could this entire Ernest Seyd bribery allegation be a hoax? Let's investigate.

According to *Wikiquote*: [337]

> In 1892 ... Frederick A. Luckenbach gave a sworn affidavit that, when Luckenbach had dined with Seyd in 1874, Seyd had told him just that story. At the time, Luckenbach was selling mining equipment to silver miners in

---

[337] http://en.wikiquote.org/wiki/Ernest_Seyd#cite_note-2

Chapter 32: Fake Quotes

Colorado. The president of the State Silver League persuaded him to give the affidavit about what Seyd allegedly told him.

However, Seyd, as it turned out, had been one of the foremost advocates of silver in England, and an expert on bimetallism. Seyd advocated for silver in all his works and had been consulted on the coinage bill because he had written a 250-page book, *Suggestions in Reference to the Metallic Currency of the United States*.[338] Here is Milton Friedman's opinion:

> Seyd was anything but a "designing bullionist." He was a British bimetallist who objected strongly to the demonetization of silver by the United States.[339]

Congressmen soon distanced themselves from the story and even issued formal apologies for their allegations.[340] Writers pointed out numerous problems with Luckenbach's affidavit and with the story of the bribery.[341] Perhaps Hermon Wilson Craven stated the most glaring question this way:[342]

> The bill dropping the silver dollar from our list of coins had passed the senate on January 10, 1871, by a vote of 36 to 14. It had passed the house on May 27, 1872, by a vote of 110 to 13. In the name of common sense, what need was there for English and German bankers to send Seyd here in the winter of 1872-3, to bribe congress to favor a measure that had already passed both houses of congress without a word of opposition from a single member?

---

[338] Seyd, Ernest (1871). *Suggestions in Reference to the Metallic Currency of the United States*. (London: Trübner. OCLC 7262411).
[339] Friedman, *Money Mischief*, p. 61.
[340] Cannon, Marion, "A Retraction from Mr. Cannon", *Los Angeles Times*, Oct. 7, 1893, p. 6.
[341] McCleary, James Thompson (June 1, 1896). "The Crime of 1873". *Sound Currency* 3 (13): 116-130.
[342] Craven, Hermon Wilson (1896). *Errors of Populism*. Seattle: Lowman & Hanford. pp. 82-89,87. OCLC 7268848

Chapter 32: Fake Quotes

Check back often for updates to Fake Quotes developments:

URL: 7.tv/2c63

Chapter 33 –International Solutions

Iceland

In June of 2010, I visited Iceland for a week. The warm welcome of the Vikings was overwhelming. The Islanders formed a group to study solutions for the Icelandic economy. This group is now called the Icelandic Financial Reform Initiative, or IFRI. I was privileged to join several members of the IFRI and I got on several radio shows which led to a string of newspaper articles.

Chapter 33: International Solutions

Iceland's tiny economy and sparse resources were also nurtured by a series of public interest savings banks. Despite a population of a little over 300,000 people and a gross domestic product of around $12 billion, Iceland is one of the most civilized nations on earth.

But then the government "privatized" the savings banks, similar to the Swedish savings banks 20 years earlier. In Iceland's case, even the Landsbankinn, which essentially was the Bank of Iceland, was privatized. For the first few years, things looked good. The economy doubled. But under the surface, the private bankers were creating a huge financial bubble.

They opened a new offshore internet bank called IceSave, targeting depositors in the UK and Holland by offering attractive interest rates for new depositors. Hundreds of thousands of new accounts were opened. Entire towns and police department pension funds put their money into IceSave, as did charities such as cancer relief funds. Using fractional reserve lending, IceSave fanned that into billions for questionable new loans.

IceSave started investing in European ventures, especially in Russia. Many now believe that IceSave actually became a money laundering operation for the Russian Mafia – all the while trading on the good reputation for solid banking Iceland had built up over the previous decades.

According to Birgitta Jonsdottir, a member of the Icelandic Parliament:

> However, when the bank was privatized, it still used the good reputation of Iceland to grow huge and do lots of criminal activities. And the owner, Björgólfur Thor Björgólfsson, he became one of the rich boys in the world really quickly – one of the billionaires. I've seen documents linking him to the Russian mafia – and his father. One oligarch that fled to the UK confirmed that Iceland was used as a money-laundering machine for the Russian mafia.

When the crash came in 2008, the big Icelandic banks were vastly overextended and quickly failed. Jonsdottir observes:

> In the 5 years time that they were privatized before the collapse, they actually grew ten times the Icelandic GDP, and when it collapsed you can

Chapter 33: International Solutions

imagine how huge the collapse was because they collapsed onto the shoulders of the nation – the taxpayers

The Icelandic Parliament at first poured enormous amounts of taxpayers' money in to try to save their banks, but they still failed. Then the government bailed out all their Icelandic depositors. But the IceSave accounts were not in Iceland and were never insured by the Icelandic government, and so they were not bailed out.

However, in the face of tremendous political pressure at home, the British and Dutch governments bailed out the IceSave accounts of their citizens, and then tried to make Iceland pay for it, at terms that have decimated Iceland's fragile economy. According to Birgitta Jonsdottir:

> The income tax of more than half of the nation – just to pay the interest of this particular loan, and then you have other loans. We would have gone in 2007 being the most developed nation in the world into a nation spending all its GDP just paying interest to foreign loans.

Inflation shot up. Icelanders soon discovered that even the principal on their home mortgage loans was indexed to inflation.

Many Icelanders saw the principle on their home mortgages double and their payments triple. This despite rising unemployment.

> The way the loan system is in Iceland is completely outrageous. Your rights as a consumer are zero.

Foreclosures mounted and the citizens rioted. They call it their "Revolution." They stormed the Parliament Square. The President was forced to call for a referendum. 93% of the people voted <u>not</u> to bail out the bankers.

The following is from a 2010 CNBC/UK television broadcast on the subject of Iceland:

> The Brits aren't exactly a shining light here about how to handle international relations.

> No, no, it's one of the worst conducted, most absurd things I've seen in a long time. I mean, it's obvious that the Icelandics cannot afford to pay this money back. What we've just seen is the first anti-bailout tax revolt here.

Chapter 33: International Solutions

Now the ruling party is trying to convince Iceland to join the European Union to be eligible for loans to save its economy. The people, however, seem unconvinced that more and more debt is the solution. Iceland now seems determined to take back their money power and not take on more national debt.

According to Jonsdottir:

> What I want to implement here is a healthy banking system where you don't have fractional reserve, you don't have high interest; the banks should not serve as mafia outlets, it should be something that is important for the communities.

Over 70% of Iceland now opposes joining the EU and some are now supporting proposals for cities to start up savings banks based on the Bank of North Dakota model to provide local credit and stop the rising wave of housing foreclosures,

> We are not part of EU yet. They are trying to put us in it. 70% of Icelanders don't want to join the EU, but the Social Democrats are in power and that is their sole mission: to get Iceland into the EU.

Iceland is proud of its democratic heritage. Iceland is home to the oldest Parliament in Europe – having met annually for over 1,000 years. For the first 800 years, the Icelandic Parliament met at the place where the North American tectonic plate meets the European plate. Called Thingvellir, Icelanders consider this a holy site – where elected government was born. Today, Iceland is the new battleground as it attempts to become the first nation in modern times to escape the serfdom of the debt money system. If Iceland escapes the rest of the world will be watching.

Hans Lysglimt – Norwegian editor of *Farmann* magazine – states:

> If you end paying this money entering into the EU to try to find salvation that way, it will only get worse. What has happened in Iceland is going to happen on a worldwide scale in our lifetime. There won't be enough money to cover all the debts.

Jonsdottir asks the crucial question:

> Why are governments pumping money into private banks? Why are they not letting them roll? Then the excuse is, 'Oh, they are too big to fail. Let them fail, please.

Chapter 33: International Solutions

The Islanders are mad. They want answers, and they want this fixed. The Icelandic Financial Reform Initiative has put up a great website in cutting-edge Island tradition. It contains complete details on their excellent proposed reforms.

URL: 7.tv/9dce

What Iceland did wrong was to let their central bank become privatized. This took away the last remaining shred of control over the quantity of money. From that day, the financial train wreck was inevitable. Once the panic came, they compounded the problem by trying to bail these banks out. They felt it was the honorable thing to do, plus they were told that otherwise, their economy would collapse and there would be no more food imports at a time when the island only had a 2-week supply. But eventually, the Icelandic people rioted in front of the Parliament building and the handouts stopped. They let the big banks go under.

Now Iceland is already back on the road to recovery, and they have learned a lesson – for the time being.

Iceland Jails Bankers
But they are not done. In January 2011, numerous bankers were arrested by Icelandic authorities.

URL: 7.tv/6c1c

Chapter 33: International Solutions

HyperScan UPDATES:

Check back often for updates to Icelandic monetary reform developments:

URL: 7.tv/2c9e

Ireland

The 2008 financial crisis also hit Ireland hard. Their money supply was also controlled by the big commercial banks. Due to a low corporate tax rate and low interest rates, the Irish economy expanded rapidly between 1995 and 2007.

In 2007, when France and Germany were growing at about 2 percent a year, Ireland's growth was almost 7 percent. It was known as the Celtic Tiger and was widely celebrated for the combination of low tax rates and fast growth. The banks grew rapidly and piled on property loans. In the early part of this decade, home prices grew at rates comparable to those in Phoenix and Las Vegas.

The banker who came to epitomize that era was Sean FitzPatrick, the chief executive of Anglo Irish Bank, which grew faster than the others by focusing on property lending above all else. He is remembered as the man who, in good times, denounced bank regulation as "corporate McCarthyism." He also turned out to be good at making secret loans to himself that did not work out.

Ireland has now taken over Anglo Irish, and it has bailed out all the other big banks.

The Irish stock market peaked at 10,364 points in May 2007. By February 2009, it had tumbled to 1,987 points, a 14-year low.

Chapter 33: International Solutions

Now, Ireland is a case study for what happens to a nation that cedes control of the quantity of its money over to the big banks, let's them counterfeit the national money by making too many loans, and then, after the crash, falling victim to the argument that these same banks are "too big to fail."

In January 2009, the famed Waterford Crystal factory laid off most of their Irish employees and moved production to a factory in Eastern Europe. The numbers of people claiming unemployment benefit in Ireland rose to 326,000 in January 2009, the highest monthly level since records began in 1967. The weakening conditions drew over 100,000 protesters onto the streets of Dublin on 21 February 2009. That same month, the approval rating of the ruling Fianna Fáil party was a mere 10%.

By Feb. 2009, the liabilities of Irish banks was estimated to be 309% of the Irish annual gross domestic product (GDP) of the nation.[343]

In March 2009 Professor Patrick Honohan, now the governor of the Irish central bank wrote a paper entitled "What Went Wrong in Ireland."

> It argues that the Tiger economy went off the rails only after joining the euro, and to a great degree because of the euro.[344]

On May 20, 2009 *The Irish Times* reported that the nation had entered a depression. The interest on the Irish National debt continues to spiral out of control. Projections are that by 2015, the National Debt will be 125% of the annual gross domestic product.[345]

Monetary reform experts in the U.K. criticized the way the Irish politicians were throwing in all the nation's money to save their failing banks.

> The present collapse of an inherently unstable banking system was the work of supra-national financiers having no loyalty to the population of any country, in collaboration with governments which have chosen to forget just who it was that they were elected to serve and whose ministers look for a seat on the boards of favoured financial institutions when they retire.

---

[343] "Irish Banking Liabilities", Davy Stockbrokers, Dublin, Feb. 17 2009.
[344] "Europe's Shoddy Attempt to Vilify Ireland", by Ambrose Evans-Pritchard Economics Last updated: *The Telegraph,* January 21st, 2011.
[345] "The Euro Area's Debt Crisis – Bite the Bullet", *The Economist*, London, Jan. 13, 2010.

> Bailing out Ireland is no solution. It simply adds to the general insolvency. Who is going to bail out the next domino to fall? And the next? And the next?
>
> Ireland itself will be the loser from this bail-out. Any vestige of independence will disappear, as the supranational moneylenders direct its economy and order it to sell off its assets in order to service the unrepayable loans. Like a third-world country, Ireland will now see its real wealth vanishing overseas, and public services cut to the bone, in order to scrape together interest installments which ensure that, however much is repaid, the debt continues to grow.[346]
>
> Any nation which wishes to remain independent should refuse to borrow billions to save delinquent banks, and, instead, lobby their representatives to guarantee legitimate deposits and legislate for all new money, non-cash as well as cash, to be issued only by public authority, free of any debt at source.[347]
>
> Gillian Swanson, Daily Telegraph website, 20-11-10

Irish monetary reformer Jim Corr addressed economics students an December 10, 2010:

> We mainly need to follow Iceland's example ... We need to default on the debt, because the debt is a scam anyway, and it's inescapable ... banks create money literally out of thin air, through the fractional reserve system and then charge interest on it. Remember what Mervyn King had to say about this "financial alchemy" in his recent speech in New York?

We'll review the Mervyn King quote that Jim Corr refers to, in three pages.

On Nov. 28, 2010, an €85 billion rescue deal was announced by the EU and the IMF, €35 billion of which would go for further bank bailouts. Shockingly, a substantial amount is to be taken from the Irish National Pension Reserve Fund as well.

On January 18, 2011, word started leaking out that Ireland was actually printing its own Euros not backed by debt. We monetary reformers

---

[346] Gillian Swanson, *Daily Telegraph* website, Nov. 22, 2010.
[347] Gillian Swanson, *Daily Telegraph* website, Nov. 20, 2010.

Chapter 33: International Solutions

suspect this was done with the approval of the EU, primarily because the EU is out of bailout money. Hopefully, this will lead to the destruction of the Euro, and the EU in general on the basis of decentralization of power whenever possible. In the U.S. *The Daily Bell* was incredulous, pointing out that the Greeks:

> ... Were forced to go begging to the IMF.... when the Greek people find out the [Irish] central bank is allowed to just print money, they are going to riot and demand tax cuts and benefits rising and massive spending. The Germans... well the Germans are just going to totally lose it. They've been told they should pay higher taxes to help the PIIGS, now they are being told the PIIGS can print EUROS at will?[348]

The problem is that the money printing can then be multiplied by a factor of 12 by the big Irish Banks, to try to re-inflate their bubble.

On January 19, 2011, Joe Higgins, an Irish member of the European Parliament told it like it is:

URL: 7.tv/2d42

On Jan. 21, 2011, I issued the following Press Release:

> I have no problem with Ireland printing its own money. Those of us in the monetary reform movement have predicted that nations would eventually have to resort to this to escape the crushing weight of the debt money system.
>
> Ireland should start printing its own debt-free sovereign money, the old Irish pound notes -- the "Punt" -- instead of Euros. Of course the bankers and their friends in the media are going to complain loudly about that and try to raise the specter of inflation to scare Ireland away from this

---

[348] "The End of the Euro? ... Ireland Prints Own Notes", *The Daily Bell*, Jan. 18, 2011. http://tinyurl.com/6yae3q4

Sovereign solution. But let me ask the Irish people one simple question: is the price of your house going up or down? So let's worry about inflation when the price of your housing starts to go back up.

Right now we are in the midst of something very unusual in economic history, if not unique; money and credit deflation (a credit squeeze) mixed in with a speculative bubble in commodities which is causing inflation in certain areas such as foods prices. These two conflicting factors are keeping us confused as to what the right course should be.

The right course for Ireland is to break off from the EU and run the International Monetary Fund out of Dublin, then reinstate the *IR£*. This is the only thing that will work. Austerity will only impoverish the Irish people further and allow the big bankers to buy up your assets and work for pennies on the dollar.

Reinstate your national money. Do not take any more loans from anyone.

Karl Denninger on the Situation in Ireland:

URL: 7.tv/9fb0

HyperScan UPDATES:
Check back often for updates to Irish monetary reform developments:

URL: 7.tv/0f70

England

Mervyn King, Governor of the Bank of England

It is interesting to know about Mervyn King. King studied at King's College, Cambridge (gaining a first class degree in economics in 1969). He also studied at Harvard as a Kennedy Scholar. Later he returned to Harvard as a Visiting Professor and became a Visiting Professor at MIT as well. There, he shared an office with then-Assistant Professor Ben Bernanke, since Feb. 1, 2006, Chairman of the Federal Reserve System. In 1998,

> King became a member of the influential Washington-based financial advisory body, the Group of Thirty. He is also the first incumbent Governor of the Bank of England to be received in audience by Queen Elizabeth II.[349]

And here is the celebrated quote from no less an authority than the current Governor of the Bank of England, Mervyn King:

> Of all the ways of organising banking, the worst is the one we have today... eliminating fractional reserve banking explicitly recognizes that the pretense that risk-free deposits can be supported by risky assets is alchemy. To work, financial alchemy requires the implicit support of the tax payer...For a society to base its financial system on alchemy is a poor advertisement for its rationality.[350]

The Bank of England (Creation of Currency) Bill

A new proposed piece of legislation is making the rounds amongst the United Kingdom's monetary reformers. Although it has not yet been introduced as legislation, it is called "The Bank of England (Creation of Currency) Bill, or simply, "The Act."

I initially heard about The Act shortly before I was to travel to England to give the opening remarks at the Bromsgrove Monetary Reform Conference in Bromsgrove, UK.

An hour later, I discovered that in the details of the new British proposal was no prohibition of national debt. This was right after I said that monetary reform rests on two inviolable pillars:

---

[349] http://en.wikipedia.org/wiki/Mervyn_King_(economist)
[350] BBC News, Oct. 25, 2010, *Mervyn Ponders Abolition of Banking as We Know It.*

Chapter 33: International Solutions

1. No more national debt; and
2. No more fractional reserve lending.

My British friends were adamant that making a proposal to the Parliament that would prohibit any further governmental borrowing would be a "non-starter." To me at the time, this was not a good argument. We have gone a long time trying to get this right, after all; why compromise, when we are just on the verge of victory, as I suspect we are?

But then, the amiable Scotsman, Alistair McConnachie and his young "Positive Money" counterpart, Ben Dyson, took me aside and explained that once the government has the ability to create money without debt, and it gradually pays off its debt with the new debt-free money, it will become clear that there is no need for additional borrowing. It was brilliant! Practical politics. So now, I fully support the British plan, though I do not feel qualified to comment on it in detail, as I do with its American counterparts.

For those who wish to read The Act in its entirety, go to:

URL: 7.tv/9cb6

Check back often for updates to British monetary reform developments:

URL: 7.tv/5f14

JRR Tolkien

According to a 1997 survey by the Folio Society, as well as a poll by the bookseller, Waterstone's, author J.R.R. Tolkien's trilogy, *Lord of the Rings,* was voted by readers as "favorite book of all time." But Tolkien also harbored ideas of monetary reform. First he criticizes bankers as the veiled backers of politics:

> The true equation is "democracy" = government by world financiers.
>
> The main mark of modern governments is that we do not know who governs, *de facto* any more than *de jure*. We see the politician and not his backer; still less the backer of the backer; or, what is most important of all, the banker of the backer.
>
> Throned above all, in a manner without parallel in all past, is the veiled prophet of finance, swaying all men living by a sort of magic, and delivering oracles in a language not understood of the people.[351]

Think back to his fictional trilogy: the Dark Lord Sauron had enslaved the people of Middle Earth through the rings of power. Could the golden rings, forged in the fires of Mount Doom, be symbolic of central banks and their power to convince entire nations to borrow their money into existence? With their unlimited power of money creation out of debt, they are able to control the mass media and spellbind the public with false solutions and rabbit trails. Tolkien then offered his surprising solutions:

> There should only be one source of money: one fountainhead from which flows the nation's blood to vitalise commerce and industry, ensure economic equity and justice and safeguard the welfare of the people... In other words, it has always been and still is our contention that the prerogative of creating and issuing the money of the nation should be restored to the State.[352]

Germany

The Monetary Reform Movement is literally springing up all around the world. Here is a brand new site from Germany called *Monetative*. At this

---

[351] *Condour* magazine, 13 July 1956, page 12, as quoted in *The Barnes Review.org*, Volume X, Number 5 – September/October 2004.
[352] Ibid.

writing, January 2011, it only has one page in English, but it is right on target. We reprint it in full because it is so interesting:

Taking Money Creation back into Public Hands

The financial crises of the recent past are rooted in the monetary system as it stands today. This system creates excessive credit that inevitably feeds speculative bubbles, asset and consumer price inflation, and results in over-indebtedness. In order to work properly, the economy needs to rely on a stable and just monetary system.

That is why we call for:

1. The full re-establishment of the public prerogative of creating money
2. An end to the creation of money by means of commercial bank credit
3. Spending new money into circulation debt-free through public expenditure.

Money makes the world go round. Who makes the money go round?

Everybody uses money as though it were self-evident. But the actual functioning of the monetary system remains just as nebulous as its characterisation as "fractional reserve system" or "multiple credit creation". This works to the benefit of the banks. They have in effect usurped the prerogative to create money by crediting 80-95% of the means of payment into circulation in the form of demand deposits on current accounts.

An increasing part of the money supply has of late fueled mere financial transactions that had no benefit for the real economy, but have caused much real damage to it. The barely restrained creation of credit drives business cycles and the stocks and securities markets into irrational exuberance - wildly overshooting in boom periods, while resulting in over-indebtedness and severe undersupply of money in ensuing crises. If banks themselves go bust, their customers' deposits and savings are at risk. If the state then intervenes to bail out the banks and vouch for deposits, governments in effect privatize banking profits, while passing the losses on to the public.

Banks act as individual companies. They are duty bound neither to macro-economic goals nor to the common interest. Leaving to them the weighty prerogative of creating the official means of payment is untenable. Money and the monetary order represent concerns of constitutional importance.

Nationalization of money, not of banking

All money should exclusively be created by an independent public authority. In the European Monetary Union this role falls to the European Central Bank and its national member bodies. They ought to be seen as the fourth power in the state: the **monetary power**, to complement the legislative, executive and judicial powers. As with the latter, the monetary power must be independent and answerable only to the law - independent from governments' and parliaments' appetite for money as well as from self-serving interests of the financial sector and other industries. In such a monetary regime, local complementary currencies and cooperative clearing systems can co-exist.

The monetary reform envisaged here is simple: Bank-money on account (today's demand deposits) would be declared to be legal tender just like coins and banknotes. The system of public central banks - the monetary power - would exclusively be authorized to create these official means of payment and regulate the quantity thereof. Money on account would thus be nationalized in the same way as banknotes were nationalized over a hundred years ago. At that time, privately issued banknotes were phased out in favor of public banknotes issued by the central bank. Today the crux of the matter is to replace the debt-laden, unstable and unsafe bank-created demand deposits by a public money base which is free of debt and interest. Today's partially nationalized money base (5-15% coins and banknotes) would fully be nationalized, not however the banks.

Government and parliament would have no say in the central bank's independent decisions on how much money it deems necessary. The discretionary additions to the money supply would be transferred free of interest from the central bank to the government that spends it into circulation under normal budgetary procedures. In recent years this has involved 200-350 billion euros p.a. within the European Monetary Union. This represented an overshooting supply, but even less money still represents very much money foregone to the public purse.

Banks and financial markets should be able to freely pursue all but one of their current activities: that of creating money by crediting it out of thin air into customers' current accounts. Banks would have to operate purely within the means which they have obtained as earnings or taken up at the money market or from their customers. Banks would hold that money in cash or non-cash in their account with the central bank.

Putting an end to the banks' ability to create demand deposits can be achieved in a technically rather simple and smooth way: Customers' current accounts would be taken off the banks' balance sheet and run separately in their own right.

Making money creation fit the public interest

Such a reform would bring about five big advantages. First, money on account could no longer disappear and would thus be safe. If banks failed there would be no reason for a run on those banks, and cashless money transfer would not be in jeopardy. Governments and the public would thus no longer be at the mercy of the banks' survival as is the case today.

Second, bounds would be set on the banks' procyclical over-and undershooting of the money supply. Before running into a stage of 'irrational exuberance' markets would run short of fuel in the form of all too cheaply available credit. Money flows would be steadier, and real and financial business cycles more moderate.

Third, the central bank would have full control of the quantity of money and would thus be able to prevent inflation by managing the money supply in accordance with real economic potentials - unlike today's credit creation by the banks which is prone to asset

Chapter 33: International Solutions 313

and consumer price inflation or to overt demonetization in times of economic stress.

Fourth, seigniorage would fully benefit the public purse and no longer be an undeserved banking extra profit. A non inflation-accelerating growth rate of the money supply is in line with the expectable growth rate of the real economy. By today's standards 1-2 per cent of GDP growth in the European Monetary Union (about 9.100 billion euros in 2008) involves an additional money supply, and thus seigniorage, of about 90-180 billion euros. This amounts to about 2-4 per cent of the total budget of EMU member states.

Fifth, and of particular importance today, governments would have the one-time chance of reducing public debt by half in a no-noise no-pain transition to the new system. The reason is that the reform substitutes central bank money on current accounts for banks' demand deposits. Most of the replacement would happen within a time span of about three to five years as old bank credits are paid back and replaced by new loans fully made out in central bank money. The necessary means for this one-time substitution can originally also be brought into circulation by way of transfer from central bank to government. Governments in turn can use the corresponding amounts of one-off transition seigniorage to redeem public debt. Demand deposits within the EMU amounted to 3.200 billion euros in 2008, in fact half of total public debt at about 6.000 billion euros.

Monetary business-as-usual is no longer acceptable. Ever more regulation and bureaucracy is not desirable either. What we now need is: replacement of bank-created demand deposits by central bank money, in finally establishing public central banks as the independent fourth power, the monetary power.

Here is their website, however, it is mostly in German:

URL: 7.tv/6b44

HyperScan UPDATES:

Check back often for updates to German monetary reform developments:

URL: 7.tv/6a60

Sweden

1789 - Sweden Tries to Escape the Debt Money System

Two years after the U.S. Constitution was signed, debt free money was tried in Sweden in 1789 – but with tragic results. To pursue a war with Russia, King Gustaf III persuaded the Swedish Parliament to print debt free money called Riksgalds. This was very costly to the bankers. Sweden had learned the secret of simply printing its own money without debt.

In 1792, only 3 years into the experiment, King Gustaf III was assassinated by moneylender Jacob Johan Ankarstrom. As is frequently the case in time of war, too many Riksgalds were printed. The quantity was not controlled. A nation will sacrifice everything for survival during time of war. So inflation ruined the debt free money experiment in

Sweden by 1834, just as it had a few years earlier during the American Revolution, again, because the quantity was not controlled.

URL: 7.tv/9a4e

HyperScan UPDATES:

Check back often for updates to Swedish monetary reform developments:

URL: 7.tv/09d1

JAK Bank

The most interesting of the Swedish experiments is called JAK Members Bank or JAK Medlemsbank. The JAK Bank is a cooperative, member-owned financial institution based in Skövde, Sweden. As of 2008, the bank had a membership of approximately 35,000.

JAK does not charge or pay interest on its loans, a principle it shares with Islamic banking. All its loans are financed solely by member savings. As of 2008, members saved 97 million Euros, of which 86 million are given as loans to other members. Administrative and developmental costs are paid for by membership and loan fees.

According to the JAK philosophy, economic instability is a result of the taking of interest. JAK operates under the following premises:

- The taking of interest is inimical to a stable economy

- Interest causes unemployment, inflation, and environmental destruction
- Interest moves money from the poor to the rich
- Interest favors projects which tend to yield high profits in the short-term, thereby creating instability.

Their website explains further:

> The ultimate goal of JAK is to abolish interest as an economic instrument and to replace it with instruments that are in the public interest.
>
> We regard receiving money in exchange for labour as legitimate; however we do not consider it legitimate to earn money simply with money. In our opinion it is unethical to lend money against interest.
>
> The use of interest also has negative effects on society. It shows up in the prices of services and goods when producers add to their prices to cover their cost of interest on loans. In an interest economy money is moved from those who have less to those who have more and thereby assets are concentrated in the hands of the few. Finally, since our modern monetary systems are debt-based and practically all money is debt that has to be repaid with interest, we have a money stock that is always growing exponentially. Anything that grows exponentially will eventually reach a breaking point. Today we have exponential growth in both real and financial assets including money.

JAK banking is made possible by a saving points system: members accumulate saving points during saving periods, they use saving points asking for a loan. The main idea is that one is allowed to take a loan for himself in the same measure he allows other people to have loans, saving into his account. For this reason (asking for a loan), earned saving points must be equal to spent saving points to ensure sustainability. If a member is borrowing more saving points than he has, he is obliged to continue accumulating so-called "*aftersavings*" during repayment period. "Aftersavings" are a fixed quota of money that one must save *after* his loan was given, so they can continue earning saving points. This way, at the end of the repayment period, earned saving points will be equal to spent saving points, and at that time he will be able to have back all his aftersavings.

JAK is growing carefully.

Chapter 33: International Solutions

We accept deposits and we give loans in Swedish Crowns (SEK). We give loans on mortgage or with personal guarantees but the property or the guarantor has to be Swedish. Hence there are few foreigners among our members.

There is growing interest in the JAK system and we do take part in international discussions on interest-free banking. However we are not seeking partners for an international expansion of JAK yet we will do what we can, with our limited resources, to convey our knowledge and experiences to parties interested in similar systems in their own countries.

JAK has been operating an interest-free savings and loan system since 1970. A bank license was obtained in 1997 ... our growth is 5 percent per year. Members' deposits finance all loans. The members have saved a total sum of € 97 million and have borrowed € 86 million. (2008) Annual membership fees and loan fees (equals approximately 2.5 % effective rate of interest) cover administration and development costs.

In combination with the interest-free savings account we have two products. Both are interest-free:

1. The (Original) Balanced Savings Loan (best suited for individuals).
2. The (New) Support Savings & Loan Instrument (for small companies and associations).

To see JAK's website:

URL: 7.tv/2bf5

Islamic Banking

Also known as participant banking, Islamic banking refers to a system of banking or banking activity that is consistent with the principles of Islamic law, which prohibits the payment or acceptance of interest fees for loans of money (Riba, usury) Islamic banking also prohibits investing in businesses that provide goods or services considered contrary to its principles.

Modern Islamic banking

Interest-free banking seems to be of very recent origin. The first modern experiment with Islamic banking was undertaken in Egypt under cover without projecting an Islamic image—for fear of being seen as a manifestation of Islamic fundamentalism. The pioneering effort, led by Ahmad Elnaggar, took the form of a savings bank based on profit sharing in the Egyptian town of Mit Ghamr in 1963. This experiment lasted until 1967, by which time there were nine such banks in country.

In 1972, the Mit Ghamr Savings project became part of Nasr Social Bank that, currently, is still in business in Egypt. The first modern commercial Islamic bank, Dubai Islamic Bank, opened its doors in 1975. In the early years, the products offered were basic and strongly founded on conventional banking products, but in the last few years the industry is starting to see strong development in new products and services.

Islamic Banking is growing at a rate of 10-15% per year. Islamic banks have more than 300 institutions spread over 51 countries, including the United States through companies such as the Michigan-based University Bank. It is estimated that Islamic banking has assets of over $822 billion worldwide, according to *The Economist*. This represents approximately 0.5% of total world estimated assets as of 2005. According to CIMB Group Holdings, Islamic finance is the fastest-growing segment of the global financial system. The Banker published its latest authoritative list of the Top 500 Islamic Finance Institutions, with Iran topping the list. Seven out of ten top Islamic banks in the world are Iranian according to the list.

The Vatican has put forward the idea that "the principles of Islamic finance may represent a possible cure for ailing markets."[353]

HyperScan UPDATES:

Check back often for updates to Islamic banking developments:

---

[353] http://en.wikipedia.org/wiki/Islamic_banking , retrieved Jan. 19, 2011

URL: 7.tv/03aa

Public Banking in India

Public banking is catching on around the world. At the peak of the 2008-banking crisis, India's Congress president, Sonia Gandhi, came out swinging in support of public banking.

Gandhi carries the most famous name in India. She is the Italian-born daughter-in-law of the late Prime Minister of India, Mrs. Indira Gandhi. After her husband Rajiv Gandhi's assassination in 1991, she was invited by the Indian Congress Party to take over the Congress, but she refused and publicly stayed away from politics amidst constant prodding by the Congress. She finally agreed to join politics in 1997 and in 1998; she was elected as the leader of the Congress. Since then, she has been the President of the Indian National Congress Party, becoming the longest serving President in September 2010. In September 2010, on being re-elected for the fourth time, she became the longest serving president in the 125-year history of the Congress party.

Gandhi was named the third most powerful woman in the world by *Forbes* magazine in the year 2004, and was ranked 6th in 2007. In 2010, Gandhi ranked as the ninth most powerful person on the planet by *Forbes Magazine*.[354]

In late 2008, Gandhi told the Hindustan Times Leadership Summit that her party had insulated India's poor from becoming "victims of the unchecked greed of bankers and businessmen." Elaborating, she said:

> Let me take you back to Indira Gandhi's bank nationalisation of 40 years ago. Every passing day bears out the wisdom of that decision. Public sector

---

[354] http://en.wikipedia.org/wiki/Sonia_Gandhi

financial institutions have given our economy the stability and resilience we are now witnessing in the face of the economic slowdown.[355]

This could be dismissed as political rhetoric, but just a few days later, the Indian Finance Minister, C.P. Chandrasekhar shocked the nation by supporting the concept of pubic banking as well.

> Public ownership of banks, besides preventing periodic economic crises, can subordinate the profit motive to social objectives and fashion a system of inclusive finance.[356]

He went on to say that India's public sector banks were strong pillars in the world's banking industry. As one report explained it:

> Three factors may have contributed to this change of opinion. First, the evidence that the managers of private banks pursuing profits had dropped all diligence and made decisions that have threatened and are still threatening the viability of leading banks in the developed capitalist countries. These include banks that the advocates of financial liberalisation and privatisation upheld as models of modern banking.
>
> Second, the recognition that the only way in which the losses made by these banks could be socialised and their viability ensured was for the government to invest in their shares so as to recapitalise them. Across the world, the response to the financial crisis has shifted out of mere measures to inject liquidity into the system to backdoor nationalisation of these banks so as to save them from bankruptcy and to ensure that they keep lending.
>
> Finally, the evidence that on an average, the public sector banks in India have weathered the financial storm much better than the private banks, including some that had been celebrated as the post-liberalisation icons of innovative banking. However, if the argument stops here, the explicit or implicit defence of nationalisation and support for public banking can only be partial and circumstantial.

---

[355] http://www.stwr.org/india-china-asia/the-importance-of-public-banking.html
[356] http://www.stwr.org/india-china-asia/the-importance-of-public-banking.html

Chapter 33: International Solutions

The report can be read in its entirety at:

URL: 7.tv/2c9e

HyperScan UPDATES:

Check back often for updates to Indian banking developments:

URL: 7.tv/5d8c

Chapter 34 – Economic Disinformation

By Nathan Martin

Do not put your faith in what statistics say until you have carefully considered what they do not say.   ~William W. Watt

By now you are quite aware that the "Federal Reserve Bank" is not "Federal," nor do they hold reserves, and not even are they a bank. The disinformation begins there and reaches out like tentacles from a metastasizing cancer to spread into most government statistics, our education system and business schools, our media, and even our history books.

The disinformation is pervasive; it causes massive misallocation of human and natural resources while working to congregate wealth into the hands of those who control the production of money – private banks. They need apparent growth (inflation) to keep their game going, without it the Ponzi of ever-increasing sums (and profit) collapses into deflation.

On the national level, all deficits add to the national debt that is financed through the Treasury and ultimately owned as an asset by the private banks in the form of U.S. Treasury Notes and Bonds. In this way the people are effectively charged interest payable to those banks via income taxes. This dynamic simply does not have to work in that manner, in effect it causes the people to pay for the use of their own money system – a system that belongs to them via Congress and not to the private banks.

Thus, the population is placed into a false box in which the solution to debt is either more debt, which is ridiculous of course, or into "austerity" – that is higher taxes and less spending. The media constantly reverberates this message – these are the only two alternatives. Reality and the right answers, of course, are only found well outside of that two-dimensional illusion.

But before any solution stands a chance of working over long periods of time, first we must be able to be honest with ourselves in

Chapter 34: Economic Disinformation

understanding the current system and we must be able to accurately measure what's really happening in the monetary system and then in our economy. We are currently living a mass-delusion created by a fog of economic disinformation.

Math is not pliable to disinformation. Inflation will absolutely destroy any currency given enough time. What sounds mundane in the short term, say 3%, will literally make a currency worthless in just a few short decades. Why would any country implement a monetary system that depends on inflation, or said another way, why would one target inflation when that inflation *will most certainly* lead to the eventual demise of that currency?

That hardly seems sane... unless you are the one who produces the money and profits from it! Thus it is vital to look through the lens of those who control the <u>quantity</u> of money when trying to make sense of the economy.

As Bill Still has repeatedly stated, WHO controls the quantity of money is far more important than WHAT backs it! Why? Because when you control the nation's medium of exchange, you ultimately end up controlling its laws, aka "The Golden Rule." This is why *who* produces the money within the economy is so vitally important to politics, and by extension world events.

Let me make that last point clear. There is a direct chain that leads from the production of money to world events! Follow the money and the production thereof. This is true because money is ultimately about *control*. He who produces the money is in *control*. Let the private bankers produce the money, they are in control, you just surrendered your sovereignty! Take loans from the IMF, surrender your sovereignty! Allow your nation to become addicted to borrowing money from China, surrender your sovereignty!

That money can be backed by seashells, gold, silver, paper, or whatever... ultimately the quantity of money can always be manipulated by those who produce it! Once the *perception* becomes pervasive that the quantity of money is out of control, and then the end of the current money system is at hand.

Thus I would propose that any system that targets positive price inflation is not sane or rational in the sense that it serves the people over the long term. There is only one price inflation target that's mathematically sustainable, and that is ZERO percent inflation.

Since there is smaller profit involved in producing a non-inflating currency, don't look for private entities to back this rational inflation target any time soon. Thus the production of money can only be rational when it is in the hands of the people who rightly own it. And who are the people's representatives? Congress – and they too must respect the math or the system will ultimately fail. Not accepting the reality of the math leads to disinformation, fuzzy thinking, people enriching themselves by cheating on the public trust and ignorance, and problems that never seem go away.

The Bad Math of Debt

Nearly all money produced today comes into existence as somebody's debt. The myth is that the government currently "prints" money. They do not, and have not for quite some time. Private banks and other quasi-financial institutions are the ones who produce most of the money. It didn't used to be this way, but today it is a fact. Private institutions make the money. They hold the debt as an asset and they collect interest on it.

This is quite different from *sovereign* money which is created when a nation produces its own money without debt.

When a nation first transitions from a sovereign money system into a debt money system, adding more credit money works to stimulate the economy as the total supply of sovereign and credit money expand, creating new infrastructure and new industry. The "Keynesian" model is to add more credit money to the economic dips in order to level things out and to spur the economy. This works in an immature economy where the ratio of credit dollars to sovereign dollars is low.

Chapter 34: Economic Disinformation

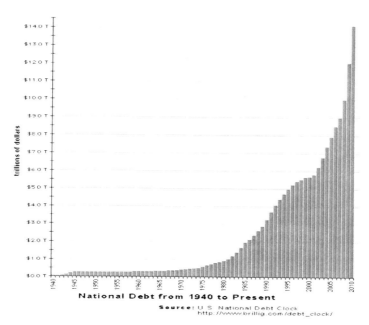

National Debt from 1940 to Present
Source: U.S. National Debt Clock
http://www.brillig.com/debt_clock/

Then the math of debt – or interest on the debt -- begins to catch up as credit money begins to outstrip sovereign money. The problem with debt is that it requires continuous *income* to service it. Once a nation's money becomes 100% credit, as is the case in the United States and throughout much of the globe now, then scarcity is assured as all that money carries interest. The interest works to consolidate the money into the hands of those producing the debt.

For everybody else, they eventually enter a condition that I term *"Debt Saturation."* That is the point at which current income can no longer service more debt. If more debt is added to a debt-saturated situation, then something *must* mathematically give way.

The United States as a whole reached the debt-saturated condition quite some time ago. Once reached, adding more debt -- as we are massively attempting to do -- no longer results in real economic expansion. Instead it results in real economic contraction, the exact opposite of what worked before! Let me make that clear, attempting to stimulate a debt saturated economy with more debt will only lead to *real* economic contraction and *higher* levels of structural unemployment!

But remember WHO produces the money! In order for *their* profits to grow, they must produce ever-increasing sums of debt, such that today the acknowledged national debt of the United States exceeds $14 Trillion!

If only it were that good in reality! But sadly it's not – there is much disinformation and fuzzy thinking here.

Even if we give this number the benefit of naively believing that's the extent of it, it is still completely unworkable math. Even the mainstream media, who is complicit in creating and disseminating economic disinformation, is forced to concede that the numbers are completely unworkable. Just taken at face value, the current advertised national debt of $14 trillion+ equals more than $45,000 of debt for every man, woman, and child in the United States (current population approximately 310 million). My family of four would thus be responsible for more than $180,000 just in our share of national debt!

Oh, but if only it were that bad! Not even close!

The never-mentioned truth is that not only are our families responsible for the national debt, but they are also the same people responsible for our state's debts, our county's debts, our city's debts, our personal debts, and ultimately because we're the end-use consumers, we're also responsible for corporate debts! Whew, it all adds up to sums so vast that there is absolutely no possible way the debt can ever be repaid. In fact, it really can't even be paid down without dramatically shrinking economic activity because to reduce the debt is to reduce the money. Math is math... it cannot be fooled. It can be ignored for a while, and that's exactly how we've been handling it so far.

Lies, Damn Lies, and Statistics

"There are three kinds of lies: lies, damned lies, and statistics."

- Mark Twain, autobiography, 1904

Another way that logic is turned on its head is when the bankers, politicians, and economists (who are trained in schools financed by

Chapter 34: Economic Disinformation

bankers), compare GDP (Gross Domestic Product) to our nation's debt! What do the two have to do with one another? Very little!

What's far more important is our nation's debt compared to our nation's income. After all, it requires income to service debts, not some trumped up measurement of production. Even using our crooked $14 Trillion current debt number, it is 583% of our nation's $2.4 trillion annual income:

Why do I say that number is crooked? For starters our government refuses to use GAAP accounting like they demand of companies within the United States. This means that we are failing to acknowledge accounts payables – future obligations and other promises that are not currently on the books, that's why it's called the "current" account deficit. Adding future obligations catapults the $14 Trillion total into the $60 Trillion (conservative figure) to $100 Trillion + range ($322,000+ per person, $1.3 million for a family of four).

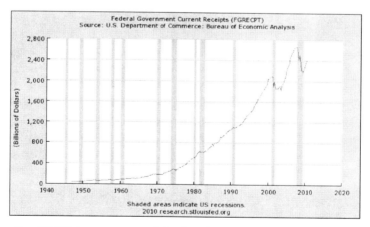

Additionally, GDP is *supposed to be* the measurement of goods and services produced in this country. This figure is VASTLY overstated for two primary reasons – this makes our debt condition all the more ominous:

1. Credit money production and derivatives, aka financial engineering, should be subtracted from GDP as creating a debt dollar only pulls future demand forward into the here and now and thus creates a future obligation. This is like taking a cash advance on a credit card and

counting it towards your personal income! It's not income, it's a loan! This single effect has masked the fact that the United State's *real* output of goods and services has not actually increased in the past decade at all. This overestimates the value of our GDP by roughly 30% to 40%.

2. Our GDP is measured in dollars and not in actual goods or services. Thus if the value of the dollar falls, it will appear that more goods and services are being created than actually are (apparent growth). For example, if the value of the dollar falls 5% in real terms, but GDP supposedly increases 3%, then real growth is actually -2%. The BEA (Bureau of Economic Analysis) and BLS (Bureau of Labor Statistics) calculate supposed inflation and then use a "deflator" to adjust the GDP number, but due to errors in the way they calculate those numbers, the net effect is to understate inflation and that overstates GDP.

The net effect of these errors is that you are being fed disinformation about the state of our economy, and about our ability to service our debts. Our nation is functionally insolvent as are large private banks.

The lie in this regard is that we are a sovereign nation and can simply print money and thus make it easier to pay back our debts and future obligation. But once debt saturation is reached and interest rates are at zero, then the only way left to cause apparent growth is to either use fraudulent accounting, or to print money. We are doing both, and both will lead to the eventual loss of confidence that will end the charade that the quantity of money being produced is under control – it is not.

Imagine that you are the largest lender to a nation. You worked hard for the money that you lent them. But that nation continues to spend money they don't have and begin to take the easy way out by printing up more money. This action devalues the money that they are paying you back with, and thus in effect they are stealing from you! Will you continue to lend your hard earned money to such a nation? Certainly not forever, and thus there are limits. History has proven these limits time and time again, yet the disinformation is overpowering.

Chapter 34: Economic Disinformation

Growth vs. Inflation

Growth and inflation are two completely different things, but the terms are often confused for one another. This is a large part of the disinformation that is laced throughout economic statistics. Often inflation is used to sell the idea that growth is occurring when in fact it is not.

A bowling ball manufacturer, for example, may build and sell 10,000 balls in one year, selling each for $80, and thus creating $800,000 in revenue. The next year they do not report the number of balls produced, but claim that sales rose to $990,000. Congratulations! If this is the only data one has, a person may be forced to conclude that they are growing their business, and one would have to conclude that demand is strong! But when given the fact that they actually produced only 9,000 bowling balls, but sold them for $110 each, then it becomes apparent that they made and sold 10% fewer products! While the company can report sales grew by $190,000 or 23%, *real* production declined! The conclusion here is different, now it could be that demand is super strong and they were setting a higher price point, OR monetary inflation is quite high. Once you have this *real* quantity information then it's easy to tell that what rose was the quantity of money, and not the quantity of product. The quantity of money in the transaction may have risen, but fewer workers will be needed with the *real* quantity of items being produced in decline.

Retail Sales Numbers

The problem is even more severe when Retail Sales are reported. These are also overstated as they are measured and expressed in dollars that are being devalued. Additionally, Retail Sales are only reported for stores open one year or longer, thus capturing only sales of stores that are open – and relatively successful. This instills substitution bias because sales at stores that have closed in the past year are not considered! This error gets larger as more stores close.

The biggest and most pervasive errors are in the way our government reports inflation data. They use "hedonistic adjustments" and a myriad of other faulty methods to make inflation appear smaller than it actually is. These errors are now famous so I won't describe them all except to say that they use these numbers to artificially hold down things like annual Social Security paycheck adjustments. And, because this inflation data is bad, almost all other data is bad too when corrections for inflation are attempted to make them "real."

Many economic data sets use "real" data. They are actually not real. This inflation adjustment error ripples throughout the data sets and winds up painting a completely false picture. Producing good retail sales numbers would be very easy with today's technology, yet we don't do it because those financing it all can't stand the truth. And everything today is marketing and perception driven. The fear is that if perceptions of weakness are evident then it will lead to more weakness. But eventually the math expresses itself, it cannot be hidden forever.

Are economic statistic errors intentional? You bet they are. They are getting worse and worse over time as one lie is placed upon the former. Some may be "adjusted" with the best of intentions by the people doing the adjusting, but this simply brings in another type of bias, that is the optimism bias. People simply don't like to report or promote bad news.

But when money interests get involved, look out!

Pending Home Sales Numbers

Organizations like the MBA (Mortgage Banker's Association) report statistics for their own economic segments. In the case of the MBA, they report Pending Home Sales and Refinance activity on a weekly basis. They are now famous hypocrites for chastising homeowners who walk away from their homes (thus returning the collateral to the bank) while they were simultaneously doing exactly that with their own corporate headquarters.

When the data starts looking bad, as it did for home sales, private organizations like the MBA begin to clam up and start obscuring the data, making it hard to examine and compare with past figures. This is disinformation step number one – a lack of transparency. The "Fed" has never been transparent and fights every attempt to force it, the latest being the "Audit the Fed" bill sponsored by Congressman Ron Paul. The "Fed" won't allow itself to be audited because it would make the fraud absolutely apparent.

Unemployment Numbers

Our unemployment numbers are also another piece of gross disinformation. The BLS induces huge errors into these reports with massive seasonal adjustments and by using phony models such as their small business "Birth/Death" model. Additionally, they also use old and outdated technology to gather information (a phone survey) when technology exists to get a very timely and accurate view. Employers are required to provide payroll information directly and thus real information could be easily compiled and reported; yet it is not.

And since so many private companies create our money, and then it is further leveraged and confused with derivatives, we have completely lost touch of our ability to even know what the total quantity of money is! Don't fall for the disinformation; "Fed" reported money aggregates are not even close to reality! What little they actually do track and report is dwarfed by what they fail to track and report, namely the derivatives within the "shadow banking industry." Truly, there is no agency that is privy to the actual total quantity of money within the system and throughout the globe. They want it that way, the more you are kept in the dark, and the easier it is for them to do as they please.

An entire book filled with the specifics of bad economic data could be written, I observe and report on it every single day. The information is there for those with the willingness and courage to look.

So, you have to ask yourself why is the data slanted, and almost always the slanting is in the direction that makes the economy look more healthy than it actually is? The answer, I believe, is readily apparent when you simply follow the trail of money back to *who* profits from it, and *who* produces the money.

Misallocation and then Turmoil

This pervasive economic disinformation leads to tremendous misallocations of resources, both human and capital. The housing bubble is an excellent example of that, causing people and resources to simply produce far more than was needed. When we are producing things we don't really need, we need to be asking ourselves what it is we're not producing but should be – like energy infrastructure.

And to keep the illusion going, interest rates were lowered to zero and kept there. Then comes the outright money printing disguised in the form of "Quantitative Easing" – which is simply more blatant disinformation by the same private organization which refers to itself as the "Fed." Their lie is that money printing in this manner is benign. It is not, as is readily apparent by the doubling of food commodity prices in the six months from July 2010 to January 2011 alone.

Real people throughout the world are starving due to these actions, yet our government fails to acknowledge this, much less take action to prevent it. People who live in poor regions are affected to a much greater degree than those who are wealthier as a much larger percentage of their income goes to pay for food. For example, approximately 40% of the average income is needed just to buy food for the average income earner in China. Imagine the effects on their lives if the cost of food doubles for them. In the United States a much smaller percentage of income goes to food, and thus we are affected to a much smaller degree. Still, those on the margins are greatly affected, a travesty of greed that has resulted in the breakdown of the rule of law.

The saying is that "desperate people do desperate things." In this manner then, the undertow of economic misallocation leads to what I term "other events." Hunger and discontent can lead to violence, revolution, and war. We are seeing these "other events" play out on the world stage now, yet few can see the chain of events leading from the "Fed's" economic and money disinformation directly to these tragedies.

Chapter 34: Economic Disinformation

Transparency, Checks & Balances are Paramount

How to stop and to prevent the spread of economic disinformation? Unfortunately it probably won't change until we change WHO produces and controls the quantity of money. However, if we look forward to the day that change does occur, then we need to be ready to create a system that is sustainable in the very long term.

Money absolutely corrupts. This makes it essential that those disseminating important economic data be neutral in regards to financial incentive. The Mortgage Banker's Association, for example, should not be the ones reporting mortgage information to the public and to investors! The government agencies responsible for reporting statistics should not be under the influence of private corporations, nor should they be beholden to politicians whose careers are dependent on winning votes (often by showering money upon their constituents). Thus, agencies that report economic statistics should be separated as much as possible from those money driven influences.

This could be accomplished by replacing the current alphabet soup of agencies with one independent agency responsible solely for the collection and dissemination of economic data.

Such an agency would be tasked with the following:

1. Compile and track all data necessary to monitor and to adjust the economy. This panel must be completely independent and without influence from all other agencies. Workers within this agency should not come from or leave to go to work within corporations who may benefit from this agency's work for a specified time both before and after employment.
2. Complete transparency is required, ALL data is made available to the public, free of charge.
3. Raw data should be made available as soon as it's available to them, no individual, firm, or politician should have access to the data before the public.
4. Statistics should be separated and reported in three categories:
    a. Raw data.

Chapter 34: Economic Disinformation

    b. Timeless data – methods should be developed to report data in such a manner that the methods of calculation can be repeated and reported consistently over time, thus ensuring that future generations can compare apples to apples.
    c. Modern data – these are data that can be improved and changed over time. However, all such changes shall be completely transparent and shall always be presented with the raw data and with access to the way in which the statistic is compiled and calculated.

But this alone is not enough. The special interests that produce the money also control our education system and our media. They also actively work to prevent good and honest scientific research in the field of economics. Again, keeping people in the dark is profitable for them. This is why the field of economics seems more like voodoo than science.

We fail to track and monitor the economy properly, we fail to do meaningful research, and then we anoint a supposed "expert" to act as God at the head of the "Fed" who is supposedly "independent." This is laughably archaic, intentionally so, and against the wishes of our nation's founders who understood the importance for checks and balances.

We should be doing meaningful research within the economy and we should be attempting to model it and the associated human behavior. We should be striving to create controls to keep the quantity of money under control – this is not impossible. What is impossible is expecting gold backing or private individuals to keep the quantity of money under control on their own. There must be transparency coupled to checks and balances if we wish to be truly prosperous over the long haul.

Nathan Martin runs the internationally recognized Economic Edge Blog at www.economicedge.blogspot.com. A former Air Force/ commercial airline pilot with 26 years of flight experience, he is a market expert with more than two decades of market experience, a financial consultant, business owner, and political activist. Nathan is the author of "Flight to Financial Freedom," "Freedom's Vision," and the www.SwarmUSA.com activists website.

Chapter 34: Economic Disinformation

HyperScan UPDATES:

Check back often for updates from Nathan Martin:

URL: 7.tv/2a18

Chapter 35 - Bonus Videos Online

I have produced a series of reports online for your viewing pleasure called *Still Reports*. As of this date, there are 17 of them.

To view the *Still Reports*, and other videos I have posted to my You Tube channel, simply scan here:

URL: 7.tv/0eec

Once you have reached the site, you may scroll down to select from the following videos (*Still Reports* are abbreviated with an "SR" notation):

SR1: Oct. 27, 2009: The State Bank option is discussed, specifically the State Bank of North Dakota as well as similar attempts in Florida and Virginia.

SR2: Nov. 1, 2009: The evidence is piling up that the coming commercial real estate crash will be an unwelcomed post-Christmas "gift" for America, which may have just as much impact as the residential real estate crash did.

SR3: Nov. 8, 2009: Unemployment hit 10.2% here in the U.S. last week, but there is a way to fix this -- only ONE way. This can work for any nation on earth.

SR4: Nov. 16, 2009: J.P Morgan Chase announced last week that it is going to hire 1200 new mortgage brokers to dish out the loans. But just who is this really helping? Could there be some similarities between today's situation and a situation J.P. Morgan found himself in during the 1907 crash?

SR5: Nov. 21, 2009: "The Secret of Oz" has been banned off Amazon.com.

Chapter 35: Bonus Videos Online

SR6: Nov. 22, 2009: Don't be fooled; this economy is going off a cliff. Even one of the biggest banks in Europe says a catastrophic world depression could hit within a couple of years.

SR7: Dec. 12, 2009: Fed Chief, Ben Bernenke's warning sounds eerily similar to that delivered by Nicholas Biddle in 1834 when President Jackson threatened to take back the power over the QUANTITY of the nation's money. Also, top market watchers see patterns in the market that are similar to those that created the market crash in the early 1930s. A big thank you to all those who flooded Amazon.com with complaints. "The Secret of Oz" is selling there once again.

SR8: Dec. 31, 2009: Part 1 of Why Gold Money Won't Work. Comments by Sec. of Treasury Geithner, President Obama, and Peter Schiff.

SR9: Jan. 1, 2010: The Fort Knox Gold Scandal.

SR10: Jan. 9, 2010: Tally Sticks - the solution to the Quantity of Money problem.

SR11: Feb. 14, 2010: Why government is good.

SR12: March 15, 2010: From the big TVA dam at Muscle Shoals, Alabama, we praise or critique economic utterances by Charles Krauthammer, Barack Obama, David Horowitz, John Stossel, Ron Paul, Ludwig von Mises, Lewis Lehrman, Dick Morris and Glenn Beck.

SR13: March 31, 2010: President Obama cancelled the NASA manned space flight program. But the cost of resurrecting manned space flight is small compared with the hundreds of billions we are just giving away and will kill American space exploration leadership forever and cede it to the Chinese.

SR14: June 15, 2010: Sweden's fight for sustainable banking.

SR15: June 27, 2010: Iceland's situation is dire, but the people of Iceland are tired of the banker's tricks. They are waking up to the fact that there is another way to run a country other than perpetual debt.

SR16: July 6, 2010: Karl Denninger, author of Market Ticker and winner of the 2008 Reed Irvine Accuracy in Media Award explains the roots of the current crisis and why real economic growth is impossible.

He explains why the stock market rebounded in 2009 and why that can't continue. He explains what needs to be done with the banks and predicts that all the big banks will fail.

SR16-2: July 14, 2010: Karl Denninger predicts the collapse of the Euro, further collapse of U.S. housing prices, and the DOW. He says Social Security and Medicare could collapse, but there is still time to stop it. Is a return to gold money the answer? Why does Ron Paul stick to gold backed money? When will the next crash come?

The Secret of Oz

As an additional feature of this book, I am providing you with a HyperScan code that will allow you to view my recent documentary film, "The Secret of Oz."

URL: 7.tv/1dbd

The film has also been translated into many languages, including Spanish, Serbian, Portuguese, and German. Versions in French, Swedish, Icelandic, and Italian are forthcoming as well.

HyperScan UPDATES:

Check back often for general updates to this book, new chapters, and important video updates on national and world events:

URL: 7.tv/5a70

Appendix – More about HyperScan®

WHAT MAKES HYPERSCAN DIFFERENT THAN OTHER QR CODES?

QR codes can provide mystery, magic, and, unfortunately, mayhem. Because generic QR codes might be generated by unknown parties, and point to unrecognizable websites (as QR codes are not readable by the human eye), there can be a risk that a generic QR code might direct your mobile device to an inappropriate web site, or one that might contain malicious code.

HyperScan QR codes were created to take your security and privacy into consideration, while still being "scannable" by most QR readers. HyperScan codes have 5 levels of security built-in, to provide a safer scanning experience:

1) Authentic HyperScan QR codes can only be acquired directly through HyperScan, LLC. Each licensed purchaser of HyperScan QR codes is registered with HyperScan, and agrees to adhere to strict guidelines as to the type of sites to which HyperScan codes can be directed. HyperScan undertakes proprietary methods to increase the likelihood that "redirects" are secure.

2) Each HyperScan QR code incorporates our trademarked design, and features the "HyperScanIt™" logo.

3) Each HyperScan QR code features a security HyperText™ code on the lower right hand corner. Other than our corporate logo, if a HyperScan QR code, in public use, does NOT feature the HyperText code, then it is not authentic; do not HyperScan it.

4) Each HyperScan QR code "resolves" to the shortest URL in the world – 7.TV. If your QR scanner, after scanning a HyperScan code, displays a web site other than 7.TV, do not proceed, as it is not authentic.

5) Lastly, the final characters of the URL within a HyperScan QR code should IDENTICALLY match the secure HyperText code on the bottom right. So, by way of example, a valid HyperScan QR code would feature a 1-5 character, case-sensitive HyperText code (such

as aB12T), and the URL your QR scanner displays when scanning the code would then read, **http://7.tv/aB12T.**

In late 2011, the official HyperScan QR code scanning application is scheduled to be released for Apple and Android platforms, providing two more levels of security, bringing the total levels offered to 7.

USING HYPERSCAN WITH YOUR PC, MAC or TABLET –

If you have a PC, Mac or tablet (like an iPad) near your reading area, and would like to see the results of HyperScan code scan on a larger screen than your mobile device. You won't have to type a long URL. Simply open your computer or tablet's browser, and type 7.tv/ followed by the 1-5 character HyperText code found at the bottom right corner of the HyperScan QR code, and press "Enter." Remember, HyperText codes are case sensitive, so type the characters precisely as you see them.

That's all. The web page, video, or graphic should load immediately. You're never more than 10 keystrokes away from the HyperScan destination designated in a HyperScan QR code.

HOW LONG WILL HYPERSCAN CODES KEEP WORKING; HOW MANY TIMES CAN THE SAME CODE BE SCANNED?

When an author incorporates HyperScan QR codes into his or her work, HyperScan QR codes remain active for AT LEAST five years following each edition's first publication date. Authors may elect to extend the functional life of their codes beyond the five-year term, by continuing to license the unique codes found in their books, and by maintaining the integrity of the links to which the unique codes direct traffic.

Each HyperScan QR code placed in a printed work is designed to be scanned successfully hundreds of times. However, the speed with which the final site is loaded relies heavily on your wireless service provider's traffic, as well as the Internet connection and traffic of the host sites to which a HyperScan QR code is directed.

Index

1907 Panic, 43
1st Bank of the United States, 98
Aldrich
   Senator, 179, 204, 209
   Senator Nelson Aldrich, 178
Aldrich Bill, 179, 180, 181, 184, 206
Aldrich Plan, 184, 185, 186, 198, 199, 200, 201
Aldrich, Senator Nelson, 178
American Bankers Association, 151
American Bankers' Association, 156, 157
American Revolution, 26, 60, 79, 315
Anarchists, 4
anarcho-capitalist, 40, 41, 42
Argentina, 22
Aristotle, 62
Article 1, Section, 28, 31, 91, 92, 96, 104, 263, 265, 270, 281
Articles of Confederation, 91
Ashley's English Economic History,, 71
Associated Press, 47, 258
AT&T, 173
Athens, 60
Attica, 58
Augean stables, 58
Austrian economist, 38, 104, 107
Bancor, 226
Bank of England, 74, 77, 78, 82, 88, 90, 169, 226, 294, 307
Bank of England Museum, 74
Bank of North America, 35, 90, 91, 99, 100
Bank of North Dakota, 248, 249, 250, 251, 252, 255, 257, 262, 263, 300, 336
Bank of the United States, 117, 119, 121, 135, 181, 182, 219
Bartlett, Josiah, 88
Baruch
   Bernard, 192, 201, 211, 217,, 225, 226, 228
Battle of Lexington, 85
Battle of Marathon, 60
Battle of New Orleans, 113
Bible, 69, 70, 72
Biddle
   Nicholas, 115, 116, 119, 120, 121, 122, 123
Black Friday, 155
Black Thursday, 227
Bond
   James, 54
British Round Table group, 203
Brooks, Mary, 46, 47, 50
Bryan
   William Jennings, 175, 193, 207
Bryan, William Jennings, 19, 159, 160, 161, 162, 163, 164, 165, 170, 191, 207, 208, 209
Buel, James, 152
Bureau of Engraving and Printing, 148, 149
BUS, 181, 219, 220
Byrns, Prof. Ralph, 16
Caesar, 66
Calhoun
   Vice-President John, 114
Calvin
   John, 71
Carey, Henry C., 129, 130, 131, 132, 133, 162
Carmack, Patrick, 274
Carnegie
   Andrew, 172, 184
Carow, Edith Kermit, 189
Carthage, 62
Carthaginians, 65
central core vault, 47, 50, 53
Chancellor of the Exchequer,, 26
Charter of Liberties, 76
Chase

Salmon P., 139
Chicago, 114, 117, 123, 147, 151, 159, 166, 167, 209, 222, 231, 232, 233, 234, 235, 238, 239
Churchill
   Winston, 228
Churchill, Winston, 26, 187
Civil War, 39, 118, 129, 137, 138, 139, 140, 143, 144, 146, 150, 151, 157, 159, 162, 169, 174, 256, 293
Clarke, Hansen, 259
Clay
   Senator Henry, 117
Cleveland, President Grover, 157, 159, 188, 190
Clinton
   President Bill, 237
   President William Jefferson, 198
Coinage Act, 102, 103, 144, 152
Coinage Clause, 79, 80, 83, 98
Col. House, 201, 202, 203, 208
Colfax, Schuyler, 129
Colonel House, 193, 202, 203, 225
Colonial Scrip, 78, 82, 291
COMEX, 167
Commanger, Henry S., 186
Communism, 67
Community Bank of Illinois, 258
Confederate Army, 138
Conlan, Rep. John B., 47, 48, 49, 50
Conservative Caucus, 29, 30
Constitution, 31, 32, 33, 35, 42, 44, 53, 62, 65, 90, 91, 92, 94, 96, 98, 104, 113, 115, 117, 149, 157, 161, 162, 180, 202, 221, 245, 253, 260, 263, 265, 267, 268, 281, 282
Continental Congress, 85, 87, 90
Continental currency, 112
Contraction Act,, 140
Council on Foreign Relations, 192, 203
Crime of '73, 145, 146, 147, 149, 151
Crown of Thorns and Cross of Gold, 159
Crozier, Alfred, 205, 206, 207
Currency Act, 82, 83, 84
Czolgosz

Leon F., 170
Daddy Warbucks, 179
Dall
   Curtis, 228
Dallas, Alexander J., 109
Dark Ages, 66, 68, 149, 150
Davos, Switzerland, 142
Declaration of Independence, 90
Del Mar, Alexander, 85
Democles, 58
Democratic Republican Party, 113
Denninger, Karl, 5, 168, 284, 285, 306, 337, 338
Depression
   The, 228
Dewey, Davis Rich, 133
DiLorenzo, Thomas J., 99, 100
discount rate, 181, 218, 226
Dodge
   Cleveland H., 184, 193
Douglas, Sen. Paul H., 238, 239
Draco, 59
Draconian, 59
Duane
   William J., 118
Durell, Ed, 46, 49
Dyson, Ben, 308
Eaton
   John, 114
   Peggy, 114
Ebeling, Richard M., 43
Edison
   Thomas A., 221
Edward III, 72
Egyptian priests of Sais, 60
Einstein, Albert, 20, 21
Eisenhower
   President Dwight D., 202
Electoral College, 118
Emancipation Proclamation, 130, 138
End The Fed, 24, 32
English Renaissance, 76
Even, Louis, 8, 143, 145, 221, 280, 326
Fannie Mae, 242
FDR, 228, 229

Index

Federal Reserve Act, 209, 210, 211, 215, 217, 218, 219, 221
Federal Reserve Act of 1913, 11, 40, 136, 157
Federal Reserve System, 1, 24, 43, 114, 137, 175, 183, 184, 186, 199, 200, 201, 202, 203, 204, 207, 208, 219, 221, 225, 227, 228, 235, 256, 262, 263, 266, 267, 268, 307
Federal Reserve System in 1913, 43
Financial Times, 34, 243
Fisher, Prof. Irving, 238
Fleming
    Ian, 54
Forbes
    B.C., 178
Foreign Affairs, 203
Fort Knox, 46, 47, 48, 49, 50, 52, 53, 54, 56, 279, 337
Franklin
    Benjamin, 80
Franklin, Ben, 291
Freddie Mac, 242
Friedman, Milton, 12, 14, 18, 19, 20, 24, 32, 44, 54, 55, 129, 142, 153, 154, 295
Galbraith
    John Kenneth, 137, 228
Galbraith, John Kenneth, 137, 184, 228
Gandhi, Indira, 319
Gandhi, Sonia, 319
Garfield, President James, 154
General Electric, 173
Germany, 20, 21, 22, 181, 230, 302, 309
Girard, Stephen, 109
Glass
    Cong. Carter, 200
Glass-Owen Bill, 200, 201, 203, 205, 206
Glass-Steagall Act, 236, 237
Goebbles, Joseph, 21
Goldbugs, 30, 88, 96, 102
golden armor of Glaucus, 58
Goldfinger, 54
Gould, Jay, 155
Graham, Frank D., 238

Grant, President U.S., 144
Great Depression, 17, 20, 39, 54, 67, 112, 142, 146, 157, 236
Greenback, 156
Greenback Party, 147, 159
Greenback solution, 40
Greenbackers, 156
Greenbacks, 25, 128, 129, 131, 132, 133, 134, 135, 136, 137, 138, 139, 140, 141, 142, 143, 145, 146, 147, 148, 151, 152, 153, 159, 275, 286
Greenspan, Alan, 35, 36, 278
Greider
    William, 114, 122
Gresham's Law, 37, 84, 281
Griffin
    G. Edward, 136, 137, 208
Griffin, G. Edward, 80, 92, 93, 96, 112, 120, 121, 173, 186, 187, 229, 294
Guernsey, 2, 3, 4, 5, 6, 7, 16, 87
Hamilton, Alexander, 98, 99, 100, 101, 203
Hamilton, Earl J., 238
Hannibal, 63
Hardmeyer, Eric, 248
Harriman
    Edward H., 170
Harrison, Benjamin, 174, 189
Hayes, President Rutherford B., 153
Hayne
    Robert, 118
Hazard Circular, 134
Heinze-Morse group, 171
Henry VIII, 72
Hepburn Act of 1906, 171
Hepburn v. Griswold, 143
Hesiod, 58
Hilton, Larry, 263
Hitler
    Adolph, 230
Holocaust Island, 8
Homer, 58
Hoover
    President Herbert, 226, 229
House

Index

Col. Edward Mandell House, 201
House of Commons, 26, 27, 71, 81
Hume, David, 81
Hunt, Haroldson Lafayette, 165
Hunt, Nelson Bunker, 165
HyperScan QR, 4, 5
Icet, Allen, 249
IMIC, 166
India, Public Banking in, 319
International Emergency Economic
    Powers Act (IEEPA), 56
International Harvester, 173
International Metals Investment
    Company, 166
Islamic Banking, 317
Jackson
    President, 113, 114, 115, 116, 117, 118,
        119, 120, 121, 122, 169, 214, 215
Jackson, President Andrew, 117, 123,
    126, 292, 337
JAK Bank, 315
Jay Cooke & Company, 144
Jefferson, 104
Jefferson, Thomas, 3, 85, 92, 101, 104,
    105, 106, 107, 109, 110, 160, 198,
    288, 289, 290, 291
Jekyll Island, 178, 180, 181, 185, 211,
    216
Jesus, 70
Jews, 70
Jubilee Year., 25
Kennedy
    Joseph P., 226, 229
Kennedy, President John F., 286
Keynes
    John Maynard, 225, 226
Keynesian, 39, 226, 324
Keyworth, John, 74
King Alfred, 72
King Augeus of Elis, 58
King Croesus, 61
King Edward the Confessor, 72
King Gustaf III, 314
King Henry 1, 74
King, Dr. Martin Luther, Jr., 238

King, Willford I., 238
Knickerbocker Trust Company, 171
Knox vs. Lee, 143
Kucinich, Cong. Dennis, 265, 270
Kuhn-Loeb & Co., 170
LaBorde, Larry, 165
Lawrence
    Richard, 121
League of Nations, 225, 226
Legal Tender, 94, 96, 128, 281
Lenin, 203
Lincoln, 156
    President, 134, 138, 139, 151, 214
Lincoln, President Abraham, 126, 139,
    159, 187, 291
Lindbergh
    Charles A., Sr., 175
    Cong. Charles A., 134
    Congressman, 182, 184, 203, 211, 218
Lindy
    Lucky, 134
Lord Curzon, 225
Ludwig von Mises Institute, 38, 40, 41,
    54, 77, 101, 143
Lundberg
    Ferdinand, 194
Lycurgus, 58
M3, 241
Madison
    James, 44, 100
Magna Carta, 76
Marshall, Del. Bob, 262
Martin Luther, 71
Martin, Nathan, 322, 334, 335
Marx
    Karl, 202
Massachusetts Colony, 79
Massachusetts-owned bank, 258
Matonis, Jon, 167
McAdoo
    William, 198, 205
McConnachie, Alistair, 308
McCormick
    Cyrus, 184
McFadden
    Rep. Louis T., 193, 221, 228, 230, 231

Index

McKinley, President William, 159, 163
McLane
   Louis, 118
Mellon
   Andrew, 229
metalists, 28, 35, 37, 144, 206
MI-5, 54
Michigan Development Bank, 258, 259
Micronesia, 12
Mises, Ludwig von, 38, 39, 40, 42, 43, 44, 54, 55, 77, 96, 101, 143, 337
Monetary Commission, 182
money changers, 58, 66, 67, 70, 71, 72, 77, 87, 89, 113, 119, 120, 123, 134, 147, 149, 155, 164, 170, 171, 175, 210, 231
Money Trust, xi, 2, 39, 42, 43, 45, 134, 158, 173, 175, 179, 180, 184, 185, 186, 188, 192, 197, 201, 204, 212, 215, 218, 222
MoneyMasters, 18, 19, 32, 274, 294
Monroe, President James, 107
Mont Pelerin, 44
Morgan
   J.P., 169, 171, 172, 173, 178, 193, 194, 217, 226
   John Pierpont, 169
   Junius, 169
Morris
   Gouvernor, 44, 99
   Robert, 99
Morris, Robert, 90, 100
Moses, 69
Mount McKinley, 163
Mugwamps, 188
My Exploited Father-In-Law, 229
Natelson, Robert G., 78, 79, 80, 83, 87, 91, 92, 94, 97, 98
National Bank Act, 135, 138
National Banking Act, 129, 131, 139, 264
National Banking Association, 136
National City Bank, 184, 193, 204
National Emergency Employment Defense Act of 2010, 265

National Monetary Commission, 175, 178
Nehemiah, 69, 70
New World Order, 203
New York Stock Exchange, 145, 228
Owen
   Senator Robert L., 201
Owen, Sen. Robert, 139, 157, 200, 201, 203, 204, 205, 206
Panic Circular, 157, 158
Panic of 1893, 158
Panic of 1907, 175, 205
Paris, 225
Parliament, 112
Patman
   Wright, 221
Paul, Ron, 36, 41
Perloff
   James, 192, 203, 215, 217, 225
   James, 192
Persian Army, 60
Philip Dru, 202
Philip Dru, Administrator: A Story of Tomorrow., 202
Pike, Rep. Otis, 51
Pittsburgh, 151
Plato, 58, 60
plutocrats, 60
Polybius, 63
post-Civil-War depression, 20, 26
Prince, Charles, 243
Princeton University, 21, 55, 142, 173, 184, 238
Program for Monetary Reform, 235, 238, 239, 242, 243
Progressive Party, 185
Proverbs, 2
Prusi, Mike, 259
Punic Wars, 63
Reforum, 2
Republic, 28, 31, 32, 65, 116, 126, 176, 245
Republicans, 117
reserve requirements, 181
Resumption Act, 147, 148, 153

Index

Richardson, William A., 145
Roaring 1920s, 38
Rockefeller
   John D., 170, 184, 226
Rockefeller Foundation, 43
Rockwell, Llewellyn, 41
Roman Empire, 67, 68, 149, 150
Roman monetary system, 150
Roman Money Supply, 150
Roman Republic, 65
Ron Paul, 20, 24, 30, 32, 35, 281, 282, 331, 337, 338
Roosevelt
   President Teddy, 175, 185
   Theodore, 170
Roosevelt, Eleanor, 188
Roosevelt, Frankli, 195
Roosevelt, Franklin, 20, 39, 47, 55, 164, 170, 171, 175, 176, 185, 187, 188, 189, 194, 195, 197, 202, 231, 235
Roosevelt, President Theodore, 43, 187
Rothbard, Murray, 39, 40, 41, 77, 78, 83, 84, 88, 101, 104, 105, 106, 107, 109, 110, 111, 112, 129, 143, 145
Rothschild
   N.M, 169, 171, 173
   Nathan, 169
Rothschilds, 169, 181
Russia, 202, 203
Ryan, Lt. General John L., 51, 53
Ryrie Study Bible, 70
Salvation Island, 8
Saturday Evening Post, 179, 205
Schiff
   Jacob, 192, 194
Search
   Dr. R. E., 67
   Dr. R.E., 66, 68, 146, 152
Second Bank of the U.S., 169
Second Bank of the United States, 118
Self government, 3, 42
Senator Glass, 208
serfdom, 3, 19, 30, 42, 66, 76, 88, 100, 194, 300
Sergeant
   John, 117
Shakespeare, William, 76
Sherman Anti-Trust Act, 170
Sherman Antitrust Act, 177
Silver Certificates, 153, 286
Silver Commission, 149, 150
Silver Commission, United States, 149
Simon, Treasury Secretary William, 21, 46, 49, 50
Skousen
   W. Cleon, 136, 171
Skousen, Mark, 107
Skousen, W. Cleon, 171, 172
Soddy, Frederick, 60, 233, 234, 243
Solon, 59, 60, 61
Sparta, 58, 60
Spaulding, Cong. E. G., 127
Stamp Act depression, 26
Stevens
   Thaddeus, 135
Stowe
   Lyman E., 67
Stuart, James Gibb, 8
Sumerians, 25
Supreme Court, 1, 33, 93, 94, 117, 139, 143, 197, 207, 216
Sweden, 22, 240, 314, 315, 337
Taft
   President, 176, 177, 216
   William Howard, 175
Tally Sticks, 74, 75, 76, 141, 337
Taney
   Roger B., 119
Tariff Act of 1789, 162
Taylor, Dr. Quentin, 146
Temple, 70, 146
The Great Depression, 228
The Hazard Circular, 134
The Market Ticker, 5
The Secret of Oz, 30, 146, 168, 249, 288, 294, 336, 337, 338
The Truth In Money Book, 134, 135, 140
Thoren
   Theodore R., 134, 135
Tolkien, JRR, 309

Index

Treaty of Ghent, 107
U.S. Constitution, 28, 31, 76, 81, 90, 91, 96, 98, 99, 143, 265, 270, 281, 314
U.S. Notes, 24, 25, 31, 117, 128, 136, 137, 143, 149, 153, 207, 263, 275, 286
U.S. Steel Corporation, 172
Underwood Tariff Bill, 217
United Nations, 225
United Press International, 47
United States Bank Notes, 136
University of Chicago, 184, 199
Van Buren
    Martin, 114, 117, 122
Vanderlip
    Frank -, 180
    Frank A., 179, 204
Vanderlip, Frank, 205
War of 1812, 104, 107, 109, 111, 113, 188
Warburg
    Paul, 183, 185, 192, 201, 208, 211, 225, 227
Warburg, Paul, 179
Warburgs, 202
Warner, Richard F., 140
Washington, George, 3, 30, 52, 58, 60, 66, 102, 105, 111, 114, 115, 121, 126, 127, 134, 136, 139, 150, 152, 158, 173, 174, 175, 176, 179, 180, 189, 206, 211, 212, 216, 219, 221, 229, 259, 260, 290, 294, 307
Washington, Samuel, 102
Waterloo, 169
Wells, Sen. William, 109, 233
Whitmer, Gretchen, 259
Whittlesey, Charles R., 238
William the Conqueror, 74
Willing
    Thomas, 99
Wilson
    President Woodrow, 208, 211, 216, 217, 225
    Woodrow, 173, 184, 185, 193, 201
Wilson, President Woodrow, 164, 201
World Economic Forum, 142
World War I, 171, 201, 217, 221, 225
WWI, 228, 230
Xenophon, 58
Yap, 12, 14, 15, 16, 20
Zoellick, Robert, World Bank president, 34

Index

CPSIA information can be obtained at www.ICGtesting.com
Printed in the USA
268344BV00002B/8/P